Building Children's Resilience in the Face of Parental Mental Illness

Mental illness in a parent presents children with multiple challenges, including stigma, self-doubt and self-blame, ongoing anxiety and depression, that are rarely discussed in the public domain. This important new book, written by young people who have lived through these experiences, as well as professionals working alongside their families, highlights the relationships between children, parents and professionals, and the emotional issues they all face.

A key focus of the book is the relationships in all combinations between the children, parents and professionals, as well as the responses to each other illustrated throughout. It will be ideal for all those working in the health, social and educational professions, as well as parents and children themselves.

Alan Cooklin has worked as a family therapist, psychiatrist, and child and adolescent psychiatrist for some 45 years. For the past 20 years he has developed the multi-family Kidstime Workshops for the children of parents with mental illness and their families, and in 2012 established the charity (The Kidstime Foundation, later Our Time) to disseminate this approach. He has published widely.

Gill Gorell Barnes has been a family therapist, published researcher, and university lecturer for over 35 years, as well as working as expert witness in the family courts for 15 years. Her focus on children in families afflicted by parental mental illness and other sources of extreme behaviour includes all varieties of family life. She has published widely.

"Describing how children and young people can do more than survive this adverse childhood experience but go on to thrive and flourish whilst supporting parents and family, written by its authors with emotional intelligence and intelligent kindness, this book is a must read for all practitioners working across the field of mental health, all health, social care, education and justice, and indeed all parents.

The impact of parental mental illness on children and young people has been a both much neglected area and where written about has had a focus on blame rather than understanding, finding solutions and building resilience in children young people and families. Now for the first time we have a book that listens to and learns from children and young people themselves. True Co-production of the lived experience of Children and Young is People is 'yes hard Hitting' whilst at the same time tender."

Dame Sue Bailey, Chair, Centre for Mental Health, previously Professor of Child and Adolescent Psychiatry, University of Manchester, President of the Royal College of Psychiatrists, Chair of the Academy of Royal Medical Colleges and Chair of the Children and Young People's Mental Health Coalition

"It's hard to draw positives from the past decade of austerity, but one has been the dawning recognition of issues, previously neglected, that underlie many of our social ills. Domestic abuse is one such issue, loneliness another. And growing up with a parent with mental illness is at last starting to win the attention it deserves.

This fine collection of accounts of childhoods overshadowed – but also, startlingly, sometimes enriched – by parental mental illness could not be more timely for policy-makers beginning to appreciate the importance of supporting children and young people living with the daily reality. It's also a welcome prompt for journalists like me to ensure the topic is firmly on the public agenda.

At a mental health and addictions charity I am involved with, people we support are encouraged to give testimonies of their challenges and recovery journeys. Recently a worker with the charity felt confident enough to give her own, extraordinarily moving, account of growing up with a mother with bipolar disorder and of how it had helped shape her career choice. 'I am no longer an insecure kid,' she said. 'I am hopeful.'"

David Brindle, Public Services Editor, *The Guardian*

"As someone who experienced parental mental ill health as a child and received no input from services, I believe it is essential that those people who come into contact with children on a daily basis are equipped to open up much needed lines of communication for them. Now in my role as a teacher

I am an advocate for increasing awareness amongst staff about the challenges that these children may face every day. This book achieves both of these goals and is an essential read for anyone working with children."

Alex Hatt, Secondary Science and Special Educational Needs
Teacher and child who experienced mental illness in a parent

"Books like this can support professionals to feel confident to look beyond the basic treatment 'task' they've been allocated. A greater appreciation of the complexity of the family lives of their patients can add an additional layer of understanding and in can lead to a difference to the way we choose to intervene leading to more person-centred and individualised care which is better received, more impactful for the patient and family and more rewarding for the professional.

Listening to, working with and learning from young carers and children living with parents with mental illness is essential for any mental health professional working in the field. Recognising, valuing and developing work with children in these families should be seen as a part of our core work that improves practice and outcomes.

Having meaningful knowledge of, and being known to the family (*Who are you? What's your job? Why are you in my house? Can you help my mum/ dad/brother/sister? Can you help me?*) can and should be integrated into our day to day practice. Its valuable to have tools to learn how to have these conversations effectively - building knowledge about what the children and young people are good at, how the family works and communicates together and supporting them to develop resilience in the face of their difficult circumstances and letting them know they are not alone.

Mental health and other health care professionals are well placed to be a consistent available adult who may have some useful (if not all of the) answers, who knows both the parent and the child. Hearing from children as to what they might consider such an adult to be like can help us focus on this area of our work.

Through their work as articulated throughout this publication, the authors demonstrate the vital importance of giving children and young people an equal place on the 'platform' to speak and be heard in their own voices and through their voices to be enabled to educate adult professionals about how we can effectively work with them and to co-create services that meet their needs. As we pursue a national programme of major transformation of mental health services this book is an extremely well-timed resource."

Chris Caldwell, D.Prof, RGN, RN (Child), PGDipEd,
Director of Nursing & System Workforce Development,
Tavistock & Portman NHS Foundation Trust

"As a young adult carer, a book that listens to young people's experiences is an essential read for anyone working with mental illness in adults and the young people it affects. It's not easy sometimes, but then life with mental illness never is. What this book does is show that listening and learning will help when dealing with mental illness."

Melissa Moody, Young Adult Carer engaged with The Children's Society Include Service

Building Children's Resilience in the Face of Parental Mental Illness

Conversations with Children, Parents and Professionals

Edited by
Alan Cooklin and
Gill Gorell Barnes

FOREWORDS BY
ALASTAIR CAMPBELL AND
PROFESSOR KIM FOSTER

LONDON AND NEW YORK

First published 2021
by Routledge
2 Park Square, Milton Park, Abingdon, Oxon OX14 4RN

and by Routledge
52 Vanderbilt Avenue, New York, NY 10017

Routledge is an imprint of the Taylor & Francis Group, an informa business

© 2021 selection and editorial matter, Alan Cooklin and
Gill Gorell Barnes; individual chapters, the contributors

The right of Alan Cooklin and Gill Gorell Barnes to be
identified as the authors of the editorial material, and of the
authors for their individual chapters, has been asserted in
accordance with sections 77 and 78 of the Copyright, Designs
and Patents Act 1988.

All rights reserved. No part of this book may be reprinted
or reproduced or utilised in any form or by any electronic,
mechanical, or other means, now known or hereafter invented,
including photocopying and recording, or in any information
storage or retrieval system, without permission in writing from
the publishers.

Illustrations and cover by Hannah Asen

Trademark notice: Product or corporate names may be
trademarks or registered trademarks, and are used only for
identification and explanation without intent to infringe.

British Library Cataloguing-in-Publication Data
A catalogue record for this book is available from the British Library

Library of Congress Cataloging-in-Publication Data
A catalog record has been requested for this book

ISBN: 978-0-367-18311-0 (hbk)
ISBN: 978-0-367-18312-7 (pbk)
ISBN: 978-0-429-06073-1 (ebk)

Typeset in Times New Roman
by codeMantra

Contents

List of contributors	ix
Forewords	xiii
Acknowledgements	xvi

Introduction   1

1 **Mental health, mental illness, the family and others: how do we think about them together?**   6
ALAN COOKLIN

2 **Parental commentary on Chapter 1**   43
LARA BROWN

3 **Comment by Juliet Brown (Lara's daughter) on Lara Brown's commentary**   51
JULIET BROWN

4 **Parental mental illness: the worst hurdles and what helped**   53
KIRSTY TAHTA-WRAITH

5 **From child of a parent with mental illness to becoming a therapist: what made a difference along the route**   69
CHINEYE NJOKU

6 **Commentary on a young adult's chapter**   81
LOU RYAN – PARENT OF GEORGIA IRWIN-RYAN

7 **Breaking out of the trap of constricting loyalty**   85
GEORGIA IRWIN-RYAN

viii Contents

8 Parental mental illness and extra difficulties for children when parents divorce   90

GILL GORELL BARNES

9 Notes from the edge: supporting parents with mental health problems   110

LEONARD FAGIN

10 Storytelling & drama: telling our stories, building resilience – Drama processes and techniques for empowerment   128

DENI FRANCIS

11 The journey from young carer to doctor: reflections on how the two roles informed each other   142

SUHAIB DEBAR

12 Keeping it together: championing young carers' rights and raising family and public awareness   147

AMBEYA BEGUM

13 A parental commentary on Ambeya Begum's and Georgia Irwin-Ryan's chapters   164

LARA BROWN

14 Not a framework, but a way to be: reflections of a school nurse   168

JESSICA STREETING

15 School-based support for young people affected by parental mental illness   183

ANITA FRIER

16 London calling – experiences with the Kidstime model in Germany   205

KLAUS HENNER SPIERLING

17 Kidstime experience in Spain   211

MIGUEL CÁRDENAS

18 Some combined tips for parents, children and the professionals who work with them   214

Index   221

Contributors

Gill Gorell Barnes has been a family therapist, published researcher, and university lecturer for over 35 years, as well as working as expert witness in the family courts for 15 years. She has specialised in family break ups, and stepfamily living as well as post-divorce work to lower conflict and improve children's resilience. Her focus on children in families afflicted by parental mental illness and other sources of extreme behaviour includes all varieties of family life. She has published widely.

Ambeya Begum obtained a degree in Banking and Finance, and later a masters in Law and Finance. Her current appointment is as a KYC analyst working with the Silicon Valley Bank in London. As the only girl, and the eldest child in a Bengali family, the responsibility of caring for her mother, who suffered severe mental illness, as well as for her family, fell on her shoulders. She later encountered the Kidstime Workshops for the children and families in which a parent suffers mental illness, and *determined to* help the Foundation, working as an 'experience' counsellor and acting as interviewer and presenter in the films made for the 'Who Cares?' schools project. She was chosen as Young Carers National NHS England champion, and has been active in and chaired meetings as part of NHS Thought Diversity programme, The Children's Society Making a Step Change initiative, and the NHS Roundtable on the needs of the Children of Parents with Mental Illness. She is now a Trustee on the Board of Our Time.

Lara Brown has a BA Hons in English and a Postgraduate Diploma in Journalism. She was a Media Reporter for *Broadcast* magazine and the Independent, freelance writer/researcher for the BBC, and a writer on Contemporary and Modern Art (and Deputy Head of Department) for the auctioneer Sotheby's. Lara subsequently retrained as a psychotherapist. She became severely ill with a bipolar episode following the birth of her second daughter, leading to numerous hospital admissions over the next seven years. Lara is married with two daughters, aged 16 and 10.

x Contributors

Miguel Cárdenas is a psychiatrist who graduated in Colombia in 1998, and gained a Postgraduate Diploma in Children and Adolescent Mental Health in London, in 2004. He works as a coordinator of the CAMHS in Sant Boi, Barcelona, Spain, leading clinical and community mental health programs. He has worked within the Kidstime workshops team in Barcelona since 2014. He is also collaborating with community projects in Colombia. He has an active interest in mental health prevention projects in childhood, and in sharing his experience in community projects.

Alan Cooklin has worked as a family therapist, psychiatrist, and child and adolescent psychiatrist for some 45 years. He developed the joint child and adult mental health 'Marlborough Family Service' over 25 years. For the past 20 years he has developed the multi-family Kidstime Workshops for the children of parents with mental illness and their families, and in 2012 established the charity (The Kidstime Foundation, later Our Time) to disseminate this approach, as well as other interventions in school and community, particularly the 'Who Cares' project. He has published widely.

Leonard Fagin works as an adult psychiatrist who has specialised in studying and developing psychological and community, including therapeutic community, approaches to treating mental health disorders as a complement to standard traditional treatments. He has been the Lord Chancellor's Medical Visitor for the Office of the Public Guardian, and is currently a second opinion appointed doctor for the Care Quality Commission and advisor to the London Borough of Hackney Social Services Family & Children Division. He started the second of the Kidstime Workshops in 2009. His most important contribution has been ways to support parents affected by mental illness. He has published widely.

Deni Francis is an actor who studied drama & sociology and uses creative techniques to tell stories, for change. She has worked in corporate, educational, penal and voluntary sector settings. She has been involved in a variety of roles in educational films, particularly concerned with domestic violence, parental divorce and LGBTQ experiences, as well as 'The Jass Story' and others with the Kidstime Foundation (now Our Time). She led the development of the use of drama in the Kidstime workshops, and has continued to be a lead trainer, both nationally and internationally.

Anita Frier is Principal at Stoke Damerel Community College in Plymouth, and the Executive Principal of Inspiring Schools Partnership, including Scott Medical and Healthcare College and Montpelier Primary School. She has built a highly regarded welfare and pastoral structure in the school over 15 years, focusing on students' mental health needs and specifically the needs of the children of parents with mental illness. The school was awarded the Healthy Child Quality Mark for many years, and was also the winner of the UK Dementia Friendly Award in 2014. She has worked closely with the Kidstime Foundation, and then Our Time, in developing the 'Who Cares?' in-school project.

Georgia Irwin-Ryan is aged 19 and obtained 10 GCSEs despite her exams being during a time of high stress related to mental illness in both parents. She attended the Kidstime Workshops between ages 11 and 15, which she confirms played a significant part in her being able to maintain her academic success, and current training. She has currently worked in an after-school play scheme for primary school children, steward at musical and other events, and now training as a nursery nurse. She writes and records music for the Platform Scheme, has published poems in a book 'The Poetry Game' and exhibited poems and photographs in an exhibition on Young Carer's experiences. She has also presented, and been in films for The Kidstime Foundation.

Chineye Njoku has a degree in Biomedical Science, masters degrees in Mental Health and Psychology and an Advanced Diploma in Cognitive Behavioural Therapy. She practised as an IAPT (increasing access to psychological therapies) therapist in the NHS for some five years. From age 10 she and her sister struggled to care for their mother's bouts of mental illness. At age 14 she joined the Kidstime Workshops. She became an 'Experience Counsellor' for Kidstime and led a 'Teen Talk' group. She is a board member of Our Time, and has been active in many roles in the charity, including film presenter, public presenter, advocate, and trainer both in the UK and Scandinavia, and both within the charity as well as outside such as on the Perinatal Psychiatry course.

Lou Ryan is parent of Georgia Irwin-Ryan. Lou was brought up in a family with a mentally ill father. Lou was diagnosed with depression at age 15 and later with bipolar disorder as an adult. In 2018 Lou was additionally diagnosed with Complex-PTSD. Unable to work for a few years due to intermittent mental illness Lou has enjoyed helping out at Family Action, as well as volunteering at various organisations such as The Parent House and Islington Pride. Lou has a love of fine art, music and reading.

Klaus Henner Spierling is a psychologist who has trained in Systemic therapy, Multi-family therapy, Marte-meo therapy and Behavioural Trauma therapy. He works in a paediatric centre in Northern Germany, where he helped to introduce the Kidstime model to his country. He describes the impetus to start Kidstime, how the team developed and which hurdles had to be overcome at the beginning and how they were solved in a roll out throughout Germany.

Jessica Streeting is a school nurse and practice lecturer, who currently works as a Named Nurse for Looked-after children in central London and as Clinical Lead for the Our Time charity. She has been a School Nurse Advisor to Public Health England and continues to support children and young people in policy writing and practice. She completed her MA dissertation on the role of school nurses in supporting children with parental mental illness. In 2011 she was awarded the prestigious title of Queen's Nurse for her work in pioneering a unique school nursing model in one high need London secondary school. She has recently written a novel to raise awareness of school nursing and was invited to speak about this at the 2019 International School Nursing Conference in Stockholm.

Suhaib Debar qualified in medicine in June 2018 and is now a junior doctor intending to train in radiology within the NHS. His family are Kurdish refugees from Iraq, and had suffered severe trauma. For many years he acted as principal young carer for his mother who suffered from mental illness, and for his younger sister and two younger brothers. His family engaged in the Kidstime workshops over a prolonged period. He used his knowledge to help other children and young people, which affected his decision to study medicine. He participated in the online film 'When a Parent has a Mental Illness...'. He has used the understandings he gained to inform his own clinical practice and development.

Kirsty Tahta-Wraith is aged 25 and graduated with a BSc in Psychology from the University of East Anglia. She now works as an assistant psychologist in Child and Adolescent Mental Health within the NHS. Kirsty attended the Kidstime Workshops from the age of 8 with her father who had bipolar disorder. She describes the support she and her family received at the Kidstime Workshops as being critical in the development of her self-confidence, as well as influencing her career choice. She is passionate about supporting families affected by parental mental illness. She currently contributes to the Kidstime Workshops as an 'experience' counsellor, and teaches across the mental health disciplines including the Think Family initiatives of South London and the Maudsley NHS Foundation Trust in 2017, a conference for the London Boroughs of Merton and Sutton in 2018, and a landmark conference on Adverse Childhood Experience sponsored by the Plymouth Excellence Committee in 2018 as well as regularly for Our Time.

Forewords

Alastair Campbell
Time to Change Ambassador

Michael Gove – a prominent politician in all UK governments for some ten years to date – championed a current populist theme: 'We have all had enough of experts'. I contend that in the worlds of politics, the media, and associated professions the world as it is needs genuine expertise more than ever. Expertise is to be valued, not derided. If I am a passenger in an aeroplane, I would like an expert pilot to be at the controls. If I break my leg, and am rushed to A and E, I would prefer that the person who examines me is an expert in how to deal with broken limbs, rather than a politician or a bloke I met in the pub.

Within broad areas of expertise – expertise in mental health and mental illness, to take an example – it is also important to have experts in narrow areas within that general field. Alan Cooklin and Gill Gorell Barnes fall into that category, experts and specialists at one and the same time. Indeed, their work is all the more important for the deliberate choice they made to focus less on the mentally ill, than on those growing up as children of someone with mental illness. I have seen for myself, in listening to the stories of young people they have helped through the Kidstime charity (now renamed Our Time) and elsewhere, the value of their work, in understanding and then helping to address the very real additional pressures in the life of a young person living with, and often looking after, a mentally ill parent.

It is typical of their approach that their book should be given over to the voices of others. One of the most important skills required of someone in their profession is the ability to listen, and to make sense of what they hear, so they can properly support and advise the people they are helping. Though expert, they do not claim to have all the answers, for in a field as complicated as this, nobody does. But what the book does is bring out the stories and the views and the voices of these three groups of people – the young person who has grown up with a mentally ill parent, the mentally ill parent to greater or lesser degrees relying on a child or young adult, and the professional seeking

xiv Forewords

to help one or both – in a way that hopefully all three can learn from each other. It is not just individuals that we would like to be able to develop resilience, but systems too, and any healthcare system will be better and stronger if the real interests, needs and experiences of the patient and those impacted by their illness are at the heart of its design. The discussions on these pages should be seen in that light.

There is a tendency in the mental health field for the focus to be on the 'woe is me, woe is us' side of life. Think pictures of children with head in hands, adults with wild staring eyes. But one of the many good things about this book, for all the sadness within its pages, is the sense of hope and optimism. Some of the young people with stories to tell of their own upbringing have now become professionals in the field. And there are plenty of examples of even relatively small actions, interactions and changes, leading to the improvement in people's lives.

It's good to talk. That is at the heart of the opening up of the debate about mental illness, the breaking down of stigma and taboo, and the discrimination that this creates. There is plenty of good talking in this book, and I am confident the dialogue within its pages will lead to a broader dialogue within families, communities and those experts so dreaded by politicians who should know better.

About Alastair Campbell

Alastair Campbell was director of communications for the last Labour Government, campaigner for mental health, writer and patron of the Our Time charity.

* * * *

Kim Foster
Melbourne, Australia

Millions of children throughout the world have a parent with mental illness; yet they're largely hidden in our communities. They quietly grapple with concerns and distress about their parent's illness, assume responsibilities in their families and try to make sense of something they don't yet understand. Their experience can put them at risk of developing their own mental health concerns. But this isn't inevitable. This book shows how we as a community can come together to support them to recover and thrive in the face of mental illness – to build their resilience.

Resilience is the ability to positively adapt to adversity such as mental illness. As a term though, it is often used to refer only to what a person can do to help themselves when they experience challenges. Yet resilience involves interactions between people *and* their environment. Being able to overcome adversity involves both a person's own skills and resources, combined with support from others and resources made available to them. It's an important message of this book that building resilience for children of parents with mental illness is a shared responsibility. The chapters give many practical examples of how everyone can help build these children's resilience – schools, community groups, healthcare professionals, and family and friends.

Stories are a powerful and courageous way to share experiences, and the children's stories here give a welcome insight into what it is like to grow up with a parent with mental illness. They honestly and eloquently reveal the struggles they experience, yet also show how the love and support of others including their parents, and information and resources provided to them and their family can help transform their experiences and trajectories. This is a unique and, innovative book in the field, with its interactive dialogues on the challenges and opportunities of parental mental illness from multiple perspectives: being a child of a parent with mental illness, being a parent with mental illness, and working with children and families where parents have mental illness.

As the child of a parent with mental illness and a professional in the field, the book resonates at both levels for me. I hope it also resonates for you, and opens up conversations with, and in, families, raises awareness about mental illness and importantly results in positive actions that communities can take to connect and intervene with families.

We can all play a role in building children's resilience.

About Professor Kim Foster

Professor Kim Foster is an internationally recognised Australian mental health nurse academic, who as a child experienced both severe parental mental illness and the privations of the Care system. She now heads a mental health nursing research unit in Victoria, Australia. Her PhD is on the experiences of adult children of parents with mental illness. She was awarded a Winston Churchill fellowship to investigate international programmes for building the resilience of children and families where parents have mental illness.

Acknowledgements

With much gratitude to the young people, parents, and team members of all the Kidstime Workshops, who have informed much of this book.

To the team of the Our Time charity, and its supporters, who have all supported the continuing work.

To Hannah Asen for lightening the stories with her brilliant cartoons.

Introduction

This is an unusual book. This is not only because its focus, mental illness in a parent, is a topic rarely discussed between children, parents, and professionals, or because it is written from the point of view of all three of these groups. It is unusual because its message is about hearing and responding to the conversations between these three groups, with the goal of developing the thinking of all of us about how to manage life in the complex family situations generated when a parent develops mental illness.

Mental illness is common – said to include as many as 50% of the population at some point in a lifetime. Popular attitudes towards mental illnesses have always been fearful, leading to avoidence and a taboo about their discussion. In the past five to ten years there has been a strong movement in the United Kingdom to challenge the taboo, and the stigma about mental illness, with attempts at government level, by the Royal Foundation, and in campaigns by voluntary and statutory bodies, to create a climate in which mental illness can be thought of as normal and on a par with any other illness. At times this pressure to consider it as normal has unfortunately meant representing it in a more benign and optimistic light than is actually experienced by those who suffer from it, or by their families. In turn this has often meant the use of a variety of euphemisms to avoid naming mental illness, such as mental ill health, mental health problems, mental health issues, and paradoxically sometimes even naming it mental health. Whilst in one sense this language could be seen as softening the blow to people suffering mental illness, as well as their families, the avoidance of naming it more candidly can act as a deterrent to people describing the full detail of their distress and disturbance, as well as – most specifically for this book – being particularly confusing for their children.

In our view, although mental illness does need to be seen on the same level as physical illness – or as defined by government and professional bodies in the United Kingdom given 'parity of esteem' – to pretend that there are no distinctions between the different kinds of illness can lead to avoidance, both of what is happening to the mind of the person with mental illness and of the distress they experience, as well as avoiding the specific impacts it can have on their children. This confusion is represented in the United Kingdom in the definition of young carers, a term which can apply to a child or young person who provides care for an ill or disabled parent. That care can be physical, mental or emotional. The rights of young carers in the United Kingdom are defined in statute, and they are entitled to an assessment of their needs to be arranged by their local authority. In theory there is no specific threshold to define a young carer in the Act of Parliament,[1] but in reality local authorities have defined the duties and 'hours of care' that they recognise. There has been no definition of the form, or amount of emotional care that a child or young person may give to a parent with *mental illness*, nor of the mental or emotional impact that their attempts to provide this care may have on themselves. It has to be concluded that at state and administrative levels, the lack of recognition of children caring for, or just being in relationship with, a parent with mental illness must represent some degree of active avoidance. This avoidance is certainly seen in the confusion of the numbers of children and young people affected. National census estimates of young carers still remain under 200,000 children and young people caring for a parent with any illness[2] (physical or mental), whilst the Children's Comissioner for England in her 2018 report[3] identified 3.7 million children living with a parent with moderate or severe mental illness.

In Australia an acronym for Children of Parents with Mental Illness was attached to both national and state services – COPMI – still used in New South Wales. As a manifestion of the confusion and perhaps avoidance of this topic, another acronym has recently been devised by a European research group – CAPRI for 'Children and Adolescents affected by PaRental mental Illness' – whilst all of the five Nordic countries have defined these children as *relatives with rights*. In this book some writers have referred to young carers, and others to children of parents with mental illness. As editors we have not felt that we should impose a standard terminology – as there is not one – but readers of this book may need to be aware of this confusion of terms and numbers, because this confusion may be playing a significant part in the failure to provide adequate services for these children, at least in the United Kingdom.

We also hope that readers will see this as an optimistic book. Young people who have had experience of parental mental illness, their parents, and professionals who have worked with them provide testament, witness and evidence of the impacts of parent's illness on their child or children, and although most of it is negative, it is not all so. Evidence about the negative impacts is easy to come by. However, both the goal of this book and the motivation to write it came largely from the realisation that quite small but appropriately targeted and timed interventions could make a great difference to a child's experience and in the long term to his or her resilience. Resilience is obviously an important concept used by most of the young adults in their chapters. However, it is also a much used term whose meaning

Introduction 3

is often both vague and various. In Chapters 1 and 8 we have looked at some specific ways of thinking about and using the concept. Realisation of the power of small interventions to have a significant impact on the resilience of this particular group of children and young people is not new. Sir Michael Rutter's monograph – *Children of Sick Parents*[4] – in 1966 clearly identified the protective effects of a child having a neutral person with whom he or she could *appraise* their situation when a parent suffered a mental illness. This appraisal was about the child's own life and his or her relationship to the ill parent, as well as some of the impacts of the parent's illness. In this book the young adults, parents, school nurse Jess Streeting and head-teacher Anita Frier, as well as the two overseas contributors, all testify to the values gained by the child from another aspect of appraisal: being able to make sense of the parent's illness and how it affects his or her mind and behaviour. As a result there is much written about explanations and their value in this book.

Two other factors in particular are addressed: the child's sense of loneliness – particularly if he or she lives with a single parent who is ill – and what is almost a craving to meet others in similar circumstances, as well as the child's need for an alternative 'anchor' to the ill parent – an adult who can make sense of the child's experience, act as an advocate or port of call in stormy times, but who is not trying to *change* or *treat* the child. The value of this combination of ingredients is referred to a number of times in the book, and the young adults and parents testify to the healing impact on themselves when they were able to access it.

What the young adults describe as needed is not difficult to provide if there is a will at legislative and professional levels. In this book all the young people, parents and most professionals have had direct experience of Kidstime Workshops. These are monthly multi-family groups of 2.5 hours for children of parents with mental illness and their parents, which are referred to in a number of chapters, but described specifically in Chapters 5 and 6. However, despite the frequent references, the book is not about Kidstime, even though the authors' experience of Kidstime has thrown much light on what is needed for the these children and young people. The development and experience of this particular intervention brought the different writers together, but what that led to was a desire to share knowledge of what happens to these children and what can be done at different levels – legislation, services, flexibility of use of professional roles, and willingness to learn about and engage in the topic – to protect the children and to build their resilience. Kidstime does happen to include the three ingredients that surveys of young people have argued were needed to build their resilience: explanation, a group of other young people who know what it is like and adults who are neutral but can be advocates. These ingredients can be provided in a number of alternative ways: the intervention being developed by the UK National Society for the Prevention of Cruelty to Children (NSPCC) – Family Smiles[5] – provides eight group sessions for young people and a parallel five group sessions for parents, which to some degree address all three

4 Introduction

ingredients. It does not appear to provide the continuing opportunity for parents and children to learn to discuss the impacts of mental illness either individually or – as we have suggested – jointly in groups. Similar models are used in seven different intevention projects in Australia,[6] a small proportion of which included some individual family meetings, although not multi-family meetings.

Another positive spin off with a multi-family model is that it encourages both parents and young people to support and challenge each other, in ways which might not be accepted by either, if they came from professionals.[7] Young carer's services in the United Kingdom have in the past had the flexibility to target their interventions to suit each child's needs. Ironically some say this is now more difficult since the Care Act created statutory assessments. Although they often included young people's groups, these rarely included the parents unless on an individual basis. Similarly young carers groups in schools have provided great relief to some young people, as described by Anita Frier in her chapter. However, because of the way many parents perceive the authority of schools, and because these young people often see their group as a safe haven, it has rarely been possible to engage parents in these groups.

Although the writers have in many ways promoted a particular intervention, it is the realisation of a different factor which can help build resilience which is the focus of this book: namely more open conversations between children and young people and their parents, supported by and including conversations with the professionals who support either. To promote this dialogue in the book we have asked the young adults (some of whom are now also professionals in the field) and professionals to review each other's contributions, include some of each other's responses in their own contributions or in some cases write specific commentaries. We have used this approach rather than publish verbatim conversations, because the points many of the family members wanted to make are very specific, and we did not want them to get lost in dialogue. The young adults who have experienced mental illness in a parent have followed a wide variety of career paths: from child care, psychology, therapy, medicine, to finance. The professionals who have written represent adult, child and family psychiatry, family therapy, school nursing, teaching, as well as psychology and psychiatry from other European countries. Therefore for the most part the conversations are virtual in this book, describing what the different young people, parents and professionals want to say to each other, as well as to hear back. There are two direct comments between parents and children on each other's ideas and experiences, and in other cases comments have been turned into a compilation of tips or recommendations to young people, parents and professionals. We asked all contributors to keep all three groups in mind when writing, and we hope that this has filtered out technical terms or jargon as much as possible. Our hope is that this book will encourage new thinking about conversations between parents, young people and professionals, and that, in turn, will lead to implementing these conversations.

Obviously to initiate these conversations will need some confidence, courage and support to get over the hurdle of what may be new and unfamiliar and will also need some ideas for *knowing how to do it.* In the final chapter of this book we have some tips or suggestions for all three groups. In some cases families may need an outside professional to help them at least get started, which raises the question of who will help the professionals. The range of potential professionals who may come into contact with families affected by mental illness is large and includes psychiatric nurses and community psychiatric nurses, psychiatrists, psychologists, occupational therapists, children's social workers, teachers and non-teaching school staff such as counsellors, general practitioners and other primary care workers, as well as many others from voluntary bodies and other agencies including the police. There is no one person who is charged with the responsibility of talking to children about a parent's mental illness, as we think becomes clear from this book. It is really the child who will decide who he or she will trust enough to talk to or listen to. Training therefore has to be a multi-professional and inter-professional issue. Moves are beginning in some professions. The Royal College of Psychiatrists has recently completed a review which we hope will lead to both a curriculum for all trainees and that all should include this thinking in their appraisals. Suhaib Debar, a post graduate medical trainee, has included similar proposals for all doctors in his chapter. Training in nursing in general, and mental health nursing in particular, needs to be encouraged. Some sources of training are listed in the final chapter of the book.

References

1 HM Government. (2014) *The Care Act,* The Stationary Office, Norwich.
2 Aldridge, J. (2017) Where are we now?: Twenty-five years of research, policy and practice on young carers, *Critical Social Policy,* 38 (1), 155–165.
3 Children's Commissioner for England. (2018) *Childhood Vulnerability in England 2018,* Office of the Children's Commissioner for England, London.
4 Rutter, M. (1966) *Children of Sick Parents: An Environmental and Psychiatric Study,* Oxford University Press, London.
5 Margolis, R., and Fernandes, P. (2017) *Building Children's Confidence and Improving Parents' Protective Skills: Final Evaluation of the NSPCC Family SMILES Service,* NSPCC, London.
6 Reupert, A., Cuff, R., Drost, L., Foster, K., van Doesum, K., and van Santvoort, F. (2013) Intervention programs for children whose parents have a mental illness: A review, *Medical Journal of Australia,* 199 (3), S18–S22.
7 Cowling, V. (Ed) (2004) *Children of Parents with Mental Illness; Personal and Clinical Perspectives,* Australian Council of Educational Research, Melbourne.

Chapter 1

Mental health, mental illness, the family and others

How do we think about them together?

Alan Cooklin

This chapter is about young people, their parents and others in their families, talking with each other about mental illness in the family, as well as talking with the professionals from different agencies and disciplines who may work with them. Part 1 discusses families, and family life, in general. Part 2 reconsiders family life in the context of mental illness in the family.

Part 1: what is a family?

In general people live in, or have lived in and left, some form of family. In my experience there are five questions which are useful to consider:

- What is a family?
- What factors in family life can help the family to become a place of safety, intimacy and care, as well as freedom?
- What factors in family life can have the opposite effect?
- What can parents, young people themselves and professionals do to improve the positive qualities of family life for the benefit of children and young people?
- What might all this have to do with mental health, mental illness and its treatment and prevention?

People commonly talk about 'the family' as though we all know what they mean, when in reality each person may mean something different. The word 'family' can stir up so many images, thoughts and feelings, which can be different for each person. Also for a particular person some of these images, thoughts and feelings may contradict each other. For example, one father told me that he grew up in a 'very close' family. However, he rarely saw his own father who worked away, he was often bullied at school, and he had never told either parent about this 'so as not to upset them'. So he was trying to keep alive the idea of a very close family, but in fact had not felt free to share his own distressing emotional experiences with either parent.

In the United Kingdom there used to be a kind of image of an 'ideal' family – a time when the census identified the 'average' family as having two parents and 2.4 children – and often represented in the 1950s and 1960s in the Ladybird books for children rather like an old-fashioned picture post card, with a mother in an apron baking cakes, a father smoking a pipe and two or three well behaved children, of course all white, middle class and fully conventional to the expectations of those times. We now know that currently over 40% of marriages end in divorce in the United Kingdom, that over 17% of stable parental couples are not married, that 22% of children are brought up by lone parents.[1] In particular boroughs the percentages may vary widely, so that in some London Boroughs the percentage of lone parents may be more than double that figure. What other research has shown is that children born into or adopted by gay couples do as well as those brought up by heterosexual couples. In addition, the multiple cultures which make up the United Kingdom now all have different perspectives on the family, on the extended family and different expectations about children's behaviour. Despite this, in some people's minds that old fashioned image of the 'ideal' family lives on, even though it is now no longer the reality of how the majority of families live, nor is it necessarily how most people want to live their lives.

So, what is a family? A family is most commonly one or more parents with one or more children, who may or may not be the biological children of either or both parents. The children, may have been born from natural sexual reproduction by both or one of the parents, by assisted reproduction with the eggs and/or sperm from themselves or from donors, or the children may have been 'carried' by, that is developed inside the body of, a surrogate mother. Alternatively the children may have been fostered or adopted by one or both parents (if there are two), or they may be part of a step-family including children from both parents, separately or together, or even from other partners with earlier partners of either or both parents...or the family may be any combination of any of these and more 'structures' or organisations. The parents may be of similar or different religions, races, cultures and they may be of the same or different genders. So from this rich variety of choices what can we take it that the word 'family' means? After all, when we say the word *family* we will expect the other person to know what we mean. So here are two possibilities:

1   A social group where some or all of the adults are committed to care for the emotional and physical needs of the children while they are growing up.
2   A group of adults only, in which some may or may not have been the children of (or children cared for by) one or more of the adults in the same group. They may share mutual giving and taking of care for some or all of their lifetimes.

Different structures and functions of a family – good and bad? An outline for parents and young people

In the first group of families mentioned earlier, there is an obvious job to be done: look after the children in the best way you can, till they grow up into adults. That includes encouraging 'Attachment' relationships – encouraging children to learn to be connected to an adult or adults they can trust, helping them to learn to manage their emotions as they discover and find out about them, as well as someone who can 'keep it together', keep routines going and create a sense of safety and stability. However, although we may hope that all of those things may happen, in the interests of the children's development, it is rare for couples to 'plan' like that when they say 'let's start a family'. They tend to have an image – a dream – of a child they want, and only when the child arrives do they begin to think about the child's own emotional and developmental needs, and the fact that even very young children may have thoughts and feelings which the parents do not expect or welcome.

The degree to which parents can respond to the young child's independent thoughts and feelings will of course vary a great deal. In many cases, especially if the parents have had a good experience of a safe and emotionally warm family themselves, they may respond in similar positive ways without

Mental health, mental illness, the family   9

really thinking – at least until some problem arises, when they may be forced to think out their response as well as what is happening to their child. If one or other of the parents has *not* had a good experience of growing up themselves, they may want to try very hard to do things *differently*. This will involve them in having to think out carefully what they think their child needs, and whether they feel they *can* respond in the way the child needs, as they may have had no good experiences of their own to refer to.

Whether a parent can put into practice what he or she thinks their child needs may also depend on whether the parent has an emotionally supportive and understanding partner. So, for this first group there is a clear job and parents could if they wish 'learn' how to do it by going to what are often called 'parenting' classes or reading a manual on child care, although the emotional part of doing the job is less easy to learn, and will also depend on the emotional supports that parent has for him/herself.

In the second family group there is no clear job, because they are living together as adults. However, there is often an expectation that the family members will all care for each other in some way and to varying degrees. That model of family could follow on from the first kind of family if, for example, the children never leave home when they become adults. This could happen for financial reasons, such as if the young adults cannot afford anywhere else to live, or for more emotional reasons: they like to have their washing, cooking and 'home making' done for them, or fear loneliness away from home. Alternatively one of the original 'parents' may expect or demand that he or she receives ongoing life care and companionship from one or more of the children. As a result one or more of the children – most often daughters in times past – may feel they should not or even cannot leave. This can also represent a complex and mutual holding together of parent and child.[1]

Safety and danger in the family

If we think that the threads, bonds and connections which hold people living together are mostly based on love and care then we have also to think what we really mean by *these* words. One common assumption is that being in a family protects us from loneliness. On the other hand some people might describe being in the family as also potentially being very lonely. Another idea is that the family is a 'safe' place. However, there may be times when a particular family does not feel safe, or even feels dangerous, emotionally or physically to some in the family. Some people will say that they can only really 'be themselves' without any pretenses or 'acting' when they are home in the family, while some people may feel they are forever having to play a part to fit in with what is expected of them by their family.

A couple – Obviously the forces which brought the parents together in the first place are likely to be different from the shared bonds which continue to hold a family together when children are born. For the couple it may have been sexual attraction, love or a conscious choice to want to start a family. Sadly, what brings a couple together in the first place may later sometimes become very painful to them or even emotionally or physically destructive, although they may nevertheless stay together. We also know that different people use the word 'love' to mean very different things. So, for the purposes of this chapter I will define love as a mutual feeling, freely given by both sides and relatively free from domination or power of one over the other – that is that both 'lovers' are relatively free from domination by the other. When that happens then both people are likely to feel free to have and express their own opinions. Of course, as they will have to share many decisions about life and living, they will also have to keep a reasonable balance between them in making decisions, and trust each other to make some decisions on their own.

The family – When those positive ingredients remain in the couple's relationship, then it is also more likely that family life can be a source of both safety and freedom for the children. When the children are young then those ingredients, as well as some intimate attachments to one or both of the parents, will satisfy most of their needs. It is later that one has to consider what the forces are that keep people together in families.

So those possible experiences described earlier can be the result of the family being organized positively as a protection against loneliness, providing some sense of security of the base where one lives, and meeting a need to feel part of a group; all positive forces which keep people together. Alternatively – as described earlier – if the family has just become their 'default' base, which avoids the fear of exploring more unknown contexts outside, they can also be forces which can lead a young adult to feel trapped. In turn this can be part of the process which sometimes 'holds' adults in their parental home.

Shaping of relationships by different cultural, social and religious beliefs

The picture of mutual affection, and equality in taking decisions, is not how the UK family has always been, nor how it still actually *is* in some families or even how in some cultures and religions it is believed it *should* be. Cultural, religious and personality factors *may* lead some people in families to accept that some people, genders and age groups have more rights to their own opinions and thoughts than others. Cultural traditions need respect, and can be *forces for good*, in that they can increase the children's sense of belonging, as well as offering a sense of security, even in an insecure environment – such as a hostile immigration environment, when a family emigrates into an unwelcoming country. However, cultural beliefs and practices have to be reconciled with what is in the best interests of the children in a family as these are defined by the laws of the land in a particular country. In the

Mental health, mental illness, the family   11

United Kingdom the laws protecting children, as well as professional ethics, require that the best interests of the children come first, wherever the courts or professional workers have to be involved about family decisions. So some beliefs, particularly promoted by extreme religious sects, or other closed groups, whether religious or secular, as well as cultural traditions which discourage mixing with other children, may inevitably limit the children's access to outside activities and positive relationships. This can then act as a constraint on their building resilience to problems in the family. While many children in regular family circumstances will have the resilience to manage different restrictions related to closed family groups, when there is mental illness in the family the restrictions may well act against the best interests of the development of the children. This is because children living with parents with mental illness particularly need as many outside contacts, activities and fun as possible to balance the sometimes extreme constrictions and intrusions which the mental illness puts on their lives. In addition they are often in reversed roles – being the protectors and carers of the family, even if not acknowledged as such by parents or professionals. As a result of being excluded from other sources of fun and freedom they are more vulnerable to extreme emotional responses in a parent with whom they may feel they are emotionally 'locked in'. It then becomes especially important that they have opportunities to develop and express their own independent thinking in a creative and age appropriate way.

Some potential problems of family 'closeness'

Consider some of the more negative forces which may keep people living in, or being more involved in, family life than is in their best developmental interests. The most obvious is economic. That can be a force on its own, or it can also become connected to other powerful forces like feelings of guilt, or a sense that someone else has the power to decide. If as a child, or as a girl or young woman, you have not been allowed to progress your education – whether for economic or other reasons such as cultural beliefs, traditions, or just because those with power in the family do not allow it – then your earning capacity will be less and you are more likely to be trapped at home for economic reasons. Similarly, if as a child or young person you have been told that you are responsible for the family's economic misfortunes, for example because your mother or father cared for you instead of going out to work, or even because your actual birth was in a sense blamed for your parent's illness or change of life-style, then without thinking you may actually accept the guilt that is being heaped on you.

Guilt can be a very strong force which may make young people in particular feel trapped, and that they have no way to 'leave it behind'. That guilt can then become a strong force keeping young people in the family. Of course that can happen with things other than money. Children can be made to feel that they are responsible for the happiness or sadness of either or both parents, and that what happens to the parent's mind depends on themselves. Or one parent can even add to that burden by making the child feel responsible in a way which is probably that parent's responsibility; 'You must always be kind and loving to your mother and not worry her by being upset or angry', or even responsible for the state of the parent's relationship: 'You mustn't say anything to Mum, cos you don't want Mum and Dad to argue with each other do you?' The child may then feel driven by a sense that he or she 'owes something'. Often that 'something' can be very difficult to define, and there is of course no logical reason for suggesting that it is a child's responsibility. However, that idea – that the child is somehow responsible – can very easily become the rule, spoken or unspoken, in some families, often without the parents intending it.

Similarly the effects of the wider family – grandparents, uncles, aunts and cousins, as well as other adults the family have chosen to give the title and status of uncle or aunt – can be forces to help free children to think and feel more independently, or alternatively they can become opposite forces pressurising the children to fit in with those adults' particular conventions and beliefs.

Loyalty as a source of security or as a trap

It is only natural that when people feel unsafe and under threat they tend to close ranks, to try to keep all their relationships and thinking inside the family, and often feel suspicious of influences from outside. This can then sometimes lead to a habit of rigid and suspicious behaviour. This suspicious rigidity can further lead a parent to demand – sometimes openly, but often by silent attitudes – that the children should be 'loyal' and adopt a similar restricted approach to life outside the family as do the parents. If the child accepts this attitude it can then mean that he or she does not engage fully with activities with others of a similar age or make close friends. Again, if there is mental illness in the family this is more likely to have a damaging effect on a child, and restrict his or her need for development of their own minds, skills and relationships.

However, as a parent and many times grandparent myself – as well as previously a child who witnessed many parental conflicts – I do know that however hard we try to keep affection separate from loyalty, we all muddle them up sometimes. There must be very few parents who have not at some time said something like 'one day you will realise that I am right about XXX, and that if you do this/go there/say this or that you will just be being ungrateful and hurting me and the family'. The fact is that most children are very 'forgiving' and can just be lightly amused at Mum or Dad 'banging on again'. This highlights how much *humour* can also be a very powerful force to help children develop resilience. However, when there is mental illness in the family, what parents say tends to get taken much more seriously, healthy humour is often much more difficult to achieve and humour may be squashed for fear of disrupting a fragile situation or in order to keep the peace.

Mental health, mental illness, the family 13

What kinds of things can make people feel unsafe and under threat?

These can be forces *outside* the family such as unemployment, local neighbour conflicts, racism or other forms of prejudice, and particularly feeling unwelcome as an immigrant. Alternatively, it can be factors affecting the people *inside* the family, such as any kind of illness or disability, poverty or a sense of having to keep up appearances when there is high conflict or family breakdown. Also, the more people feel the need to hide things they think will lead to prejudice or stigma – which could also be about illness or disability – the more they believe these will not be understood by friends or neighbours. This is then likely to lead to their feeling more isolated and disadvantaged, which is a particular risk when a parent suffers from mental illness. Stigma and shame, which add to the pressures on the family, are described graphically by different writers in this book.

Specific family 'secrets', about something which is seen as a source of shame or stigma to the family, may particularly lead the children (and also one or more of their parents) to feel cut off from possible friends and school mates. Secrets can have the effect of creating much confusion and of even making things worse, as in this example of a family I worked with.

The parents were first cousins, and the children were under orders that no one should know. The effect was to lead to an expectation that any information about the family should be 'sacred' and not talked about, regardless of whether it had anything to do with the parents' relationship. This led to the parents hiding a minor criminal act by one of their sons, even although the act was something they disapproved of, and would normally report. The effect of the 'secret' was then that the whole family got into trouble and experienced shame and stigma for something quite unrelated to their family relatedness as cousins. So the family 'culture' of hiding the truth had in effect led to one of the son's and then the whole family getting into trouble with the law.

What families need to work towards – some general family living hints for parents

There is evidence that the mental health and development of the children in families is best when certain elements are present – and by definition provided by the main carers, whether these are parents, grandparents, elder siblings or other relatives. These are:

- The relationships are careful, caring, and emotionally warm
- Recognition that different people, genders and age groups may have different opinions, and that the right to have and express different points of view are respected (even although the parents or carers may have to have the final say)

- Different opinions should not be confused with lack of love – beware the idea; 'if you don't agree with me you don't love me (or respect me, care for me)'
- The children are aware of and can mostly accept, or at least respect, the limits or rules that the parent/s or other carers have set and agreed about, and can understand what the rules are, and why
- Rules should be limited to what is necessary for family life to run reasonably smoothly and for the children's safety and development, but should not be unnecessary or excessive
- Children are encouraged to have relationships and activities outside the family as well as close relationships within the family.

These guidelines give pointers to what can help children develop resilience to adversities, and problems they may have to face. As none of us can do it all perfectly, under normal circumstance most children cope easily when their parent or parents slip up a bit. When there is mental illness in an adult in the family, some of the principles, described earlier, can become much more crucial, but at the same time much more difficult for the parents to follow. It can then become much more difficult for children to treat their parent's eccentricities and quirks with humour because:

1 They are likely to watch much more (or too) closely what the ill parents say and do
2 They may be much more vulnerable to being affected by the ill parent's mood and behaviour

Some pointers for all families – to put these principles into practice:

- Encourage debate and discussion of different points of view

This does *not* mean encouraging the children to argue about everything, but *does* mean encouraging them to think about decisions and even be allowed to suggest alternative decisions, even if they *do* need to obey the parent's final decisions for the safe and the smooth running of the family. It is important that a reasonable level of listening to what parents say does not get confused with discouraging the children from thinking out solutions themselves.

Parents also need to...

- Hold your ground about what really matters

The key words here are 'what really matters'. It is helpful for any parent to decide (or if there are two of them agree) on what really matters in terms of their own beliefs, principles and what they think children need. This means

Mental health, mental illness, the family   15

separating out their own key rules and principles from those that do not really matter to them, but have been chosen because of someone else's (such as their own parents) traditions, or assumed public conventions. Obviously, any responsible parent will take a strong position about anything which threatens the safety of their child. Therefore

- Avoid conflicts about unimportant matters or 'bees in bonnets', and choose carefully what you decide to argue about

This means that it is best for parents to try to avoid rules which it is difficult to make understandable to the children, especially if another parent disagrees with them. Imposing rules which cannot make sense to the children will lower their respect for both the rules, as well as for the parent's authority. It is best to try to avoid arguments where one's own pride or 'honour' as a parent feels at stake, and try to stick to those which really matter for the children's safety, development or for the smooth running of the family.

- Warmth and pride are key tools for change, and coldness and shame are potent for remaining stuck

While this is obvious it is often forgotten both by parents, as well as by some of the professionals who try to help them. If, as a parent, you feel good and proud of your family, and see other people as having warm feelings towards you, you are more likely to be willing to consider other points of view and therefore more able to be flexible in your thinking and actions. If on the other hand you feel ashamed or that other people are cold towards you and critical of you, you are more likely to stick to what you know, dig your heels in, and reject any point of view other than your own.

- Avoid confusing disagreements by your children with 'betrayal' of affection

A lot of pride, based on upholding a particular set of family traditions with a preoccupation about 'family unity', rather than pride about the children as they actually are, can lead to an emotionally cold or even cruel atmosphere. When children are encouraged and supported in developing their own points of view, and in thinking for themselves, even when they may hold a number of different views from their parents, then home life encourages the development of their minds. This, in turn, helps to develop their resilience to distressing events. However, when a child does disagree with his or her parent it is important that the parent does not confuse this potentially positive behaviour with disloyalty, or with not loving the parent. It can of course mean that a child may disagree with the parent about some rule or aspect of discipline, but provided the child can respect and follow the 'important'

16   Alan Cooklin

rules, this does not need to be a bad thing. As discussed later, this can be doubly important for a child who is being affected by the negative thinking of a parent with mental illness.

- Be open about your own feelings as much as possible

Many parents may be fearful about their children seeing their true feelings, either about themselves or a sibling, or about other aspects of the parent's life, including the parent's own childhood experiences. Often it can be helpful for a child to see clearly how his/her parents feel about things, provided the child's own emotional life is not 'flooded' by that of the parent. To learn about the parent's feelings may be better than just trying to impose rules which make no sense to the child. Obviously, it is important not to overload or invade a child or young person with what they cannot use, or what may confuse him or her – such as the parent's sexual life.

- Beware of your child becoming a 'parent' or 'couple caretaker'

This is not easy and not always possible, especially if the child or young person has caring duties for one of *the parents* or for the household. If that has to be the case then it is important to acknowledge the work the child is doing, as well as the fact that when doing the work s/he is not really in a child's role. It is important that as a parent you do not feel ashamed of what your child is contributing, can be open about it and celebrate your child's achievement, at the same time as trying to minimise those things he or she has to do which are not appropriate for a child of that age. However, it is very important that your child is not asked or expected to mediate between the parents, or take a position on one side or another about the parent's relationship with each other.

- If the parents are in serious conflict or separated then work hard to avoid the child/young person becoming a 'go between' or communicator with, or about, the other parent

Letting the child become a 'go between' or asking the child to pass messages between the parents, or even asking the child questions about the other parent – which can easily happen when the parents are separated – is one of the most damaging things that can happen to the child's emotional development. This is because it trains him or her to become a sort of referee of others, while ignoring the skills he or she needs to learn about relationships for him or herself (see Chapters 7 and 8).

Take account of your particular family structure. For example:

- In a lone parent family, be aware of the possible pressure on the child to become the parent's principal friend and emotional support

Lone parent families are now the second most common family structure in the United Kingdom at 22%, with married couple led families at 60%. There can be a temptation to think and talk about the lone parent family as though it were the same as a couple led family. There are positive elements in lone parent families; there is no confusion of authority between the parents, the child is not caught up in conflicts between the parents, there is a much lower risk of violence in the home and often there is the freedom and some need for the child to learn more household skills and responsibilities. What the child lacks in the lone parent family is the value of different perspectives and points of view between adults, where the child may also find it easier to develop his or her own mind and feel less pressure for loyalty to a common 'view', because the intensity of the relationship with a single parent is diluted. With two parents attention has to be shared between the children and each other. It can be useful for a parent living alone to be aware of and maximise these positive elements of having just one parent, as well as to be aware of and try to mitigate the negative ones. This will obviously be easier if a parent on their own does not suffer loneliness and has emotional supports from friends or 'outside' partners.

- In a re-partnered ('step') family, recognise and acknowledge the difference from a 'first time round' intact family

When parents from two separating or divorcing families get together to create a step-family, the upset and pain of the separation and divorce process often lead the new couple to feel they must try to recreate something which almost pretends to be the same as the original families one or both of them had before. This can then lead a step-parent to feel they must try to be exactly as (they imagine) the original mother or father should have been. This can also mean that they do not acknowledge how confusing the (usually) unwelcome changes in arrangements and authority will be for their step-children. It is important to recognise that the situation is now *different*, and that any authority that a step-parent has over step-children must be specifically delegated by the original parent. Also this authority must only remain as long as that parent delegates it, and respect has to be earned by the new step-parent rather than assumed. This all needs to be made clear to the children from both sides of the previous families.

- In a re-partnered ('step') family, openly discuss the children's experience of changes in their ordinal positions (i.e. who is oldest, youngest, middle)

It is important for both step-parents, as well as the original parents, to be aware of, and respectful of, the changes the divorce or separation has made to the different children's views of themselves and of their rights, privileges and responsibilities. One example of that change is when an eldest child is suddenly treated as a younger child because of the arrival of older step-children, or conversely that a youngest child suddenly finds that he or she is no longer the youngest and is expected to treat another young step-child as more in need of nurture. All these changes, as well as how they may affect the lives and feelings of all the children, are best discussed openly with the children.

General principles for professionals doing family work, relevant to all families

It can be useful to:

1 Get the family together, if you can, or if not at least think about all the members in the family, even if they are not in the room with you
2 Help the family recognise positives in each other, particularly in those so far only described in negative ways

When people in families get stuck, in solving problems, in responding to changes, and particularly changes in children's development or growing up, then very fixed, often negative, or 'stuck' attitudes can develop about particular family members. This especially can happen in families where there is mental illness, because the illness both makes everyone on edge and interferes with the usual ways of solving problems.

A professional who thinks about what is good as well as what is going wrong, and insists on eliciting different positive views of *all* the family members from *all* of them is more likely to be able to help the family change those fixed images.

3 Assume that there may be different and valid points of view between different family members

This may seem obvious, and in fact most parents from many cultures will – if asked specifically – agree that there should be the freedom in *the family* for different points of view on many topics. However, in the reality of the actual relationships, and specifically the power relationships between men and women and between generations, that freedom to think differently may not be obvious. The danger for a professional is then to assume that there is a unified 'family' point of view. Rather, *the professional* needs to help *the family* negotiate an acceptance of the existence of possible different points of view.

4 Challenge any of the observed assumptions around 'if you don't agree with me you don't love me'

Mental health, mental illness, the family   19

This point has already been touched on. Particularly in situations in which a child has had to take on more responsibility than is optimal for his or her developmental age, then it is very important that *the child* is encouraged to voice and respect his or her own thinking. In that case it can be very destructive to *the child's* development if his or her different thoughts are interpreted as either disloyalty or as a lack of, or withdrawal of, love.

5   It is a good idea to challenge assumptions about power and rights – in the adults or in children

Although in the United Kingdom there is no legal entity of *parent's rights*, there are responsibilities which as a result do give parents certain rights in order to carry out the tasks of bringing up the children. When power and authority are seen by all as for the benefit of the children's development, it can then be benign and positive. In some traditions – whether related to religion, race or culture or just the tradition of that family (or even the tradition of just one member of that family) – the exercise of power by one gender over another, or the unthinking and automatic exercise of power over the children, can be constraining and detrimental to the childrens' emotional and educational development. The professional then needs to find ways to open up discussion within the family about the bases of power and authority.

6   Demonstrate that some level of conflict can be faced usefully

Of course violent conflict is not useful or safe within any family. However, the capacity to reconcile different points of view and to resolve conflict is an important skill for children to learn in their family. Sometimes parents have had experience of violent conflict during their own growing up, or have grown up in families in which any disagreement is greeted with fear and disapproval. The professional may then need to get some acknowledgement of *different* points of view, and to demonstrate that these can in the long term actually lead to more creative, and less fearful, outcomes.

7   To challenge invalidation of experience – that is remarks such as saying to a child 'you did not really mean this or that...you did not feel upset, sorry, sad, cross, angry...you don't care for me etc.'

This is perhaps the most difficult of three principles to define and illustrate, if only because when parents do not validate their children's experience or actively invalidate it, they are usually unaware of doing it. Obviously parents do not want too many feelings expressed which might 'rock the boat' of the smooth running of family life. The problem is that often children offer up expressions of feelings about all sorts of things to their parents, not necessarily assuming that that parent can remove the feeling or solve the

20 Alan Cooklin

problem, but just to get their perception of what happened to be recognised, and their feelings acknowledged. That is an important part of emotional development and plays an important role in the child learning to regulate his or her own emotions as he or she develops. Therefore, if the parent even unintentionally says something like 'you did not really think or feel that, or you had no reason to think or feel that because what you saw and felt was untrue' that can over time seriously undermine the child acquiring the skills for regulating their own emotions.

8   Create an environment where it is easier for a child to think and respond rather than avoid any self-expression

Many children are alert to try to give adults what they think the adult wants. That is something they have often learnt from school and to some extent from parents. As a result they will be reluctant to engage in a conversation or express any personal point of view or feelings unless they can be confident that they know what is expected. As a result many children may find 'open' questions – 'how do you feel about…' – as actually inhibiting, and they may freeze up and feel almost paralysed to respond. The adult (especially a stranger or professional) will then often become anxious and, if the child is silent or withdrawn, may respond by 'over-talking'. Many children may find it easier to respond to multiple choice questions such as 'So was it that you feared Dad might get angry, or he might get upset, and was it that you just held everything in so you didn't get too upset…or are those all wrong?' In fact that way of questioning will encourage confidence or courage in some children, who can then respond 'It wasn't any of those…it was just that…etc.'. Obviously it is important that a professional demonstrates, in their choices of answer, some awareness of what a child might be experiencing in that particular situation.

Where possible avoid:

1   Making any assumptions that the way the family has defined a problem in one individual is a useful one

When parents and/or children seek outside help it is often surprising how much they at first appear to agree on how the problem should be defined – e.g. this child or this parent is or is not at fault. In fact even the person who appears to be being blamed for the problem often seems to agree that he or she *is* to blame. Often these very *fixed* attitudes have continued for a long time, despite the fact that that way of looking at things has continued to leave them all stuck. A professional who is asked to help needs to seek a different way of thinking about the family relationships if they are to be useful in helping the family move forward.

Mental health, mental illness, the family 21

2   Accepting any one person's definition of what is happening/has happened

Part of helping the family members to find a different way to think about their relationships and problems is to show that each person can have a different point of view, all of which may have some validity.

3   Colluding in conflict avoidance of uncomfortable topics

Often how people think about their relationships can become very stuck when they fear that any disagreement or conflict will in some way be dangerous and either 'break up the family' or at least will upset the way the family members have become used to talking about themselves – e.g. 'We are all very close' when this ignores some serious differences of opinion. A professional then needs to help them see that different points of view can be helpful and constructive.

4   Assuming that those who speak little or none do not have a valid view
    to express

Often conflict in a family is avoided by only one or two people speaking for the others. When those who speak little or not at all are encouraged to express their own point of view – e.g. this could be a 'silent' child or a 'silent' parent – then it can help all the family members begin to think differently.

These few principles may be familiar to many family members and practitioners, even if they have not always been easy to implement. As I have suggested this difference can result when people see threats to their safety and stability, whether this threat is seen as coming from inside the family or outside; people then tend to stick to their old 'traditional' ways of managing family relationships, ways that have come from either their own family or cultural traditions, which may however have got them into a tangle in the first place.

Part 2: some ideas about health, and physical and mental illness in family and other relationships

First, what is meant by illness or disease. These are words we all know and yet they can have very strong feelings attached to them, as well as much confusion. We can feel sympathy for someone suffering a disease, because it hurts or harms them and it is usually seen as being out of their control, and not at all their 'fault'. We also know that some people may say 'I am ill' or 'you are making me ill' when they are experiencing extreme emotional upset. In fact the word 'Illness' in the fifteenth century used to mean 'moral weakness' or even 'wickedness'. Unfortunately there can often still be such questions about understandable and distressing states of weakness – 's/he is just putting it on...needs to pull him/herself together...stop thinking about his/her self so much' etc. when some people talk about mental illness. If they are not seen as ill by family friends and others, then they may be seen as just 'weak' – showing 'bad' behaviour or even just 'bad'. In some cultures this 'moral' idea may be taken even further, so that the ill person's behaviour is explained as their being 'possessed by evil spirits' (Chapters 5 and 12). If on the other hand the ill person is recognised as ill, then does that mean they have to be perceived by family friends and community as a totally passive victim of the illness and have no responsibility for any of their behaviour? Mental illness can change what people feel and see around themselves, as well as how they think about what they see and feel. Nevertheless, many people struggle to maintain some responsibility for how they feel and behave. A significant number of parents who suffer from mental illness have recounted how they can often control much of what they say, as well as how they behave, when they know it is affecting their children. Our tendency to think about a whole range of physical illnesses from infections to cardiac, respiratory and gastrointestinal disorders as something being done to the person, where he or she is a kind of helpless victim, is rarely the whole truth. We all know that much of what happens to our health, and how we live, is partly or potentially under our control, although less so the more the family is blighted by poverty. An obvious example of this is the huge changes in lung cancer and respiratory diseases since people took on board the risks of smoking. So, in that sense, in both mental and physical illnesses there are aspects we cannot control, and aspects over which we can, if the circumstances are right, exert some control and take some responsibility for what happens to us.

So why do we get so confused about illness when we are discussing mental illness? Part of this confusion may be because of our tendency to split the mind and the body when we think of illness. Someone who is very emotionally changeable, with extremes of expressed emotion, someone who is angry or depressed, confused and having difficulty managing their life, is most often seen as emotionally weak, or even undeserving of sympathy, rather than ill – even when a level of mental illness may be the basis of their behaviour. That way of thinking has been much challenged by the recent campaigns against the stigma associated with mental illness. However, many people who behave in unpredictable ways are still seen as weaker, and also as a result often see themselves that way. If, however, we think of the mind and body as one entity, working together, then thinking about mental and physical illness in these separate ways loses its meaning. If all categories of mental and physical behaviour do not have to be split up and one can then see that extreme physical and mental states and behaviours can be common in ordinary everyday life, then mental illness itself becomes a less frightening idea. However, these states may become more visibly extreme in mental illness. This is illustrated later in what I have called the 'Wheel of causality'. *That is a way to think about causes, although the effects of mental illness – whatever the cause – can still be devastating* to the person experiencing it, as well as to those close to him or her.

Both mental and physical experiences are peculiar to each individual

Consider how our brains are responding to, and constantly processing all of our experiences – physical and mental – in ways which make those experiences understandable to us as humans. The way the brain does this is probably different from most or all other animals, because it allows us to think about the things that happen to us, give them categories, such as good or bad, construct some kind of explanation of what the experience means or its cause, as well as reach some kind of conclusion about how to respond: perhaps to try to increase it if pleasurable, or reduce it if not. For some experiences, such as pain or major discomfort, nearly all of us will go through a similar process and reaction, although we may find different meanings or explanations for the pain. On the other hand different people can feel quite differently about similar experiences, give them a different meaning and react quite differently. So very loud music can be pleasurable, and generate good feelings inside some people, and they will think of it as positive and good. Even if it harms their hearing over time, they may want to stay close to it. For other people it may be unpleasant, or even painful, and they may try to move away from the sound as quickly as possible, an example of how we may think differently about the same *physical* experience.

The same thing will happen with a *mental* experience, where different people can experience the same things in different or even opposite ways. So one person may enjoy feeling peaceful and quiet, with little happening around him or her, whilst another may find that boring and isolating. However because mental (including emotional) experiences come partly from inside our-selves, and partly provoked by our relationships with others, how we think about the meanings and explanations, and how we all respond, will vary in a more complex way. For example, a demand for an affectionate hug or cuddle may be seen by one person as a welcome show of love, whilst it may be seen by another as a demand and an expression of a wish to control. One person may experience a flood of ideas as an exciting source of help to move forward on a project, whilst another person may experience it as being overwhelming.

Because medical knowledge is so easily available on the internet, many people can now have a picture in their minds of how their *body* works, and by monitoring their physical feelings with this knowledge in mind can often make more sense of their physical experiences. However, this mental map of the body commonly does not include, as perhaps it should, a map of how the *mind* works and what affects that working. As a result it may be less obvious that how we feel and think can affect not only our brain development and functioning, but also how our body works, and its vulnerability to illnesses of many kinds. So when we think about our bodies we need to think about our minds and vice-versa.

Developing a mental map

Because thinking about mental processes is often more complicated than thinking about physical processes, and because habits of bringing up children often do not encourage them to develop their own mental map, there can sometimes be a tendency to think and talk about mental processes as though they were physical. Often language encourages this, as it offers many physical metaphors for mental experiences such as 'my heart dropped'[2] when someone is shocked or very disappointed or 'I had butterflies in the stomach' when someone is very anxious. Because many people find the idea of disturbed mental processes or mental illness to be frightening, they may express their distress or even perceive it, and believe in it as something physical. They may also see this way of talking about what they feel as being less subject to stigma or feeling ashamed.

As a ten year old caring for his father on his own, Aron had to face this confusion on his own. He had never heard the term *Young Carer*, although that was what he was, and he was confused about his father's illness and treatment, as the mental aspects of it had never been discussed with him. As a result he was often very confused about how to respond to his father's complaints about his heart. His father did suffer a mild heart complaint, which was stable and of no medical concern. He also suffered severe depressive episodes – with negative thoughts, low energy or motivation to do anything – obsessive compulsive disorder – with obsessive negative thoughts and rituals, as well as occasional psychotic episodes – when he would become suspicious, paranoid, as well as deluded about events around himself. As no one had explained any of this to him, all he heard from his father was about his heart complaint, which he described as more severe and painful whenever he felt more depressed or distressed. With no explanation a child can see a parent as unhappy, bad tempered, or withdrawn or perhaps complaining of some physical pain or problem, with no map to make sense of it. Alternatively the child might see the parent behaving strangely, overexcited or very suspicious, and *doing* things the child cannot make sense of.

Unfortunately, in our current cultures, many parents and well-meaning professionals may feel they should *not* try to explain to children what is happening to their parent in this situation, believing that this is to protect the child from hearing distressing information. This is a strange idea, given that the child is likely to be more distressed from seeing or hearing the parent's upset *without* any understanding of what is happening. In fact there is good evidence that children can manage all kinds of stressful or even traumatic events the more they can understand the source of their stress. There is also specific evidence that children who have a good understanding of a parent's mental illness show less mental health disturbance in themselves.[3,4]

The importance of a good explanation for children – a message to parents and professionals

So when a parent develops a mental illness it can be helpful for both children and their parents to have a realistic 'map', a model of what is happening to the person's mind, to help them make sense of what is or has happened.

26   Alan Cooklin

Unfortunately, both because of people's fear of and the stigma still associated with mental illness, the explanations in both public and private talk and 'gossip', as well as in the media, are often very misleading. People often talk of 'it runs in families' – as though inheritance was the main or even only cause – leaving the children feeling they were the subject of a kind of 'curse' from which they could not escape. Alternatively children are often given an explanation such as 'it is caused by a chemical imbalance in the brain' which does not offer a child or parent any map of what may have happened and why. This one is also very misleading, as it gives the impression of being scientific, when it is not. Some would call this kind of explanation as based on 'scientism' – or pretend science – rather than true science.

So consider how a clear and *visual* explanation of mental illness in a parent might make the experience less frightening for a child.

First it can help the child to feel less helpless when things are difficult. By having a picture in his or her own mind the child can both feel that things make more sense, and by understanding the process the child may feel reassured that the episode of illness can be time limited, and does not have to continue 'for ever'.

Second it can help the child to look at the ill parent in a more *objective* manner. Obviously how much a child can be objective about his or her parent's behaviour will be dependent on the child's age. However, in the Kidstime workshops we have found that even some children as young as three years old seem to gain relief when they have a picture of, and a name for, their parent's episodes of disturbed behaviour. Sometimes they repeat the name and talk of the picture more as a kind of mantra which they use to reassure themselves.

As a result when things are very upsetting, the child will be able to see this as part of an understandable illness, rather than his or her fault. In addition the teams running the Kidstime Workshops[5–7] have found that by helping a child to be aware of what is going on *inside* their parent, when that child is living with the parent's behaviour and emotions, he or she is more likely to be able to keep some genuine affection for the ill parent, without having to be so caught up in the disturbing things their parent may say or do.

Feeling caught up in a parent's mind often means to a child that s/he must be at least partly responsible for the parent's illness, and that therefore s/he must almost accept and join in with how that parent sees the world. A child may need to be helped to separate his or her own mind more from that parent's mind before s/he can develop their own mind as a separate entity. This can then allow that child to have their own view of the relationship with the ill parent. Many parents are quite unaware of how much most children feel it is in some way their fault or responsibility when things go wrong in the family. When they can recognise this, and acknowledge it to their child, such recognition can play an important part in helping the child to feel freed up to use his or her own mind more constructively. This process could be called *recognising, labelling and confirming* the child's experience.

So what is a good explanation?

A good explanation needs to be as neutral as possible, not blaming the ill parent, but also not denying the human effects of the illness, and particularly the way the illness interacts with the person's relationships – in both directions. It may be useful for parents to know that how well they can function as good parents is not necessarily connected to their particular diagnosis. Some parents with quite mild mental illness may have great difficulty in meeting their children's emotional needs, whilst some with diagnoses of more major mental illness may function very well as parents during their well periods, and even struggle to do their best during the bad times. Even when their ability to function as good parents *is* undermined by the illness, it does not have to be permanent and can recover when they recover from the illness (Chapter 4).

However, a parents' recovery of their ability to act as good parents will be much encouraged if they can talk openly with their children about what happened to them when they were ill. So in the work we have been doing in the charity Our Time we have not focused so much on explanations of specific diagnoses, but rather on how each parent can function practically, socially and emotionally – despite their illness (Chapters 4 and 5).

We have learnt much from working with a large number (in excess of 800) families over the course of nearly 20 years. An important piece of our learning has been that a good explanation to children needs to be visually imagined in the child's mind for it to have meaning. It also needs to offer the child an image (almost a kind of video) of what may be happening in the parent's mind. This can then help the child not to feel so involved in those aspects of the parent's mental processes which they can now better understand are not really their business. An example of an explanation is given later in this chapter, both through an exercise and via reference to the short film on the Our Time website, 'When a parent has a mental illness…'.[2]

Both parents and professionals need to know that explanations to both children and older young people may need to be repeated, sometimes many times, because when children are having to cope with high levels of emotion, it can be very difficult to take in new ideas, even if they are welcome ones. These explanations also need to challenge children's irrational self-blame, so they do not need to take outbursts of anger or sadness by their ill parent so personally, even although sometimes these outbursts will in fact be directed at the child.

What is known about what triggers a mental illness?

Professionals of different disciplines continue to argue about how to think about mental illness. Some stress the vulnerabilities that people inherit, whilst others focus on how each of us responds to different stresses at different points in our lives, as well as the social, cultural, racial and religious influences on how we interpret and respond to these stresses.

Some have called this kind of argument 'Nature versus Nurture', as though one side of the argument needs to win. This kind of thinking can be misleading and may have been responsible for some of the serious misunderstandings about mental illness. Many people have now talked instead about the Gene-Environment interaction that causes mental illness. This is better. It means that we accept that all of us are born with some strengths and some weaknesses carried through our genes, and that some combination of particular stressors with particular inherited vulnerabilities can – again only in some situations – lead to illness. But even this may not give a full picture of how that would work.

So, what follows is an attempt to create a fuller picture. It may seem a bit more complicated, but trying to oversimplify things can often lead to misunderstandings and make things *more* difficult to understand.

Imagine a big wheel turning. It could be like an old fashioned water wheel in a mill or even a wheel on a bicycle turned upside down. Then imagine different forces acting to turn the wheel at different points. At each point the different forces will make the wheel turn faster.

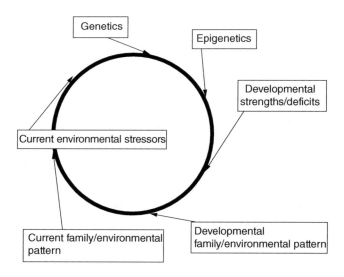

The wheel of causality.

So if we now think of the wheel as our mental processes, the speed of the wheel can represent either good (healthy) or bad (overwhelmed) mental processes. The diagram shows six forces which can be positive or negative.

Mental health, mental illness, the family   29

Genetics refers to the effects of our genes on how we feel and behave. Our genes are like strips of very complicated 'memory' – a bit like computer memory on a hard disk – which are all held together on long strips of material called chromosomes. We inherit different parts of these from each of our biological parents, and they control what we inherit from the nucleus – at the centre of – each cell in our body. Apart from one or two rare genetic illnesses, such as Huntington's Chorea, our genes do not carry a particular mental illness from one generation to the next. It is true that you may see some mental illnesses being more common in one family than another. However, the effect of what is inherited is very complicated. Say someone in your family has had bouts of depression and manic excitement, which may well have led to a diagnosis of Bipolar disorder. They may have inherited a tendency to unstable moods. However, those mood changes are likely to have also been influenced by how calm or erratic their parents' moods were when they were first learning about their emotions. This may have led to a very un-calm family atmosphere, which, in turn, will have also affected the stability of their own moods again. What our genes can carry are our particular strengths and weaknesses. So some will be stronger at maths, whilst others will be better at art or music. Some may find strong emotions difficult to process, and tend to avoid situations which stir these up, whilst others may actually seek out situations which bring strong emotions and passions. Similarly, some of us may easily get upset tummy or bowels, whilst others may get colds and infections more easily.

Epigenetics is a relatively new science, and we are still learning how it works. Basically it means that some things we do in our lives – such as drinking a lot of alcohol – can have an effect on our unborn children, grandchildren, or even great grandchildren. This effect may be good or bad. It may even for example give the later generations some protection from the effects of alcohol. However it is not inherited directly through our genes but through a number of other parts of the chromosomes or other parts of cells.

Developmental Strengths and Deficits refers partly to the effects of genetics and epigenetics, plus the effect of our early environment – whether from our relationship with our mother, father, or other carers – on the strengths we develop in our early years, as well as the things we have more difficulty with. So as a result some children will race ahead with their school work, but be shy and find it difficult to make friends. Others will find traditional school work difficult and be good at sports or arts subjects.

Developmental Family and Environmental Pattern refers to our family and other contexts where we experience emotional relationships – which could be school, sports teams, clubs, etc., and the effect these have on our emotional and mental development – good or bad. This pattern can be made up from very small and simple things, repeated again and again over time, like someone understanding how you felt when something upsetting or puzzling happened to you, rather than laughing at you or criticising you. Or it might just be someone noticing and appreciating small helpful things you did or said inside the family. When you actually think about your family it can be surprising to realise that you can probably almost guess how a conversation in the family would develop, who would say what, in what tone and even how the conversation would end: with agreement or understanding, with stony silence or with someone flouncing out of the room. Although you could guess what would happen, as presumably so could the others, it is quite likely that none of them was aware of that or had thought about it, before say someone outside the family has pointed it out.

Current Family and Environmental Pattern as a grown up may be a bit more surprising. People tend to think of their family experiences as part of growing up and in the past. However, even as an adult the same or a similar pattern may still be continuing. Many mature adults find that although they are adults in their usual lives, when they go 'home' to visit their 'old' family they often find themselves, as well as the others, behaving in similar ways to when they were children or adolescents. Sometimes that can be pleasant or funny, but sometimes, depending on how they felt as they grew up, they may find it embarrassing, it may make them feel less confident and it may even stir up some of the same feelings they had as a child. For some people re-experiencing some of those old family patterns – and being reminded how they felt as children – especially if the relationships *now* are very similar to the relationships *then* – can be quite disturbing and can make some of their current life stresses feel much worse.

Current Environmental Stressors refer both to upsetting things coming from inside either the mind or body of the person, and those coming from family and other relationships, from work, or even more from *lack of* work, from social pressures such as stigma over race, gender choices, sexual preferences, disability. It includes physical illness and positive or negative physical sensations. In fact it includes everything that a person experiences from both inside themselves interacting with all aspects of their outside environment.

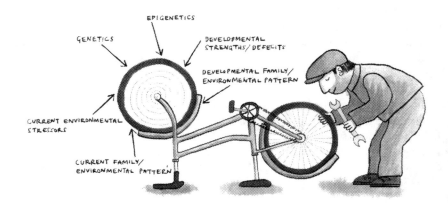

Any of the six factors can drive our mental processes either positively or negatively. One reason it is drawn as a wheel is because most of these factors can also affect each other and increase or decrease the overall effect. So obviously your genetics will affect the possibility that you may also inherit some traits through epigenetics, and both will affect how people in your family respond to you, and as a result affect how you experience the family atmosphere. Old family patterns will affect how you experience current ones, and all of these will, in turn, affect how different current stressors affect you. So all of this is happening to all of us. The effects can be both strengthening and stressing, but we do not all develop mental illness – even although we know that nearly 50% of us will develop some level of mental illness at some point in our lives. So what distinguishes a mental illness from just extreme emotions or mental states?

Learning skills and techniques to regulate our emotions

All of us will sometimes experience extreme emotions, but the question is what tips those over from something we can manage – however upsetting they be – into illness? It is true that some people will have a stronger tendency to develop a particular illness, but a tendency does not mean they have to develop it. One way to think about it is to consider the *skills* we develop, as we grow up, for *managing and regulating our emotions.* We usually learn these techniques both through observing how people we love – parents, carers, brothers and sisters, or friends – manage their emotions, plus through these people recognising the kinds of emotions we have felt, and helping us find words for those emotions. It is through being able to put feelings into words, so that they can be understood as having meaning, that we also learn not to be so scared of our emotions. As that happens our emotions become more manageable, and more a part of ourselves that we can find acceptable. For that process to happen we need to feel that our emotions have been acceptable to another person – usually a parent or carer – and being helped to find words for them, just like when a parent says to a little child having a tantrum or being glum; 'you are cross today... or sad etc.', is an important part of that process. For people who have had difficulty learning these skills, for whatever reason, they may have tried to learn to just control their emotions instead. This can work up to a point, but it can sometimes have a negative effect on some parts of their body, which will be different for different people. It can also become an enormous strain when their stress levels become too high. A parent with mental illness can be part of an emotional environment in which it is difficult for a child to learn about, and learn how to regulate, his or her emotions. How much this happens will depend in part on the child's age when the parent first developed the illness, and there are also many other situations in which this can happen.

32 Alan Cooklin

Here are four common effects of not having learnt how to regulate one's emotions positively:

1 Choosing *extreme control* of one's emotions as a way to try to regulate them
2 This can lead to *negative effects on one's body* and make one vulnerable to certain illnesses
3 Becoming more *vulnerable* to stressors
4 Experiencing emotions and moods often in an extreme form, and sometimes being out of control

The healing power of good relationships

Fortunately, people can still learn more positive ways to regulate their emotions later in life, either through later positive relationships with a spouse or partner or through various kinds of therapeutic experience. The potentially healing power of a supportive spouse in this situation was described by Sir Michael Rutter in 1980.[8] When this happens it can also lessen the effects of what are often called 'Psycho-somatic' illnesses such as some stomach and bowel disorders, some skin and respiratory disorders and many others. As we develop more positive ways to regulate emotions we can then often become less vulnerable to stressors.

When feelings, thoughts and moods become more than a person can manage

Let's now think what can happen when high levels of emotion, thoughts and other forms of arousal tip over into illness. Both our bodies and our minds have a great capacity to adapt to changes. For example our body temperature can stay almost the same even if we move from sub-zero temperatures into maximum tropical temperatures. Similarly, we have all to some extent developed techniques – to varying degrees – which allow us to adapt to unexpected new situations without changing our whole way of thinking and personality. This works up to a point, but each of us will have a point where our coping strategy turns upside down and becomes another stressor. For example if our mind and body are used to responding to sudden stressful changes by going into what has been termed fight/flight mode, then our heart rate increases, our adrenaline level increases, our blood supply to parts that do not immediately need it – such as our gut – is diverted to heart, muscles and brain, and we become hyper-alert. This is a response of the body which prepares us for 'flight or fight' to face a particular crisis, and for that incident it can be protective. However, if this continues for too long or happens too frequently, and this becomes our 'normal' state, then what was a protective state can lead to a more vulnerable state. In that state our heart is overworked, we produce too much adrenaline, as well as another hormone called cortisol, which together can have negative effects on our bodies, and our hyper-alertness can make us hyper-sensitive, suspicious or even paranoid. A positive strategy for an acute episode has led to the opposite effect if repeated long term.

Using the wheel metaphor, the wheel can spin too fast for us to control it any longer. So, one could then define that state of things, spinning out of control, as a mental illness. Of course, it will affect different people differently and while some people will be able to withstand enormous levels for stress before it all goes out of control, for some it will happen much more quickly and in response to lower levels of stress.

An approach learnt through the work with the Kidstime Workshops, and ways that professionals, parents and children themselves could use the ideas

In the work with the Kidstime multi-family workshops over some 20 years the kind of explanations described earlier has been a central part of the work.

The model of explanation used is illustrated with a group of children in the Our Time video (https://ourtime.org.uk/resource/when-a-parent-has-a-mental-illness). This film also used an exercise with the children to illustrate how people can cope with overload and also:

1   How anyone can become overwhelmed – in this case by voices
2   How when we are in a mentally healthy state we can select which voices and sounds we choose to hear, so that we do not become overwhelmed

34   Alan Cooklin

Below is an illustration of the exercise used in the film:

> Stand in a room and all talk at once. The amount of sound will be all the noise each one of you made added up. One friend should be selected (without the others knowing) to keep saying the name of one of the others, but no louder than the others. He or she will, probably hear their name quite soon, even though the other sounds were louder.

This can be done with a name or trying to describe a film or a story. The explanation then continues:

> This is because our brains can sift out or sieve out or filter out (whichever word you like best) the things we need to pay attention to. Otherwise our minds would be overloaded and couldn't work at all. We think that there is a part of the brain which does this job. But when someone has a severe mental illness they often can't choose what to hear, so they may hear everything or only bad things. So you can see how their mind could then become very jumbled up with strange thoughts and ideas which don't fit. This can happen for three main reasons:
>
> 1   their brain is just having to cope with too many ideas, worries, feelings and everything, so that it just can't filter out what is important
> 2   because in the person's early life they have had just too many things to cope with, so that they have too many feelings and ideas going round and round inside their mind, to cope with any new ones
> 3   because the bit of the brain that does the sifting out or filtering, is not working properly. We do not know exactly why that happens to some people, but that part of the brain does seem rather more vulnerable in some people. That does not mean that those people have to get a mental illness, because it needs the other stresses for that to happen, and anyway there are ways to protect your brain from 'overload'. In fact if your parent has had a severe mental illness, it is likely that he or she will have been given medication, and one of the ways that that medication can work is by helping the brain 'filter' to cope."

We have found that the advantages of using this model include:

1   The notions of overload and being overwhelmed are easily understood by children
2   It is a model which describes a process in the brain rather than a theory of a cause
3   Having this model in mind allows the child to understand the range of internal and external factors which might lead to such overload

Implications for family and professional intervention: the Kidstime model

As Chineye – then aged 17 – puts it:

> I know the sieve or the filter doesn't explain everything about how it feels or even what happens when someone has a mental illness, but for me it has been a helpful way to understand what might be happening when my mum gets so muddled or confused.

One mother wrote:

> I am so proud of my daughter, she is having a maths test in school tomorrow and just told me she was going to her friend to prepare for the test. She originally planned to invite her classmate to our house – in former times she would have cancelled the learning altogether and looked after me, feeling bad. Now she said "Mum, if your filter is not well at the moment, I better go to Anna – we can do the learning there". This would never have happened without Kidstime. For me it is a great relief to see that my daughter can now concentrate on her needs, not feeling guilty and trying to care for me – this makes me feel much better as well.

Were these ideas were too complicated for young children? A few months after this explanation had been used in one of our joint parent-child

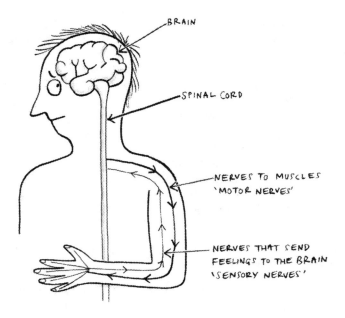

seminars, the children created a drama in which they were the professionals explaining to other children. In one case an eight year old boy and girl – both playing social workers – offered two other young children the following explanation:

> Here's a picture of the brain (and they drew their version of the brain and spinal cord on a white board, which was fairly accurate if quite "original").

> We're going to tell you what happens when someone gets a mental illness. The brain can't stop stuff from coming in. It just fills up and she gets very muddled and can't think of anything else.

As an older young person puts it 'Its so simple really, but it helps you think about what has been unthinkable…it made all the difference to feeling I had a mind myself', and another 'It made all the difference that it was visual, based on pictures so you could have a picture in your own mind instead of just the anger, upset and chaos'.

Another advantage of this model of understanding how parents can become overwhelmed is that it has helped some parents to apply similar thinking to their children – how to protect their child from becoming overwhelmed, when before they were often just paralysed by guilt.

Children see and hear, but may need help to make sense of it

Many parents, as well as some professionals, are often surprised to discover that their children – even from a few years old – can be profoundly affected by their parent's mental state. This is partly because the parents have often tried to hide what was going on in their minds, and are then unaware of how much the children observe. They are also often unaware of how much many children try to take on responsibility to correct things in the family which seem to be out of balance. However, although nearly all children are affected, some will more easily overcome the effects or 'bounce back' from them. This ability in some children has often been called *resilience*. It is an important ability, particularly because there are simple things which parents and professionals can do to help children develop it. [See tips for parents, children and professionals below.]

Resilience: what is it, and how to encourage its development in children

There are many definitions of resilience but a simple one is: 'the ability to be happy, successful, etc. again after something difficult or bad has happened'.

Mental health, mental illness, the family   37

This capacity to 'bounce back', to not be overwhelmed or permanently discouraged by unsolvable problems that a child may face, was first described in relation to adults in the United States who had a mental illness themselves and managed to 'bounce back'.[9,10] The goal here is to consider what may increase the child's own capacity to be aware of his or her own need to protect him or herself and find ways to do it, and to distance him or herself from the invasive elements of the parent's emotions and behaviour. The original focus of the study of psychological resilience by Norman Garmezy[11,12] was of factors in a child of a parent with schizophrenia which might protect him or her from developing the illness. It does not mean that for example living with a parent with mental illness may not be stressful or emotionally painful, and may in some ways be harmful, but it does mean that one child can keep resilient and can recover and make their own life despite the struggles, whilst another child might become demoralized, depressed or give up. Psychological resilience has been defined as the child's capacity to successfully adapt to adversity in ways that do not damage him or her, despite challenging or threatening circumstances. This capacity can be as a result of his or her own individual characteristics or temperament – rather than shared cultural factors – and it may be specifically in relation to particular kinds of adversity, such as parental mental illness, trauma or loss,[13,14] rather than other traumas.

There are many factors which can promote or encourage the development of resilience in a person. One is the sense of feeling loved and confident about oneself as an infant, which may have been the case for many children of parents with mental illness, despite what later happened to that parent. Another factor is whether the child had alternative trusted people he or she could feel safe with to talk to. These people could be another parent, a supportive older sibling, uncle or aunt, or family friend. There are also the obvious things throughout a child's life: continuing supportive adults (teachers and others included), friends and social groups, skills such as football or other sports, athletics, drama and dance groups. The acknowledgement by a trusted adult of the strengths or skills that children have developed, both those listed earlier as well as their caring abilities in the family, can also play an important part in strengthening self-esteem. Children also develop their own individual pathways that help maintain their resilience, made up from good moments in their day or week. Play, being able to go out to play, and even knowing *how* to play if you had not had the habit, has been mentioned by children and professionals alike as important. However other than physical play, being able to play mentally with ideas that have got stuck or emotions that may have become very rigid are also skills that a child in this situation will gain from. Humour has been mentioned before in this chapter as having a protective function, but being able to see the funny side of things or to be more light-hearted about matters that had seemed all too serious is one way in which mental play can begin.

For a child to feel free to become more light-hearted she or he will be helped if there is:

- a trusted adult and/or group of friends with whom she or he can joke or engage in banter – provided it is not at the child's expense – about some aspects of the child's life
- some message or indication from close adults that the child can be affectionate to an ill parent, but does not have to be reverent, or take what the parent says as *sacred*
- some message or indication from an adult that it is OK for the child to be *silly*, or engage in word-play and ideas, and have imaginary worlds of their own
- an adult and/or brothers and sisters, who can engage in thinking and play at the child's own level

There is no one specific way to help a child to appraise, reflect and form a more independent and objective view of themselves and their life. Rather this will depend on the child's level of self-esteem as well as all the other factors we have discussed in this chapter. There are a number of elements of the approaches to talking with children, as well as creating explanations which we have found to make a positive difference.

- If adults – including professionals – can talk with children, not lecture but engage with *their* minds and what *they* know as well as offering alternative ways of seeing things and reacting. This theme has run through this chapter in the form of explanations that have been advocated. However there has often been reticence among many professionals to engage actively in discussions with children – especially young primary school age children. There may be some irrational fear accentuated by uncertainty about how to approach a discussion with a young child, including cultural appropriateness, which inhibits some professionals. This is a topic I have explored previously.[15–17]
- The professional may have to abandon many of the behaviours commonly associated with their usual role, and engage 'on the level' with a child. This may mean engaging in a combination of serious and humorous banter, which allows the child to trust that the adult is not just seeking that the child does what he or she (the adult) wants, but is prepared to 'play' with ideas at the child's level and not expect the child to fit in with the professional's *wisdom*.
- The professional may have to find ways to engage in the child's own version of humour, or particular way of thinking, and encourage that as well as the child's ability to play with ideas.
- This may mean allowing the child to change the subject, make verbal or play puns and appear to avoid the worrying topic. The professional

Mental health, mental illness, the family 39

needs to be able to hold the topic in mind and re-introduce it in a manner similar to the child's way of moving away from it.

- *The explanation specifically needs* to discover what the child knows and understands, offer adult knowledge to fill in the gaps or to give alternatives to unhelpful ways the child may be thinking (such as blaming him or herself), which can lead to a discussion of how the two sets of ideas can come together. The professional needs to discover:

- What the child has noticed about the parent's behaviour and any changes?
- What the child thinks about it or understands about it?
- What if anything has been explained, by whom and what the child thought about the explanations?
- How as a result does the child think about the parent's behaviour as an illness, as the parent just being cross, angry or sad, or does the child think he or she is to blame?
- What are the child's thoughts, worries and fears about what may now happen in the short term – to the parent and to the care of the child – and to what degree can the professional honestly mitigate these?
- What are the child's ideas about the long term; will the parent get better, get worse, stay in hospital or die? Will the child suffer the same/ a similar illness?
- What are the child's ideas about how the illness has/will have affected his or relationship with the parent. What may need to happen for the child to trust the parent as a carer of him/herself again?
- Can the child still feel some affection for the ill parent without having to agree with the parent's ideas which may have been affected by the illness?
- Can the child be helped to think more for him or herself?
- What can the child see that may have changed both about his/her role in the family and his/her relationship with the ill parent as a result of the illness?
- Are there some things the child would like to see change in their role and relationship with the ill parent?
- What kinds of things has the child been expected to do, wanted to do or decided to do that might be the job of an adult or an older sibling as a result of the parent's illness?

In many cultures young children may still be thought about as recipients of the ideas or behaviour of adults – good or bad – rather than active thinking participants in their own right, with their own minds. This way of thinking can also inhibit adults from talking to children about distressing dramas in their parent's lives, which may nevertheless have left a deep impression on them. Sometimes it is as though some adults think about young children as though they cannot hear or see, or will 'forget' anyway. I can recall quite vividly being about 3½ years old when *my* parents were having a furious row about money. I remember going on my own down some steps into the garden to visit a neighbour's family with whom I felt safe. Returning about ½ an hour later I remember seeing my grandfather sadly trying to stick together some pound notes that had been torn in two. I would have felt so much less anxious if someone had talked to me about it. In Kidstime a little girl of three suddenly exclaimed 'My mum does "crazy" and I don't like it', after which she was greatly calmed when some older children began to talk about it and explain it to her. This is one of the most important effects of the children's part of the Kidstime groups, where events which may have seemed *crazy* to a child can be made to feel more understandable just through being talked about with other children.

Learning from ACEs – hints for parents and professionals

When children do feel overwhelmed by a parent's mental illness it can become what is now termed an adverse childhood experience (known as ACE). Some ten factors which can affect a child's life as he or she grows up have been widely researched and found to be especially important. They include things like abuse and neglect, but also family violence, high conflict separation and divorce and misuse of alcohol or drugs by the parents. However, it is encouraging that it can be easier to help a child develop resilience to mental illness in a parent if other adverse factors are not present, than it is to prolonged exposure to other adverse childhood experiences. That is both because most parents with mental illness often try to make it up to their children when they are well (Chapters 4 and 5) and because the negative effects of how the parent behaves when he or she is ill can be helped by talking to the child about the illness and how it has been affecting the child. This is one reason why it is so important that children *do* have an adult to help them sort out their thoughts. It also really helps to ensure that the child is not left alone and can talk to other children in a similar situation.

In fact repeated surveys of children and young people who have a parent with mental illness have consistently come up with three things they want or *ask*:

1   An *explanation* which gives them a real understanding of what is happening to their parent, what the treatment may do and how they as children should respond
2   *An adult they can talk to, and call upon* – not a therapist but a neutral advocate or companion in times of acute stress, who can also encourage the child's independent thinking
3   *Some way* – such as a group of young people in similar circumstances – *to feel they are not totally alone*

And it is really important that these *asks* should be listened to, respected and responded to.

This chapter has included some tips for professionals working with families in general. Specific tips for professionals when there is mental illness in the family will be included in a chapter at the end of this book: 'Some combined tips for parents, children and the professionals who work with them' contributed to by Ambeya Begum, Lara Brown, Chineye Njoku, Georgia Irwin-Ryan, Kirsty Tahta-Wraith, Lenny Fagin and the two editors, while Suhaib Debar includes some recommendations for medical training in his chapter, and Kirsty Tahta-Wraith includes further specific ideas for young people in her chapter. For training resources see the end of Chapter 18.

Notes

1 An extreme form of this was illustrated in a famous documentary film 'Grey Gardens' about the reclusive life of the aunt of Jackie Kennedy (wife of the famous American president who was assassinated) and her 60 year old daughter.
2 https://ourtime.org.uk/resource/what-does-it-mean-to-have-a-parent-with-a-mental-illness/.

References

1 Office for National Statistics. (2017) *Families and Households*, Office for National Statistics, London.
2 Krause, I.B. (1989) Sinking heart: A Punjabi communication of distress. *Social Science & Medicine*, 29 (4): 563–575.
3 Raphael, B. (1986) *When Disaster Strikes: A Handbook for the Caring Professions*, Century Hutchinson, London.
4 Falcov, A. (2004) Talking with children whose parents experience mental illness. In *Children of Parents with Mental Illness. Personal and Clinical Perspectives* (2nd edn) (ed. V. Cowling): 41–56. ACER Press, Melbourne.
5 Cooklin, A., Bishop, P., Francis, D., et al. (2012) *The Kidstime Workshops; A Multifamily Social Intervention for the Effects of Parental Mental Illness: Manual*. CAMHS Publications, Evidence Based Practice Unit, London.
6 Cooklin, A. (2013) Promoting children's resilience to parental mental illness: Engaging the child's thinking. *Advances in Psychiatric Treatment*, 19: 229–240.
7 Wolpert, M., Hoffman, J., Martin, A., Fagin, L., and Cooklin A. (2014) An exploration of the experience of attending the Kidstime programme for children with parents with enduring mental health issues: Parents' and young people's views. *Clinical Child Psychology and Psychiatry*, 20, 406–418.
8 Rutter, M., and Quinton, D. (1984) Long-term follow-up of women institutionalized in childhood: Factors promoting good functioning in adult life. *British Journal of Developmental Psychology*, 2: 191–204.
9 Werner, E.E., Bierman, J.M., and French, F.E. (1971) *The Children of Kauai*, University of Hawaii Press, Honolulu.

10 Werner, E.E. (1982) *Vulnerable but Invincible: A Longitudinal Study of Resilient Children and Youth*, McGraw-Hill, New York.

11 Garmezy, N. (1973) Competence and Adaptation in Adult Schizophrenic Patients and Children at Risk. In *Schizophrenia: The First Ten Dean Award Lectures* (ed. S.R. Dean): 163–204. MSS Information Corp., New York.

12 Garmezy, N., and Streitman, S. (1974) Children at risk: The search for the antecedents of schizophrenia. Part 1. Conceptual models and research methods. *Schizophrenia Bulletin*, 8 (8): 14–90.

13 Masten, A.S. (2009) Ordinary magic: Lessons from research on resilience in human development. *Education Canada*, 49: 28–32.

14 Rutter, M. (2008) Developing concepts in developmental psychopathology. In *Developmental Psychopathology and Wellness: Genetic and Environmental Influences* (ed. J.J. Hudziak): 3–22. American Psychiatric Publishing, Arlington, VA.

15 Cooklin, A. (1989) Making connections through talking with children: From the 'return of the repressed' to 'dialectics'. *Journal of Family Therapy*, 20: 153–164.

16 Cooklin, A. (2001) Eliciting children's thinking in families and family therapy. *Family Process*, 4 (3): 293–312.

17 Cooklin, A. (2013) Promoting children's resilience to parental mental illness: Engaging the child's thinking. *Advances in Psychiatric Treatment*, 19: 229–240.

Chapter 2

Parental commentary on Chapter 1

Lara Brown

On Alan Cooklin's chapter

I hope to bring together some of the themes that might be useful to parents who have had experience of mental illness, as well as sharing part of our journey as a family. I am a mother of two daughters (now 16 and 10) and my husband and I have been together for 21 years. I have a diagnosis of bipolar disorder, which had been relatively mild until my youngest daughter was seven months old, when we were suddenly catapulted into crisis, as I became psychotic for the first time in my life. As a result our family saw and experienced things we could never have imagined.

Mental illness often instils terror in people's minds and is still one of the last taboos. Add the idea of mentally ill *parents* (who are sometimes seen by society as breaching a 'duty of care' over their children) into the mix, and it somehow becomes even more difficult to talk about. Yet in my view, it is *talking* that can make all the difference to families with experience of parental mental illness. The question is this: what is it that we, as parents who have suffered with mental illness, can do to help and support our children both to understand their experiences and to recover from them? What are the principles to highlight from these chapters and how might they help us to better understand our roles as parents who have faced these mental health difficulties?

I found Alan Cooklin's chapter to be a very useful piece on how families are defined today, and how mental illness can impact on family life. It works well to look at ordinary families first as then the later information about how mental illness affects the family and more specifically the children within it is put into context. It is also helpful to relate the developmental needs of the child to family structures in general, as this is a key to understanding how things can go wrong.

It's important, as Alan points out, that we as parents hang on to the fact that *none of us is perfect*. Good enough is enough, but when you are mentally ill it is hard to know what 'good enough' looks like. One of the things I felt as a parent who'd become mentally ill was massive guilt – that I was letting the girls and my husband down, that I wasn't there to nurture them and look after them as a mother should when I was in hospital and that therefore they would automatically be horribly damaged. *I think the idea that we try to do our best as parents, and that this does not necessarily stop when we become mentally unwell, has actually helped to lift that burden of guilt.*

How we hold onto strong bonds of attachment to our children is and was central to the whole subject of parental mental illness for me and for my family. Alan explains that those bonds to 'significant adults' that children trust is vital to development and a sense of safety and hence regulation of children's emotions. I was extremely lucky to have a husband who was not only a committed and very capable 'single parent' (during all that time) but who also built on an existing bond with my daughters that only strengthened over the years, and helped to give them a sense of safety. We were also very lucky to be able to afford live-in support, which meant that my husband could continue to work to support the family economically.

But the truth was that I had a significant attachment rupture to deal with myself on my return from the hospital after three months away, and this rupture only grew with subsequent admissions. The reality for me as a mother was that the trust I had nurtured with my children and held so dear had been shattered – I needed to build it back up gradually with the children, and that was a challenging process of understanding that meant I had to be extremely patient and could not expect to be let in straight away. I appreciate that this was also partly because my eldest daughter particularly had had to hold many things in for a long time. The reality for us was that our bond had been damaged and the children in different ways felt abandoned and horribly let down. I was helped by having done a lot of learning about attachment, separation and loss in my Psychotherapy training and kept reminding myself that we had always held in mind the idea of *rupture and repair*. Nothing, however, prepared me for the reality of it being played out in my own life, which I never expected and found very upsetting and difficult to deal with.

For us as a family, the issue was that once my Bipolar illness had been triggered hormonally it was episodic – I would function well in good periods but then have to be admitted into hospital. I never had extreme outbursts of sadness or anger or heard voices, but at its worst as I went into hospital I *was* delusional and would behave oddly, watching the clock, or saying that I could speak German and Japanese, or that I knew celebrities, for example, when I quite obviously couldn't and didn't. That was very upsetting for the children. So the challenge for the girls and I was that I'd seem well but then would suddenly disappear, undermining all the work that we had done to bond again. As my youngest daughter said: 'It's like I love it so much when you're here, Mummy, but then you're gone again and I can't let myself trust it'. At one point she wrote on the side of her bed: 'I miss my Mummy'. For my elder daughter, who was almost seven when I first went into hospital, it

was about mourning the mother she'd had, and then wrestling with her difficult feelings when I was back, because I wasn't the mother she remembered
and the bond had been so damaged that she couldn't let herself believe in it
any more.

One point that Alan makes to parents is to be very careful of your
child(ren) becoming a 'parent' or 'couple caretaker'. The idea is that guilt
can trap young people and make them feel responsible emotionally for their
parent(s). Many chapters that follow in this book show how that process develops. My husband *was* forced into the role of single parent while I was in
the hospital, a role which he rose to extraordinarily well, and I was suddenly
'missing' from the family, which completely changed the dynamics. Though
my daughter(s) never had to care for me, their father or the household *mate-
rially*, the eldest one did somewhat have to step into the role of mother, having to grow up before her time and 'be okay', as well as in some ways having
to be a friend to her Dad. She also had to look out for her sister more than
normal and take on a huge emotional load of responsibility. This entailed
putting her own emotional needs to one side in order to lessen the stress
on her father and support her sister. There were many things in our case,
however, that helped the girls: my husband's very solid, efficient and consistent parenting, tasty cooking and his sense of fun and humour were all
sustaining. That, and the support of our extended family and close friends,
played a very important role in helping the girls develop and maintain that
'resilience', despite the fact that they were missing 'mother love'. I suppose
what I'm expressing is to do with being lucky enough to have had a 'well
husband/partner' to keep things on the road, but also other mother figures
who the girls could turn to and talk to for comfort – despite the fact that
figures could clearly never replace me. The stigma and shame attached to
mental illness can make children and young people affected feel 'other', and
maintaining a sense of 'belonging' in the family can help to counter that.

The Mental Processes Wheel (and it spinning out of control) that Alan
describes is a very clear visual way of representing the inter-connected factors that can lead to mental health problems and how they can affect one
another. I like the way he says 'mental illness' and tells it like it is. Too often
I hear people saying they have 'mental health', which seems to me to skirt
around the problem, as if people are scared to call it an illness. In my view
this can then lead to more stigma and 'hiding' and doesn't make it easier for
parents or their children.

How we coped and what helped us as a family

One of the things that we hung onto as a family was keeping routines going,
with the live-in help when I was in hospital, and I think maintaining these
routines when I got home helped to give us all – especially the children – a
feeling of safety and stability.

My husband really encouraged debate and discussion, and worked on normalizing the experience we were going through, so that the girls were given support to develop their own points of view. *That* helped to maintain a feeling of safety and security which went some way to countering their hyper-vigilance and sensitivity to my behaviour. Alan shows that when parents – and professionals – mistakenly 'protect' the child from distress, not talking about their parent's illness, it makes them more vulnerable. In fact evidence shows that when children understand they can better manage stress and trauma, meaning they are less likely to have mental health problems themselves. One of the key precepts we learnt from Kidstime was to give children a good explanation, and talk openly, and it's something we really must try to remember as parents. Open talking helps to develop their resilience.

This links to something else that Alan makes clear: while parental mental illness is considered an 'Adverse Childhood Experience' (ACE) for kids affected, we should be encouraged as parents to be aware that it may not be as damaging as other ACEs, as 'making it up to the children, when they (*we*) are well', and the ability to talk and process what has happened can both make a huge difference. Reading that actually changed the way I felt about the impact of my illness on the children and made me feel less negative.

Kidstime helped both my daughters in different ways. Why? My younger daughter for the first time had friends to talk to whose parent(s) had the same diagnosis, and who automatically understood her experience. For both of them there was a sense that talking, 'making sense of' and being open could help to build confidence and a feeling of belonging. For me, knowing that they had the support of other people who understood what they had been through was a huge relief. Later, understanding that this could help them build 'resilience' helped to set my mind at rest about the possible future effects on them of having had to deal with my mental illness. These monthly workshops were literally the only place where there were people from different disciplines – Child and Adolescent Psychiatry, Psychology and Family Therapy, Drama and Social Work – all communicating with each other and working with the children and families. It was a genuinely multi-disciplinary approach that was healing for the kids.

In our experience, Kidstime offered children an image and explanation that not only helps them feel safe but also counters some of the damaging things they might hear publicly. In our case this included dire genetic prophecies: my daughter was once told by someone from a local agency who was supposed to be helping her that she would 'get' my illness. She was really upset and frightened. Alan discusses the idea of genetic inheritance and argues that kids of mentally ill parents should be given a clear understanding that the illness is not inevitably handed down. A 'tendency' does not mean they are going to develop the same disorder. Understanding this is crucial to helping them manage their feelings, because otherwise they can feel 'cursed'. I believe that all children coping with a parental mental illness should be offered this 'map' of what is going on inside their parent, including the fact that inheritance is only one of many factors, as Alan says, so as to separate their experience out. It was 'recognising, labelling and confirming' my elder daughter's experience that helped her so much. It transformed a very negative experience into something positive that she could 'own'. If she had not had that, I believe something extremely upsetting and potentially traumatising could have become scarring.

These are some of the ideas and hints from Kidstime/Our Time that we've found helpful in our family.

- Giving a clear explanation of the illness
- Being open about what's going on
- Suggesting that they find a supportive adult they could trust to talk to
- Giving them access to other children/young people to talk to in similar circumstances at the workshops
- Acting out some of what was troubling them dramatically, which was very powerful
- Helping to take away the responsibility from them, but also encouraging them to feel proud of their achievements

Finally, family therapy, from a gifted, sensitive and highly skilled practitioner (not connected to the Kidstime group), made a huge difference to us as a family and to me as a parent. I only wish we had had access to it sooner. It created a safe place where we explored the impact that mental health difficulties and Bipolar in particular could have on our identity as a family and our relationships. We discovered a lot about our own resilience and closeness as a family, and the way in which working to strengthen and repair our relationships contributed to long lasting recovery.[1] It was vital to acknowledge how my husband and our daughters had been affected by my illness, and to work together to repair and strengthen my attachment bond to the children. We have spent the last few years building up the trust that had been broken and healing the attachment issues I discussed earlier. We also explored in depth the whole concept of *recovery* and what it meant for the family. The effect has been extremely curative, and we feel very fortunate indeed as a family to have been able to work with someone who understood that we were ALL important. This links, of course, to one of the points Alan makes to professionals. I really hope others affected can be supported as we were.

Points I'd like professionals to take on board

Develop a whole family approach

There often tends to be no real understanding of how mental illness affects the whole family, rather than one mentally ill person. I suspect that especially since the swingeing cuts on mental health services clinicians in different areas tend to behave as isolated individuals, and neither 'joined-up thinking' nor linking between services is encouraged. The family is a complex system that has many inter-related influences but sadly there seems to be little understanding of this among mental health professionals.

Support for the 'well' parent would be useful – if another parent is present – so that s/he is not so alone when the ill parent is in hospital. My poor husband had to deal with a massive crisis that came out of the blue and had never happened to us before. In my case, it was my first experience of being hospitalised under 'section', and we were all in shock. Having access to clinicians who understood us as a family – linking to the above – as well as being aware of issues around parenting would have made all the difference. We didn't get it until very much later when we started family therapy.

Adopt a more holistic, person-centred approach in general

More of a holistic, person-centred approach would have helped me keep some confidence as a parent, at the same time as managing what was happening to my mind, especially when I was vulnerable and trying to cope as a parent. Only one of my care coordinators, who came on the scene later, had children herself, and shared her experience with me in a really encouraging way. This made her able to be extremely supportive, sensitive and understanding of my role as a parent. It would be useful to 'pair' parents with support workers who have some parenting experience themselves. Speaking to her helped me to fight the isolation I felt when I was mentally ill. When you are a parent it is doubly difficult because you often feel guilty about not being a 'normal' mother for your kids. Some kind of honest, specialised intervention to help battle the stigma and shame that I experienced as a parent would have been really helpful.

Research

The triggers for my illness are now being seen as very hormonal, not just post-childbirth, but in the run-up to, and as I entered, the menopause. There urgently needs to be more research into, and understanding of, hormones and how they interact with mental health problems for women, hopefully leading to better treatments.

Give basic information to the family

Being offered a leaflet or some kind of advice at the time of the crisis which outlined how to give a simple but compassionate explanation to the children of what was going on would have helped us manage the stress as a family. My husband did explain it to them, but I think it would have really helped him to have a 'blueprint'. Because I was going in and out of lucidity once I was in hospital, I worried a lot about the children. Knowing that someone was helping them to understand what was going on would have been invaluable.

Alan talks about bringing professions together in a 'mutually cooperative framework' – this *did not happen* in our experience. The so called interconnection of the professional matrix in mental health services is woefully infrequent. Nor was there any understanding among mental health professionals that my illness took place in the context of the *family*. In fact, *Kidstime* was the only agency in which complementary professionals worked in a holistic framework. It was not only refreshing but helpful.

Points on behalf of children and young people

1   *What might reduce their sense of responsibility for their parents and their feelings?*
    Offering them an explanation that helps them to understand what is happening to their parent, how the medication works and how they are affected. Finding a trusted adult(s) they can talk to and approach in times of stress, to support them and help them think for themselves.

2   *What might reduce their sense of guilt?*
    Making sure that they have someone they trust who can explain that they are NOT responsible for their parent's illness in any way, and providing the opportunity to get together with a group of young people in similar circumstances – such as the *Kidstime* workshops – to help them feel they are not totally alone. Once the parent has recovered, if possible encouraging open conversation about the crisis, and making clear that it is the *parent's* illness and never the fault of the child.

3   *What might help them carry on with their own lives and develop their resilience?*
    Being honest with them so they know the truth and can make sense of it, and get on with their lives. Making sure, if they have siblings, that they are able to understand and support each other. Helping to boundary and 'hold' extreme emotions for them without patronising or 'babying'. If the illness is episodic and the parent has got much better, then making sure that they have some conception of recovery (see endnote[1]) and what that might mean for them. Then it is about letting go of something so they can move on.

I hope to have brought together some of the themes that might be useful to parents who have had experience of mental illness, as well as sharing part of our journey as a family. Hopefully we can help our children by taking on board some of the hints that have come out of many years of experience with the *Kidstime* approach to help them build confidence and resilience for the future.

Note

1 The term recovery has been used in a confusing number of ways within mental health care practice. It is most commonly used to denote a sufficient degree of improvement of symptoms, rather than to define a 'cure'. A common definition would be: amelioration of symptoms and other deficits associated with the disorder to a sufficient degree that they no longer interfere with daily functioning, allowing the person to resume personal, social and vocational activities within what is considered a normal range. See also Lara Brown's personal description in editor's note from her comments on Ambeya Begum's and Georgia Irwin-Ryan's chapters.

Chapter 3

Comment by Juliet Brown (Lara's daughter) on Lara Brown's commentary

Juliet Brown

On reading my mother's chapter, I found it interesting to see how she tried to help my family, my sister and I in particular, to deal with the confusion and stigma around her illness. I had no idea of the extent to which we were in her thoughts at that time. For my sister and I, our visits to the hospital were scary as we saw our Mum as a completely different person, which made it difficult for us to imagine her considering us and our feelings. I agree with my Mum that it is essential for not only the children of a mentally unwell parent to have support but also the well parent. Regardless of the amazing help given to my sister and I through Kidstime and other sources, without the continuous support of my father I'm not sure how I would have coped with my mother's absence and illness. In addition, without the help given to my mother, she would never have been able to return to the role of parent to my sister and I, allowing us both to be children again.

In my experience the best way to help children dealing with a parent's mental illness is to be as brutally honest as possible. Even though as a parent you may want to sugar coat the truth in order to protect your children, it actually does the opposite as it creates a stigma and sense of fear around the topic that is completely unnecessary. As a child I knew when adults were hiding the truth from me, and not only did it destroy the trust I had with those adults, but it made me even more confused and scared about the illness my Mum was facing.

It's important to realise that there are different kinds of 'looking after'. Even though I was never told it was my responsibility to protect my family, there was always a lingering sense of duty that I had from an early age that I had to be okay for everyone else to be okay, and I would hide my emotions and feelings from my younger sister and my Dad in order to take some of the stress from them. Emotionally, I always felt responsible for my sister because a nanny could never replace the bond between her and my Mum that I felt I had to fill for her to grow up normally. This made it even harder when my Mum would return from hospital and I would be forced back into the role of child after becoming so accustomed to the role of parent.

I think the sense that I needed to look after everyone, even if I didn't actually physically have to do much, is extremely hard in a different way. This backs up a key issue faced by people dealing with mental illness that a mental feeling is seen as not as important as a physical one, just because physically I wasn't having to pay bills or look after my Mum, emotionally I was a parent.

Chapter 4

Parental mental illness
The worst hurdles and what helped

Kirsty Tahta-Wraith

Introduction

This chapter is written based on my lived experience of parental mental illness. I was raised by my father who had bipolar disorder. He became a single parent to my sister and I from when I was two years old. This was a result of a custody case between him and my mother which resulted in my father getting full custody. My relationship with my mother subsequently became intermittent, and at times non-existent, due to her own difficulties. Therefore much of my experience of being parented was within the context of a serious mental illness. My father's illness impacted him, his parenting and thus me in a number of ways. This can be split into the effects of experiencing intense, isolated episodes of psychosis and the effects of living with the more day-to-day symptoms of bipolar disorder such as low mood, sleep disturbance and hypomanic phases. As is the nature of bipolar disorder, my father's symptoms and therefore their impact on my sister and I were changeable with regard to their intensity, duration and after-math.

54 Kirsty Tahta-Wraith

This chapter will touch upon specific experiences and their effect, though it focuses more generally on my reflections of the cumulative impact of my father's illness ('the hurdles') and the experiences which helped mitigate them ('what helped').

It is important to note that my family received specialist support for my father's mental illness in the form of a multi-family support group named 'Kidstime Workshops'. We attended these workshops once a month when my sister and I were between the ages of 8 and 15. Whilst intermittent, our attendance there is a large part of 'what helped' as it laid the foundations for much of the family-level and individual protective factors I detail in this chapter. Thus, I will refer to aspects of the Kidstime model throughout with the disclaimer that, whilst not intended to be the focal point, they are important contributions to building resilience and thus future success for the children who took part in them.

Hurdle 1 – no explanation

A central hurdle, one which I conceptualise as the root of many other hurdles resulting from my experience of parental mental illness, is the *lack of sufficient explanation received and thus lack of 'real' understanding I had about my father's illness*. I quote 'real' because whilst I now know I had an insightful and sensitive understanding into his mental state for my age, much of this was misjudged and fantasy based, as this chapter will highlight. For, as children do, I created unrealistic, story-like narratives in the absence of the facts.

Having no explanation meant I grew to fear my father's illness, it was the unknown. I knew that he had 'Bipolar' but nothing more. I knew it was an illness but I did not know what a *mental* illness was. My understanding was that illnesses were physical with visible symptoms, that they were bad for people, made them struggle and less able. Whilst my father *was* impacted by his illness, he was the only example I had of parenting and thus I experienced him as 'normal'. This blinded me to his 'real' symptoms as a younger child. I was therefore constantly on the look-out for evidence of this illness, for signs of him being or becoming unwell. This vigilance remained unanswered for a long time because I did not know what I was actually looking for. I did not know that, in fact, what I was looking for was in front of me the whole time. This left behind a sense of impending doom regarding when and how this 'illness' might surface.

This, in addition to the 'hurdles' discussed later, contributed to a constant underlying state of anxiety. It also resulted in me misinterpreting unrelated things as symptoms of his bipolar disorder and overestimating their consequences. For example, my dad had a chest infection, 'was *this* the illness they told me about? Was it finally happening? What happens next? Can it be cured? It must be bad. I bet this is going to get really bad. Is he going to die?'

The fact that I experienced my father as 'normal' did not mean I was unaffected by his behaviours and emotions. His more extreme states, high or low, were of course unpleasant to experience. Regardless of their intensity, I often felt to blame for his changes in mood and responsible for solving them. I would attribute these changes to the tiniest of things I had done or not done, for example 'did I say that too harshly earlier?' or 'I should have just offered to do that for my sister so he didn't have to'. I would also hash out different scenarios which might bother him and possible ways of resolving them, particularly in an attempt to soothe or busy myself during longer periods of his more obviously expressed difficulty such as anger or withdrawal. As you can imagine, this added to my state of anxiety. These conclusions were *so* illogical, yet *incredibly* easy and tempting to make when confused about my father's behaviour and, most crucially, in the absence of another explanation for his difficulties.

What helped hurdle 1? – a simple, clear explanation

The key things that helped me develop a 'real' understanding of my father's illness were receiving an explanation which, in turn, soothed my anxiety around it. The Kidstime Workshops gave us a general, age appropriate explanation of mental illness, what contributes to it and what it can look like to others. It was also relatively simple. The workshops were somewhere where, as a result of frequent, open conversations about mental illness, I became increasingly comfortable talking about my *own* experiences of my father's illness. This was crucial in facilitating my confidence, in raising my own questions about it, and thereby having them answered. In summary, an explanation enabled me to understand the 'real' root of my father's difficulties and thereby prevented me from blaming myself for them.

Receiving the accurate and understandable information about mental illness at Kidstime replaced the harmful misconceptions I had about mental illness with facts. It enabled me to realise, on my own, much of what I had misunderstood about my father's illness and largely corrected my assumptions about my influence on his behaviour. The continued conversations about mental illness and our experiences of it meant that any distorted ideas that were particularly entrenched or newly developed eventually came out in some way. They were either raised explicitly by myself in conversation, or, recognised over time by professionals running the workshops. This provided the opportunity for the adults around me to address them and provide the accurate information or reassurance I needed to correct them. *It is important to note that, to replace the more entrenched/reinforced schemas, a consistent approach over a considerable length of time was necessary. It mostly did not change after one explanation.* Kidstime staff often noticed the young peoples' concerns or misconceptions and immediately and directly challenged them in the group, often referring back to the set explanatory model of mental illness used in the workshops. Indeed, over time, the explanation became a reliable and credible model of understanding mental illness for my family. This was also the case for ideas I was not aware of and therefore did not explicitly raise.

Learning from each other: parents and children in multi-family groups

The Kidstime Workshops educated parents and children on the common anxieties experienced by children of parents with a mental illness. They also provided parents with different ways of thinking about and explaining their own behaviours to their children. *This was also powerful in changing my understanding.* In addition to the issues raised by staff, my father also heard the concerns I raised *myself* at Kidstime. This made him aware of *my* worries and gave him a chance to address them, something that I was unlikely to have approached him with in private. The staff modelled effective ways of addressing such concerns and he drew on these along with his own approach, to contest and help me change my mindset. For example, he might do this whilst at the Kidstime Workshops through interjecting in the discussions to tell me something was not my fault.

The discussions at Kidstime gave my father insight into how I was experiencing his behaviour. This is something he was previously unable to do as his illness made experiences intense for him and meant he had to struggle to not just focus on himself in those times. The discussions gave him this other discourse (at least) in the back of his mind, which made him more able to take a step back and say, for example, 'what I am doing right now is nothing to do with you' or, more powerfully for me, provide an alternative explanation for his behaviour or expressed emotions. At Kidstime, he learned the theory. He came to understand the importance of verbalising an explanation for his distress which he then put into practice at home with me. He did so even when he may not have understood why he was reacting in a certain way himself. He was able to keep my experience in mind and prioritise it through providing some alternative explanation. In retrospect, this change in his approach was incredibly powerful in changing my own assumptions – even when I knew exactly what he was doing.

Hurdle 2 – viewing my father as defined by his illness

As a result of seeing my father unwell or reduced in some way, I came to view him as somewhat defined and limited by his illness. My father's illness had a range of presentations. He was diagnosed with bipolar disorder almost 20 years before I was born due to alternating periods of stability, depression, mania, psychosis and many hospital admissions. Whilst I may not have known it, I experienced most symptoms of my father's illness in my early years. Though, overall, and

Parental mental illness   57

particularly compared to before I was born, my father was relatively stable. His periods of mania were the least frequent and they were not severe enough to come close to requiring a hospital admission (i.e. psychosis) until my teenage years. My father then had two episodes of mania that developed into psychosis, first when I was 13 and again when I was 15. In both instances my father became increasingly unwell over many weeks and remained at home. He was then sectioned in a psychiatric hospital for 4–6 months, followed by some months of recovery at home (living with my sister and me).

My father's periods of low mood and anxious states meant that he frequently sought emotional support and reassurance from me. As noted, this was our 'normal' dynamic which I was very used to and so, on a conscious level, I felt relatively un-impacted by his distress then. Upon reflection I know that this had a cumulative impact on my view of my father and my appraisal of his ability to support me. I believe the thing that had the largest impact on me was the distress and delusion I witnessed during his acute psychotic episodes. His vulnerability during these events lead to me viewing and treating my father as vulnerable and less capable *overall*. In this sense, I came to view my father as defined by his illness. This created a number of difficulties for me.

Seeing my father in incredibly vulnerable states during the most acute phases of his illness made it very difficult for me to view him as a possible source of support. My father was genuinely unable to support me in those periods. However, this also impacted me long term as, even when he was well, I came to struggle in seeking support from him or accepting any support which he tried to give. Also, more widely, this led to me developing similarly limited expectations of other adults.

Seeing him that unwell and, being unable to do anything about it, was the most acutely distressing thing I had experienced in my life. Therefore, each time he was unwell I was in a dilemma of needing care from him the most I had ever needed it, whilst he was simultaneously least able to provide it. I was also aware of this whilst it was happening and this intensified the hopelessness I felt. Feeling so stripped of care from him in a time that I needed it most meant I came to not expect support from him at all. This even bled into times when he was well or times when I did not actually need that much from him. It had been so hard to need, but be without the support when he was most unwell that I effectively 'decided' on some level that I was not going to attempt to obtain support from him at all, in order to avoid feelings of panic, loss, fear, abandonment and hopelessness upon realising I could not have it.

What helped Hurdle 2? – re-discovering my father's supportive abilities

The environment created by the Kidstime Workshops *was extremely valuable in reframing my view of my father as an adult capable of providing support.* The groups comprised multiple families which created a dynamic support network with everyone supporting each other. Every workshop, adults and young people came together for a group discussion of various topics or common difficulties. Within these, parents supported other parents, young people supported other young people, parents from one family supported the children from other families and children provided advice to adults from other families. I therefore witnessed my father provide support to others, both young people and adults. This empowered him in my eyes, disproving my previous assumptions. This *gradually* encouraged me to view him as a credible source of effective support. It also drew my attention to just how sophisticated his caregiving skills were, as I witnessed him show careful consideration and real insight *towards other adults with mental illnesses*, and therefore arguably more complex needs, than your average Joe.

Also important to note is that, at Kidstime, there was no real hierarchy amongst the adults (clinicians and parents). During the discussions and beyond, the 'unwell' adults were presented as experts on their situations on a par, or even with more specialist knowledge, than the 'professionals'. It never felt like the clinicians were instructing the parents on how best to parent. Rather, it always felt like any changes were initiated from the sharing of advice between the parents in the room and that the staff were simply facilitating a space within which the parents refined their natural abilities. If it had felt like the staff were teaching the parents, it would have fit into my already undermining view of my father, rather than worked towards reversing it. As *a result of this environment, I was able to rebuild my schema of my father, and thus adults more widely, as supportive and reliable.*

Hurdle 3 – fear of my father becoming ill again and being unable to seek support from him for myself

The impact of seeing my dad in very vulnerable states impacted me in a number of ways. Under Hurdle 2, I addressed how this affected my view of him as a possible source of support. Hurdle 3 explores how seeing my father experience such distress created great fear that his mental health would deteriorate again. In turn, I overestimated both the fragility of his mental health and the impact I could have on it. This caused difficulty in two ways. First, I largely went without parental support. Second, as touched on earlier, feeling able to impact my father's mental state (whether for the better or worse) was a source of great responsibility and thus anxiety.

I have explained that seeing my dad very unwell meant I came to perceive him as very vulnerable. In practice, this meant I could also treat him as fragile and unable to do certain things. I therefore leant on him much less for emotional support, *particularly regarding my own difficulties related to his illness*. My protectiveness towards him and not wanting him to deteriorate became the perfect excuse to prevent me from seeking support from him for the strain I realised his illness was putting on me. This became a barrier in the way of my father having any opportunity to address this and alleviate this pressure. Despite what I said in the previous hurdle, even once I realised my father was perhaps more capable than I thought he was through seeing him support others, I still struggled to *actually* go to him with my 'stuff', my rationale being that, even if he was capable of support, he was still vulnerable. I did not want to be the one to push him over the edge and so I effectively continued not to fully utilise him as the supportive father he was able to be.

Over responsibility: my fantasy of having the power to keep him well

I also attempted to fill the gaps left by things I assumed he was unable to do, both emotional and practical tasks. I effectively took on a parental role in my family. For example, I undertook domestic responsibilities, stepped in as a supportive figure for my sister and would often take charge of decisions/ daily situations all of which, upon reflection, likely felt undermining and controlling to my father and wider family. This ultimately created further distance between my father and I, as doing it myself made it even less necessary to look to him to do these things. This gave him less opportunity to prove me wrong, thereby reinforcing my over-estimation of his vulnerability. Also, the longer he stayed well whilst I was doing these things, the more entrenched my distorted narrative became. This hidden narrative, known only to myself, was that I was keeping him well by doing these things and was therefore responsible for him staying well, and would thereby be responsible if he became unwell.

What helped Hurdle 3? – my father realising the impact of his illness on me and then seeking support from him

Whilst under Hurdle 2 what helped was watching how my father could be supportive and helpful to other parents in the groups, *Kidstime also helped me to make use of this view of him myself and experience receiving support from him in practice.* The core focus of the Kidstime Workshops was to help young people and their families identify and understand the ways in which parental mental illness impacts upon children and the risks this poses. Difficulties faced by children of parents with a mental illness were addressed frequently, either symbolically through drama or through more explicit group discussions. As a result, over time I could no longer pretend to my father that I was unaffected or pretend to myself that my father did not realise these difficulties also applied to me. In addition I identified with concerns expressed by other young people at the group and learned through witnessing professionals address these.

I was therefore gently and gradually pushed into confronting my fears, into addressing the fact that I was struggling with him and into seeking and receiving support for this from him. Believe it or not, despite how much I may have convinced you or my child self, this did not result in the spontaneous combustion (or hospitalisation) of my father. Whilst I may not have been aware at the time, this *proved* to me that my Dad could 'take it' and support me. This enabled me to continue sharing my struggles with and getting support from him in practice – both long term and regarding difficulties unrelated to his illness.

Hurdle 4 – preoccupation with the needs of others: The 'to do' list and the 'little martyr'

As touched on under Hurdle 3, one of the things attending the Kidstime Workshops helped me to realise was that I had great difficulty putting my needs first. In my mind there were lots of things I could not go to others for or rely on them to do. I therefore ended up with this endless 'to do list' of practical and emotional tasks that would not get done if I did not do them myself. Overall, this made me very preoccupied and it would therefore often simply not occur to me to prioritise myself or my 'things' above this list.

These 'things' ranged from small to large, and not doing them ranged from relatively inconsequential to rather costly. For example, I would not seek emotional support from my father if I was having difficulty at school. I might choose not to go out with friends, or I would feel I could not spend time on school work or revision because I assumed I needed to help my sister or dad with something instead. Even if I did 'put myself first', it was often laden with unpleasant guilt or anxiety which created its own difficulty. For example I would be easily distracted whilst studying. I joke now that I had the mindset of a 'little martyr mummy' who must always look out for others despite the cost to herself. Due to the idea from such a young age that my Dad needed so much support from me and due to how long this went unchallenged, this mindset of support and self-denial was deeply entrenched. The adoption of this caring, martyr-like role is likely to be the most enduring impact of my father's illness on me. I tend to adopt this role in other relationships and have worked very hard to change this.

What helped Hurdle 4? – encouragement and support in recognising and then changing my role

The key to me becoming aware of and then overcoming this hurdle was (again) the Kidstime Workshops. Despite it not necessarily being the natural order of things, the staff never shied away from acknowledging the fact that children of parents with a mental illness often take on a more responsible, indeed 'parental' role in their families. I was therefore able to realise the ways in which this applied to me and my relationships. Importantly however, *this role was not simply accepted as necessary and unchangeable.* Workshop staff sent a gentle, yet clear message to families that this was not 'okay' or 'normal' and that is damaging long term if not changed. This was an uncomfortable message to receive at first. It felt shameful to admit to ourselves that this was happening in our family and, in line with my strong protectiveness towards my father, I found it excruciating to acknowledge this in front of him and others. In doing so, I felt that I was undermining and embarrassing him.

Shifting my familiar mindset: learning to become more 'selfish' and not always put others first

Beginning to challenge and change the caring role I had in my family was also threatening to me as it was all I had ever known and brought me a sense of purpose, capability and much comfort. The anxious mindset that lead to me playing out this role, the idea that I had to do it as no one else would or could, was deeply entrenched and thus difficult to shift. Attempting to behave differently therefore meant facing a deep fear that things would fall apart if I did not do this which added to the anxiety, especially at first. *However, the workshops acted as a consistent, monthly reminder to be 'selfish' and of the importance of making this change.* Naturally, a shift in long-held roles in our family did create some tension and conflict. Kidstime acknowledged this may happen and provided a space for us to express and work through our grievances. But the solution we were always supported to reach was that the children must learn to put themselves first regardless, and that it was worth it in the long run.

I feel it is important to convey that this 'lesson' has to be taught early as it was not easy to learn and, putting this into practice still does not come easily to me. I still find myself putting myself in the role of the carer and others as needing care, and am still frequently tempted to prioritise (what I assume are) others' needs before mine. An example of this, despite years of practice and encouragement from my family and Kidstime, was when I chose to move away from home for university. At the age of 19 I thought I had cracked it. I saw myself as a shamelessly independent young woman who was flying the nest, and who could now always prioritise herself. I convinced myself that, just like my friends, this was my time to go off and explore and there was no reason not to. However, my father then experienced a manic phase. During this time he took a course of anti-psychotic medication to prevent it developing into full-blown psychosis so it was not as bad as it could have been. I quickly became convinced that I had to stay at home. Not only did I assume he could not cope living alone, I also told myself that it had to be me that stayed at home and supported him. It did not even cross my mind that my sister could offer support as she was moving away for university too and so, in my eyes, needed to be protected from this. I therefore applied to and almost changed my university choices to ones in my city, despite always dreaming of moving away and absolutely falling in love with my first choice university in a different city. Here, I almost put my father's and my sister's needs, not just before, but at a real cost to my own needs.

The message I aim to convey here is that had I not had that consistent message drummed into me, life would likely have been very different, as even with that message these decisions were extremely hard.

Hurdle 5 – the shame of being different

As is natural as you grow older, I became increasingly aware of friends' families and compared my own with theirs. This resulted in me feeling very different to them. Their parents worked, my father did not; their parents therefore lived in larger, prettier homes, my dad did not; their parents cooked elaborate meals and kept their houses clean and tidy, my dad did not; their parents woke up early and made them breakfast, my dad needed to sleep until later in the day because of insomnia and strong medication. Their parents went to doctor's appointments on their own, my dad asked me to go with him; their parents went away for work trips, my dad went away for psychiatric hospital admissions. You get the picture? I could not help but be aware of these differences and they became particularly evident in my teenage years – a time when comparison is rife and any differences feel huge and automatically negative. Over time, feeling different as a result of comparing myself to others turned into me holding the assumption that I was different to others before I even knew anything about them. My mindset was 'difference equals bad' and being lesser than others. Being the odd one out and therefore being 'less' than others became my default position.

Luckily, I hid this feeling well. I am very sociable by nature, so I was invested in developing friendships. Therefore, on the surface, I did not let this get in the way. Underneath it was a different story though. Underneath I felt a lot of anger towards my situation and my father for not being 'normal'. I did not feel good enough in comparison to others and developed real shame about my family's situation. I was incredibly anxious that friends, or just anyone at my age, would find out that I was 'different' and consequently view me as 'less' than them too. This made me feel like I was living two separate lives to some extent which was incredibly unpleasant.

What helped Hurdle 5? – daring to share and feel like your true self, a long journey

Perhaps the only way to remedy feeling like the odd one out and the shame that this creates is to spend time with others with similar experiences. This is what Kidstime did for me. The groups were a community of young

Parental mental illness 63

people with shared, unique experiences. We often discussed feeling different to peers and hiding aspects of our lives from friends. Most young people shared the view that others our age would not understand, even if we did show them things, due to our roles at home being so inappropriate to our age. We were able to build relationships, not in spite of, but because of the roles we had at home and the fact that we could identify with each other. I did not spend much time with people from Kidstime outside of the groups, but whilst I was with them I felt I could be my genuine self and this is not a feeling I otherwise experienced. The group and relationships built there therefore became a sanctuary to me.

The groups were also a source of alternative information as I found that not everyone hid their home lives so determinedly from friends. Those that 'dared to share' did not report being met with hostility, ridicule or rejection. This surprised me and created a curiosity as to the reactions my friends would have if I shared more of myself with them too. This was not enough to immediately overhaul my approach to friends and meeting new people – but it did give me the boost I needed to try. Whilst I still struggle with sharing parts of how I grew up with new people, my friends know most things, enough for me to feel that friendships are no longer tainted with hidden parts of me. This has been a long journey, requiring much practice and resilience. It is also important to emphasise that the experiences I have now shared with my (wonderful) friends have actually lead to them expressing great admiration and respect to me, a far cry from the judgement and criticism I once expected.

Hurdle 6 – low self-esteem, being constantly self-critical and the ongoing buzz of anxiety

During my early teenage years, as a result of growing more aware of how different others' home lives were from mine I became acutely aware of how this caring role I had in my family was inappropriate for my age. I felt two things, *resentment and low self-esteem*. I begrudged the fact that I could not be carefree and guilt free when doing things for myself like studying and socialising. I felt like I was missing out and the more I focused on this, the bigger and more unpleasant this feeling became. This ranged from rather consequential things such as 'I would have better friendships if I did not feel so guilty when spending time with friends', to less consequential; 'I would be able to feel more switched off and properly relaxed when watching television if I was not so distracted by the list of things I (felt I) had to do'.

Second, this had a negative impact on my self-esteem and belief in my own efficacy – i.e. my confidence in my ability to do things well. This long list of things I had to do or think about was endless and always in the back of my mind. It was never soothed or settled by the completion of a task as my mind was always onto the next one. This created a general level/buzz of anxiety in me and led to me becoming very self-critical. I felt like I was constantly juggling more than I could handle which left me with a sense of hopelessness that I would never get everything done. *Whilst the content changed over the years, this list and feeling like I could never complete it existed from a young age.* It is a feeling I believe to be very important in building self-confidence. The feeling has gradually lessened as I have learned to allow more space for myself, away from my family, for things that I enjoy and make me feel good about myself. However, there has always been this feeling deep down that I am ultimately not as able as other people (who had less to worry about), that I am not as good at things and that I may not succeed in what I want to do.

What helped Hurdle 6? – celebration of my achievements as carer and an alternative parallel narrative

Kidstime helped me re-frame this view of myself and offered a convincing, much more empowering alternative feeling. The group discussions drew everyone's awareness to what it felt like to be the child of a parent with a mental illness, the stresses we may feel and how this could get in the way of our lives. However, it was always clear that the main focus of the groups, and the rationale for their existence, was to recognise the burdening nature of young carers' roles and celebrate their triumphs in spite of this. This shifted my focus from what I was not doing and how this compared with my peers. It shifted me from the 'martyr' narrative of focusing on the cost of my caring role, to celebrating my 'hero': role. The difficulties faced as a result of my fathers' mental illness were addressed enough for me to feel heard and validated.

This was not done in a pessimistic, hopeless or indulging way. The staff effectively laid out each and every hurdle we had and all the extra little things the young people felt they must take care of, in front of everyone, so that we and our parents knew exactly how much we were contending with. Then, month after month, they made a point of openly discussing the successes and achievements young people had made. This created a real culture of celebration of the young people and their achievements, from the staff, other young people and crucially our own parents. *My father adopted this into his parenting style and carried this with him long after we stopped attending the groups.* I know that he always felt proud of my sister and I, but there was definitely a difference in how openly he expressed it to us after attending the workshops. At times of expressing pride, from birthdays to finishing exams or getting into university, he always made reference to things I had going on when I was younger and how far I had come despite it. Here, consistency over time and the fact that it was coming from someone I loved dearly and sought approval from the most (my parent) meant it sunk in the most. Now, I believe it. Now, I own what I contended with when I was younger. Now, I feel proud and grateful for what I dealt with and who it made me. I now feel impressed by my younger and current self.

Parental mental illness 65

The workshops therefore helped me turn my view of myself as someone who had a number of deficits in my life, as explored earlier, into someone with unique strengths. It did not feel like the staff were naively encouraging us to feel this way. Rather, this idea was introduced by other young people at the groups, mostly those older than me. In group discussions with the young people, they reflected about the fact that they had had to grow up quickly, but this would often lead to them expressing that they actually feel ahead of their years and thus their friends in many domains, from awareness of emotions and mental health, emotional intelligence and empathy, understanding and supportiveness towards others, ability to cope with stress, to knowing things about household bills that their friends had no idea about yet. From this grew a widely shared feeling of gratitude for our experiences due to the skills and sophistication it gave us along with the idea that, on the whole, they would not change their experiences as it made them a better person. This is something I still strongly identify with.

Hurdle 7 – responsibility without power and the paradox of power and helplessness

My father's periods of more acute illness resulted in a strong sense of being out of control. This is a general feeling and does not apply to all areas of my life. However, the seemingly unpredictable nature of his illness in general became a harsh realisation during these episodes and, due to the important role I played in his care at these times, this therefore left me with an overall sense of knowing my life could become significantly different very quickly, at any time, and there was essentially nothing I could do about it. This feeling co-existed with the aforementioned feeling of me being a powerful influence on my father's mood discussed under Hurdle 1. The contradictory nature of the two feelings is apparent to me now and, upon reflection, was an incredibly confusing and frustrating place to be in.

The involvement of social services: a further disempowerment

Feeling very responsible for my father and able to impact him day to day, yet ultimately not feeling able to control my surroundings, and the frustration this caused, were both compounded by my interactions with services; those who *were* able to 'do something about it', when my father was most unwell. In summary, during his second episode of psychosis in my life time (when I was 15) my father was still living at home, though he was becoming increasingly unwell and it was clear to me that he needed hospitalisation imminently. Whilst at home with my sister and I, my father was not sleeping at all and was in an almost constant state of delusion, experiencing distressing hallucinations and paranoia which resulted in uncontainable behaviour such as believing our block of flats was on fire and trying to warn our neighbours of this at 3am, or running away at night. During this time a mental health service called the crisis team were visiting our house once each day to assess his mental state and help manage his medication, in an attempt to prevent him being admitted to hospital. They required my sister and I to monitor his medication intake and effectively administer it ourselves as he took his medication more frequently than the once daily visits from them. They also needed an abundance of information from us about what and how much medication he was taking and great detail about his mental state and behaviours. As he became more unwell and so less manageable at home, I made it clear to members of the crisis team that my father needed to be hospitalised. I would make this abundantly clear each time they visited, explaining why and that I did not feel I could keep him safe. I effectively begged them to take him to hospital and out of my hands. Despite this, they did not do so and did not explain why. It took a further week and numerous distressing incidents for him to be sectioned and hospitalised. The day this happened, my sister and I got home from school and were met by our Aunt and social worker who told us the plan was to live with our Aunt until our father came out of hospital. My sister and I objected strongly to this for many reasons; mainly, we just did not want more upheaval in our lives. We just wanted to stay in our familiar surroundings and routine and continue going to school, just as we had been doing in the weeks leading up to our father's admission. However, we were told this was not an option and so went to live with our aunty. Our social worker was of course following the law and could not allow 15 year olds (under 16) to live alone. He did explain this to us and we both understood this on a rational level. However, my experience of the whole process was that we were being 'handled' and carted off by social services like two incapable, helpless young children.

This was similar to my experience of the psychiatric services in that I felt like I was not being listened to or allowed to have a say. *However, this stood in stark contrast to the expectations of the psychiatric and social services whilst my father was at home, as they expected us to provide 24/7 care to an incredibly unwell adult man and report back to them whilst fending for ourselves and still attending school. It just did not match up.* So, when I was told I could not stay at home *without* my father and the arguable risk he posed to us, I felt used and abused by the services. I was outraged. I had not seen that coming. This speaks for itself as to how I was made to feel *even more* out of control of my surroundings. It undid a lot of the progress that attending the Kidstime groups had helped me achieve in trusting and feeling understood and respected by professionals. It also strongly fed into and confirmed my belief that I was not good enough, and that others did not see me as capable as the services did not let me influence decisions about my father's care or my own living situation.

What helped Hurdle 7? – a reminder of my strengths

Fortunately I was able to access the Kidstime Workshops which restored *my sense of agency and reminded me of my strengths and capabilities.* Whilst it took a while, staff at Kidstime validated and helped me to process my experiences. They helped me to understand why services had the response they did. For example, they reminded me of the legalities of being under 16 and educated me about how bed availability works in the psychiatric inpatient hospital system and how this is likely to be why my father could not be hospitalised sooner. They also helped me to recognise my successes despite being in such a difficult situation; such as being able to assert my needs with services and continuing to go to school and study for my exams. This helped me feel less like a passive victim and reminded me of my core capabilities.

The staff encouraged the young people in the group to produce an initiative named an 'advanced directive'. This was a plan made by each family regarding what would happen to children in the families if the parent became unwell or had to be hospitalised. This involved going through the options available in a crisis and creating a plan which prioritised children's preferences in multiple possible eventualities, whilst taking into consideration the limitations to these based on rules and regulations of services involved. Children were therefore made aware of these and how this could impact their choices in *advance*. In doing this, it felt like the professionals at the workshops were effectively asking *me* to teach *them*. This meant that I not only felt like I had more of a handle on my own future situations, but so much so that I could help others too. This was incredibly empowering and did wonders for my self-esteem.

My personal conclusions

A core theme in experience of parental mental illness is *anxiety*. Anxiety runs throughout all of the hurdles detailed in this chapter, which I summarise again here with their solutions

1 Fear of the unknown and anxiety, followed by later having an explanation
2 The feeling that I was to blame for my father's difficulties (as a result of the absence of other proper explanations), followed by the power of an alternative viewpoint and discourse in debunking that view
3 My inappropriately limited expectations of my dad, followed by relief at being in an environment in which he could show his more capable side. This also led to more hopeful expectations of other adults
4 Preoccupation with always looking after others, followed later by learning to put myself first

5 Not feeling good enough and developing an alternative narrative (learning to celebrate the achievements of carer)
6 Changing the balance between power and helplessness as my understanding changed and self-confidence developed

Overall, the centrality of feeling heard is 'what helped' me to overcome the hurdles I faced as a result of my father's mental illness. In my experience 'feeling heard' captures the idea of feeling not just listened to, but also prioritised and understood. Through making me feel validated, feeling heard was the essential first step to realising difficulties and then wanting to change.

I have used the experience of attending Kidstime Workshops to analyse and describe my path to resilience. To professionals (of whom I am now one) I would say 'hold in your mind my description of how attending Kidstime made me feel; how empowered, respected and prioritised I felt as a result, and do all you can to leave the children you cross paths with, with the same feeling'. This can be done by providing them with an explanation about their parents illness they are able to understand or something as simple as asking them what they think should happen. In both you are letting them know they are important and sending the message that in your view they are capable of dealing with something they are managing day in day out. Maybe then they will see themselves as capable too. There is a high chance that other adults they meet are ignoring them and by doing so are implicitly sending the message that they, as children, are not capable. This fear of not being capable, which I hope came across in this chapter, was my biggest fear all along.

Chapter 5

From child of a parent with mental illness to becoming a therapist

What made a difference along the route

Chineye Njoku

London and Nigeria: different cultural lenses on mental illness

My mother developed a mental illness when I was born and at the time my father thought that her mental illness was underpinned by supernatural causes that required a spiritual intervention. My mother struggled with her illness for two years when my father decided to search for a spiritual intervention in Nigeria. He relocated the family (mum, sister and I) to Nigeria when I was two years old from the United Kingdom. Whilst in Nigeria, the traumatic experience of religious exorcism caused her health to deteriorate further and so she decided to move back to the United Kingdom. I was four years old at the time. My father also left Nigeria a few years later, leaving my sister and I behind with his relatives as he felt my mother was not well enough to look after us in the United Kingdom. Whist in Nigeria, my sister and I had to look out for each other. The conditions we found ourselves in placed a lot of strain on our relationship. However we endeavoured to be there for one another, especially in times of crisis. I particularly struggled to process the way in which my mother was described. She was often referred to as a lovely woman with 'madness'; and this created an image in my mind of an insane and unkempt woman with no sense of control or dignity. I avoided talking about her, as it was easier that way. It was difficult for me to process having a 'mad' mother. The belief at the time was that 'mad' people are possessed with spirits. I could not quite process what that actually meant but I knew it was something I ought to be ashamed of. I became more subdued. I remember bursting into tears whilst waiting to be picked up after school and a student asked where my mother was. I simply ignored the question and walked away, perhaps because she evoked a subject matter that I learnt to avoid cognitively.

In 1999, I was reunited with my mother in the United Kingdom. I was now nine years old and seeing my mother for the first time in five years. Meeting her after so many years resulted in an implosion of emotions that I couldn't fathom; it was a mixture of some excitement and some confusion. I had never experienced my mother's illness first hand, and could not make sense of my mother's countenance. I couldn't understand why she stared at us so vehemently and struggled to connect emotionally. Despite her very peculiar demeanour, I was simply happy to be finally reunited with my mum. It was also a relief that she was not the insanely, unkempt, scary looking woman that I imagined.

Living with foster parents

My mother experienced a relapse the week we arrived in the United Kingdom and her social worker decided that we could not live with her. My aunty could not accommodate both my sister and I, so we were separated. My sister stayed at an aunt's house in Milton-Keynes, while I stayed with another aunt in London. I remember being downcast about the decision to separate us, as well as not being able to live with the one person, my mother, I had yearned to see for many years. Nobody asked how I felt, so I was silent. I felt my opinion was unimportant, so I decided to do as I was told and endure the hurt in silence. I was enrolled into primary school. My demeanour began to change at school; I became increasingly sombre and unobtrusive. I was successful academically but struggled socially as I was withdrawn and always quiet. My English teacher noticed that something wasn't quite right. I received a lot of attention from her that I had never really received from an adult, and this made me feel that someone genuinely cared about my well-being. I gradually disclosed what was happening in small tentative doses. She, in turn, never got involved in my personal life, but was there to listen to me and often ensured that I got involved in the fun activities at school. My mother's health improved and she was eventually discharged from the hospital. I was finally allowed to live with her. I completed primary school with very good grades in Mathematics, English and Science. I was thrilled to move on to Secondary School, but was slightly apprehensive about the prospects of making new friends. The difficulties I encountered strained the relationship with my sister, and we argued a lot. My aunty blamed us for my mother's illness and she often said that my mother was ill because my sister and I argued a lot. Subsequently, anytime we discerned that my mum was experiencing a relapse, we would ensure that we were on our best behaviour, the house was immaculate and we saved our arguments for when she was not in the room.

The impact of having a mother with a mental illness

Growing up, my mum did her best to ensure that we were not hugely impacted by her illness. When she was well, she took excessive measures to make up for her time in hospital by ensuring that she met our practical needs.

From child to becoming a therapist 71

Her way of expressing her love to us was by feeding us and always wanting to be around us. She seldom told us no and tried to give us whatever we asked for. However, she was often unwell and that meant that I was responsible for the practical tasks such as grocery shopping and doing the house chores. My mum had a schizophrenia and bipolar disorder diagnosis; as such, she had episodes of mania and depression. When she was depressed she would stay in bed crying all day and would lose interest in her daily activities. I felt guilty not being around to comfort her when she was depressed, and so I would regularly decline invitations to go out with friends, just so I was available to console and keep an eye on her. I found it emotionally and mentally draining. I came to realise that my mum's mood rubbed off on me. I was down when she was depressed and happy when she was happy.

My mum's depressed mood usually transitioned into mania. She would suddenly be filled with so much energy and have a virtually irresistible desire to talk constantly. In her manic phase, she would talk loudly, incoherently and emphatically. She experienced hallucinations and delusions. This frightened and confused me as I could not recognize her and struggled to communicate with her. She had racing thoughts, which made conversations with her disjointed and illogical. I was often embarrassed by her and avoided her meeting any of my friends during this phase. I recall a relapse occasion where I was on a bus with her, on our way home from grocery shopping. I sat on the top deck while she sat at the bottom deck. When the bus reached our destination, I heard my mum scream my name from the top of her lungs asking me to get off the bus. I felt so humiliated. I felt my face heat up instantly; I was filled with rage and didn't know what to do with myself. I sprang up, catapulted down the stairs and ran out of the bus with my head down. I felt very cross at my mum, all I wanted to do at that moment was hide. There were many instances like that where my mum embarrassed me and was completely oblivious of her actions. It was therefore difficult to be upset with her, as I knew her actions were due to her illness. There were times where I would purposely avoid doing things with her, particularly when she was unwell, to avoid being humiliated by her.

When my mum was in her manic phase of bipolar disorder, she had insomnia and did things that often had disastrous consequences. For example she would spend the whole day out of the house and when she came back home, she spent the whole night cooking. She did not cook quietly; she made a lot of noise with pots and cabinet doors. The slamming doors, aroma of the food and noise from her banging pots often woke me up. This was difficult for me as I was sleep deprived and consequently I struggled to stay awake and concentrate during the day at school.

My mum often went missing. I recall the first time she went missing; she wasn't home when I returned from school but I didn't think anything of it as I assumed she went shopping. However, as night approached, I became increasingly worried; I called her phone on numerous occasions, there was no answer on the phone. I was home alone. Trying to stay calm, I called most of my family members in London, but no one knew her whereabouts. However, when it was nearing 12am and I hadn't heard from her, I became extremely worried. I was flooded with a coalition of ideas in my mind as to what could have happened to her. I called the police. They attended the flat, asked me a few questions and took a photograph of her. Much to my relief, she was found a couple of hours later. The police returned with my mum; I could tell from her swollen, red panda eyes that she was exhausted. However, she was filled with so much energy and excitement; I knew I was not going to get any sleep that night. I immediately took advantage of the fact that the police were present and administered her medication in their presence to avoid any resistance from her. The police informed me that she spent the whole day on bus rides and a concerned bus driver contacted the police. After that occasion, my mum went missing a few times but I soon learnt not to get alarmed as she often found her way back home, albeit it was quite difficult managing my worries and anxieties.

My mum relapsed at least once a year and we got used to different faces from the social services who came into the house to speak to my mother and arrange for her to be hospitalised. They would often engage us with small talk and evade conversations relating to my mother's health or how we were coping with the problems at home.

Discovering Kidstime and play

Although I had a disjointed and distant relationship with the social workers, I have to admit that the best thing they ever did for my family was to refer us to the 'Kidstime' workshop. I do not remember the exact details of my first day at the project, but I remember that I felt very welcomed and free. I was free to laugh, free of responsibilities, free to have fun with the other kids there and I felt comfortable being a child. These were privileges that I seldom received at home. The importance of play has been vastly documented; play is essential for healthy brain development. Through play, children learn to socialize, communicate their thoughts and emotions and ultimately develop new competencies that increase their resilience and confidence.[1] Knowing that there were other children who also had a parent with a mental illness was a source of consolation for me; it gave me a sense of liberation that I cannot explain. I felt normal. The short and simple lessons conducted on mental illness that were part of the workshop made me realise that mental illness is just like every other illness in the sense that a part of the body stops functioning to its full capacity (in this case the brain), and is restored when it receives the appropriate treatment. These lessons helped erase the ideas that my mum was 'mad', which were fed to me by some family members, as well as in part from my culture and to some extent my religion. My mum had an illness like everyone else, which is beyond her control; this therefore made her normal. Yes she had a mental illness but was also a responsible mother.

What I gained from Kidstime

What stood out for me about the Kidstime workshop was the members of staff: a psychiatrist, a social worker, a dramatist, a support worker and a family therapist. They truly cared and took genuine interest in the families that attended the Kidstime workshop. The Kidstime model allows children to experience connection to other people. I connected with families with similar experiences as mine, and professionals who truly cared. As humans, connection gives purpose and meaning to our lives and this is particularly crucial for children. Children of Parents with a Mental Illness (COPMI) would have experienced many embarrassing and traumatic moments that may cause them to withdraw, become ambivalent or develop an overwhelming sense of responsibility, which may in itself have devastating consequences in the future. Children need connection with friends to develop normally and studies have shown that children with fewer opportunities to develop are less likely to develop cognitive abilities. COPMI children may experience too many moments of disconnection. My mum struggled to emotionally connect with us, especially when she was ill. I recall two occasions when we had to go into foster care because she was too unwell to look after us. Throughout our stay in foster care we could not visit my mother for various reasons; whilst I eventually got used to not knowing how she was, I worried excessively about her. I often thought about how she was and hoped that she was treated well in hospital. Kidstime gave me a strong sense of connection; I felt like I belonged to something.

Being seen and heard

Kidstime allowed me to be vulnerable and be truly seen. On reflection, the main reason why I avoided attention was because I did not want to talk about my difficult experiences. Talking about my experiences meant feeling the painful emotions that these memories evoked. It felt easier to cognitively avoid and dissociate from these memories or anything that triggered the memories in my mind. I genuinely thought that avoiding talking about my experiences would ensure that I had the headspace to focus on my education and other activities. Ultimately, I did not want to feel sad; I thought I could selectively numb sadness. I have now learnt that emotions cannot be selectively muted. Difficult emotions have to be felt, in order to be processed. The Kidstime staff gave me the attention I needed even though I tried to blend and avoid standing out. The environment was a safe space to be vulnerable and for me, being vulnerable was talking about my experiences. Seeing other children and parents open up about their difficulties gave me the courage to be vulnerable enough to talk about my own experiences. I developed a sense of belonging when I started to feel worthy of belonging. It was a setting where people truly knew me and made me feel special despite my family circumstances.

The conversations about mental illness provided an explanation for mental illness using simple, age appropriate and effective language, which is an achievement because mental health/illness is such a complex and misunderstood phenomenon. Having an explanation helped me realise that I was not to be blamed for my mother's illness. It helped me understand that my mother is actually normal; she has an illness just like everyone else but her illness has a strong mental component. I was skilled up with the language to describe my mum's illness, which to me was my own positive ammunition to use against those that were misinformed about mental illness. I learnt what to do in a crisis situation – I was told the numbers to call and who to contact. Although I still felt that I had some duty of care towards my mum, I was no longer burdened with an overwhelming sense of responsibility. I could reduce the amounts of things I did for her without a huge sack of guilt weighing on my shoulders. It was suddenly embedded into my mind that I was not responsible for her illness and it was reaffirmed that her unique mannerisms were due to her illness, which were definitely beyond my control. This helped reduce my levels of anxiety significantly.

Advocacy

The Kidstime staff acted as advocates. I remember a relapse episode when I was 15 years old where my sister contacted the crisis team because it became apparent that my mother was relapsing. They attended our flat and assessed my mother; when they left they soon contacted us back stating that she was not ill. We were quite worried about her health deteriorating further if she did not get immediate help. We then informed a Kidstime staff, who contacted the crisis team and requested for her to be assessed again. A psychiatrist from the crisis team assessed her and confirmed that she was indeed unwell; he reviewed her medication and she was eventually hospitalised. I recall another relapse episode where my mother was in hospital and the social workers gave us some money for food. We soon ran out of money and barely had any food left; we did not have our social worker's telephone number. So we contacted a Kidstime staff who made contact with the social service on our behalf. A social worker immediately came round to check up on us; we had different professionals attend the flat until we were eventually placed in foster care.

Being in a strange home and the constant worry of not being able to visit my mum in hospital affected my performance at school. My foster carer was generally okay; she ensured that we had food to eat and we got ready in time for school. She was placid but did not try to develop some kind of relationship with us. It was conspicuous that her job was to ensure we ate and had somewhere safe to sleep. She rarely spoke to us and there were a few occasions where she wasn't home when we came back from school and I would have to wait outside for hours for her to return. We did not have mobile phones at the time so there was no way of contacting her. I didn't feel I could say anything to

From child to becoming a therapist   75

her, as I was simply grateful we had somewhere to live. I started hanging out with the wrong crowd in year 10 and getting into trouble for sneaking out of school at lunchtime. Nobody in school was aware of my personal life. I did not want any attention; I just wanted to blend in and be normal like the other pupils. I knew I was on the wrong track as my grades were plummeting, but I did not know how to break away from friends that were a bad influence on me. The turning point for me was when my Secondary School English teacher, Mrs Johnson, noticed that I was being bullied and stood up for me. She asked for me to come and see her in her classroom during the lunch break. I was nervous, as this teacher was known for her strict, 'no nonsense' approach to teaching; yet I was determined not to divulge any information. Nonetheless, I obliged and went to see her. She expressed her concerns to me. She told me that she knew I was an 'A grade' student and perplexed at the gradual decline in my grades. She told me that it was not too late to turn things around and requested to know what was happening at home. I felt the iceberg in my heart melt, she told me what I needed to hear, and I burst into tears. I gradually felt I could open up and speak to her about things at home. She then planned with me things that I could do to get my grades back up again and stated that she would speak to my other teachers with my consent about giving me some extra support in loosening ties with the group of friends having a bad influence on me. To cut a long story short I totally broke away from the friends I was hanging around with, my grades started to improve accordingly and I moved back up to the top set in English.

After about six months of us being in foster care, my mum recovered and we returned to my mum's house. Her recovery lasted for almost a year and when I was 16 years old we both decided to go on holiday to visit my grandmother in Kenya during the summer holiday. We only intended to be in Kenya for two weeks. Kenya was beautiful and the people were a joy to be around. After a week in Kenya, my mum began to display all the usual signs and symptoms of her illness. We did not take any medication, as neither of us anticipated that the excitement of seeing her mum would cause a relapse. My mum's health deteriorated rapidly; she became extremely manic. This was the worst I had ever seen her. I asked my uncle to take her to the hospital, but he was hesitant; he said he did not believe hospital treatment could treat mental illness. Instead he and my relatives resorted to giving her traditional herbal treatment. It was obvious that their 'herbal cleansing' was redundant as my mum soon got out of control. After two weeks in Kenya, I had to make the difficult decision to go back to London, as I had to commence preparations for my GCSEs. My mum was too sick to come with me so she stayed behind. I left Kenya in fear of what was going to happen to her. It was difficult getting my mum back to London, as she was too unwell to get on a plane. I didn't know any of my mum's social workers, so I contacted a Kidstime staff and he got in contact with the social services; they liaised with my aunty in Kenya and insisted that they took her to hospital in Kenya.

76 Chineye Njoku

My mother's psychiatrist liaised with the doctors in Kenya about what medication to administer. That was a really stressful period for me, as I had to cope with mum being unwell and worrying that something bad was going to happen to her, as well as prepare to sit my GCSEs. Thankfully, I received a lot of support from the members of staff at Kidstime and my teachers at school. I achieved very good GCSE grades.

Genetics, the environment and creating possibilities

Kidstime creates an environment conducive for a child's development, which consequently builds resilience. Studies show that resilience is rare where adversities are continuous and extreme, and not moderated by factors external to the child.[2] Thus, the adults in a child's life must positively influence the way in which children cope with adversities. It is also imperative that professionals make a mental note of what aids resilience for both the parent and their children and encourage them to take-up the resources available to them. Encourage parents to connect with their children through reading and playing.

Genetics is not deterministic; it codes for proteins and not behaviour. Parents shape their children's experience by providing an environment that is conducive for healthy emotional and psychological development. If a parent is unable to parent due to a mental illness and thus unable to shape the child's environment, this could lead to some behavioural difficulties within the child. Genes do not fix behaviour in a rigid fashion but establish a range of possibilities that depend greatly on environmental influence. Children need to read, play and laugh with reckless abandon; ultimately they should be protected from the difficult facets of life and only experience these in small manageable doses. I had to grow up before my years but the Kidstime workshop provided me with the opportunity to be a child again. I played and laughed with the other kids there; it was my safe haven.

Children are born with a very basic mental structure (genetically inherited and evolved) on which all subsequent learning and knowledge are based. Children learn best in an environment, which allows them to explore, discover and play. Play is not simply the act of engaging with a list of play activities; however it has more profound sustained positive impact on children. Play is a medium by which children can practice behaviour without concern for its consequences. It enhances language development, social skills, creativity, imagination and thinking skills. Doris Fromberg[3] suggests that play is the 'ultimate integrator of human experience'. This means that when children play, they connect aspects of their past experiences, which includes things they have done, seen others do, read about or seen on television. They use these experiences to build play scenarios. The integration of these different types of behaviours is key to the cognitive development of young children.

As I got older, I got better at noticing the signs and symptoms of my mum's illness in its early stages and became more confident in holding firm conversations with the crisis team insisting that my mum was seen sooner rather than later. The crisis team was brilliant as they responded swiftly over time and developed a healthy patient-professional relationship with my mum. At the time I wasn't really aware of my responsibilities or how much of my personal life was being neglected; I just got on with it. It wasn't just practical responsibilities like the house chores that I had to adopt; I also had some emotional responsibilities.

Building resilience

Children are hard wired for struggle and discomfort. There's no doubt that the Kidstime workshops helped me build resilience. I consider resilience as the ability to bounce back after having a tough time. The positive adults in my life helped me bounce back and recover from adversities. My exposure to a positive environment compensated for my previous difficult experiences. In addition, I had other hobbies that helped me survive my difficulties. I loved drawing and writing songs. My hobbies helped me focus my attention on something other than my problems; it was my great escape from the struggles in my life; I could get lost for hours in my paintings and songs and it induced great happiness within me. I had my religion, Christianity, which gave me a strong sense of hope. I had hope that my future was going to be better than my present. I was also a member of the choir at my secondary school and part of a gospel band in church.

It also really helped having caring teachers. As I explained earlier, my English teacher in primary school was very attentive and acted on her instincts that something wasn't quite right with me. She kept asking how I was until I gave her an answer. In Secondary School I went from being a very driven and determined student in all the top sets at year 7 to hanging around the wrong group of friends and bunking off classes in year 9. My strict, no nonsense Secondary School English teacher helped me get back on the right path. Thanks to Mrs Johnson, I attained very good grades in Secondary School.

The very caring professionals that I had come across hugely inspired me; I therefore felt an enormous desire to give back. I felt I had found my calling, although I wasn't quite sure exactly what profession I wanted to go into; I had an idea that I definitely wanted to work with individuals/families where there was a person with a mental illness. I wanted to help build resilience. I volunteered at the charity and pioneered a teen group along with an adult social worker. I discussed my dilemma about what career field to go into with one of the kidstime staff; this informed my decision to complete an MSc in Mental Health and Psychological therapies. Upon completion of this course, I made an informed decision to become a psychological therapist. I now work as a cognitive behavioural therapist for the NHS.

My message to professionals

A service is nothing without the people that work within it. Whilst the NHS is better than health systems in comparable countries, it is not perfect. You may therefore encounter time constraints and staff shortages that may hinder you from staying as long as you would like with your clients. I work for the NHS so I understand how easy it is to become preoccupied with managing risk rather than being preoccupied with the factors that keep children safe. So I have nothing but sympathy for the social workers and the other professionals that do their job in autopilot mode without stopping to connect with us. Social workers, psychiatrists, nurses have such a difficult job. They have a high caseload with very little time and encounter many constraints that may hinder them from working to their full potential. Nevertheless, I would like to celebrate the social workers/teachers who made an impact, the ones that followed their instincts and acted upon their sixth sense. I am so grateful for the one's that took some time out to simply ask how I was, how I was coping with school and ultimately validated my experience.

We spend a lot of time training and learning about different techniques, strategies, and state of the art medicine, but my message is this: do not underestimate the power of basic human connection.

- Ask questions; ask the mothers and fathers in your care how they are and book follow up appointments. Ask if they have other children and what kind of support they have around them.

From child to becoming a therapist 79

- Refer families to local services that you think could be of help to them. Referring a family to a service might just be the transition point. A random social worker that I only met once referred us to the Kidstime workshop and the rest is history. It is therefore imperative that you maximise every opportunity with your patients because a short meaningful encounter could be a lifeline.
- Children also need to be clear about what services they have been referred to and be given a point of contact.
- You can help build resilience. Your actions should therefore positively influence the way in which children cope with adversities. When you ask questions, make a mental note of what aids resilience for both the parent and their children and encourage them to take-up the resources available to them. Encourage parents to connect with their children through reading and play.
- Don't underestimate the power of empathy and connection.
- Children need an adult to be their advocate. In my case it was my English teacher and the Kidstime workers.
- The young carers are also experts on their parents' illness. It is therefore important that the professionals involved communicate with the children and consider the young carers opinions on their parents' illness as it might help them feel heard.
- The professionals involved need not just to communicate with the children but also with each other, by holding meetings with the mental health workers and children's social workers both present.
- It is not always about medication and hospital. I strongly believe that the best treatment for mental illness is a combination of medication and holistic therapy.
- Foster carers should encourage a warm and caring relationship with the children under their care. This could help create a sense of belonging, respect and self-esteem for the children. Children do not only have material needs but also emotional needs; they come with thoughts and emotions and should therefore be listened to. A good relationship is the solid foundation by which children develop resilience and foster carers should view themselves as drivers of that honest caring relationship. They can break the ice by enjoying a shared, creative and leisure activity together. Children also need someone to look up to and foster carers may well be a role model.

Culture has remained a recurring theme for me and here are some of my arguments:

1   Make children aware of their rights and the services they receive, as they are more likely to lack knowledge of their rights/what they are entitled to. For example I was unaware of the services I was entitled to. I did not know that I could access counselling in the NHS and this was not offered to me.

2   Understand the family's culture so that the service is tailored towards each family. So what I mean is that staff should be alert and observant. Thus, observe the family's values and traditions. For example, it may be a family tradition to go to church on a Sunday or mosque on a Friday. Ensure that meetings are not arranged on those days. When families notice that they are being respected for who they are and what they believe in, they are more likely to be receptive and take part in developing a rapport with the professionals.

3   Service barrier – This is linked to the first point in that patients/carers may not speak English, thus may not bother enquiring about the services available to reduce any inconvenience/complication. It is therefore important for the staff to make it their duty to ensure the client's family is fully informed of any development in the service they receive. Sometimes patients/carers may avoid receiving a service due to the prejudice within the community. They may fear that someone within their community would find out that their loved one has a mental illness. Thus, explain confidentiality to them.

4   A large family does not in itself mean that sufficient support is available. It is easy to assume that because the young carer has a large nuclear or extended family that they are receiving emotional and moral support. Most people are not very well informed about mental illness and stigma very much exists even within families. For example some of my family members thought that my sister and I were to be blamed for my mother's illness and some still believe that mental illness is due to sinister causes. Thus, try to explore the family's cultural or religious beliefs about mental illness.

Carers from an ethnic minority background may feel that it is their duty to look after their parent in order to abide by their cultural/religious beliefs. They are therefore less likely to ask for help even when they desperately need it. It is therefore essential that they are encouraged to make use of the services available to them so that they can gauge a balance in their caring role. Lack of appropriate service may lead to feelings of isolation and forced dependency on family.

References

1   Mahoney, J.L., Harris, A.L., & Eccles, J.S. (2006). Organized activity participation, positive youth development, and the over-scheduling hypothesis. *Social Policy Report*, 20, 1–31.

2   Cicchetti, D., & Rogosch, F.A. (1997). The role of self-organisation in the promotion of resilience in maltreated children. *Developmental Psychopathology*, 9, 797–815.

3   Fromberg, D.P. (1990). Play issues in early childhood education, in C. Seedfeldt (Ed.), *Continuing issues in early childhood education* (pp. 223–243). Columbus, OH: Merrill.

Chapter 6

Commentary on a young adult's chapter

Lou Ryan – Parent of Georgia Irwin-Ryan

As a parent who has been mentally ill for the majority of their life, it is very difficult for me to be objective about my illness. I think that I'm being fair, understanding and supportive of my children, but the reality is that mental illness makes it very difficult for anyone to be that way. I was once told that mental illness is a selfish disease and I was very offended. However, it *is* selfish, because the symptoms ensure that the patient is cocooned in their own feelings, no matter how much they wish it weren't the case.

Reading Chineye's account of her childhood makes me realise just how difficult it is for children to cope with a mentally ill parent. I was also the child of a mentally ill parent and have now, in turn, become the parent with mental illness. I thought that my own experience as a child had educated me as to what it's like for my children, and perhaps to an extent it did. However, Chineye's account has made me realise that each child has a very different experience and may need different types of support. The cornerstone of any support, though, has to be communication. This is where Kidstime has played an integral role. Throughout Chineye's teenage years, it was obvious just how much of a positive effect Kidstime had. Kidstime is a catalyst for communication between children and their mentally ill parents. The Kidstime staff are also professionals who listen rather than judge. This is essential to help children in their development – it is crucial mental and emotional support.

Living with a mentally ill parent is confusing and frightening for children. They don't understand what's going on and they can't ask their mentally ill parent because they are the cause of the child's dismay. In addition, if there is a second parent who isn't mentally ill, they often are overwhelmed trying to cope, so that they are at a loss to know what to say to the child. Kidstime gives a forum for all parents, well and unwell, to attend and discuss mental illness with their children. It also gives children a safe space to speak their truth as to how their mentally ill parent's behaviour affects them and makes them feel.

It's also important to note that when a parent is mentally ill, the extended family and/or close friends of the family can very often take on caring roles for the children. This was brought home to me in Chapter 1 by Alan Cooklin. We have to ask ourselves – 'what is a family?' This is because illness of any description can disrupt the parent or parents' ability to care adequately for the children and so other members are brought in to assist. This extended family unit can be essential to keep stability for the children. However, the children can often be aware that perhaps their friends at school don't have this sort of arrangement and can be unsure of why they are different. As Alan discusses in his chapter, in reality there is no 'average' family. Although there are many different possible structures to a family unit, there can be no doubt that for the children to feel safe and secure in their home life there should be a 'social group where some or all of the adults are committed to care for the emotional and physical needs of the children while they are growing up'. This is where I found Kidstime to be invaluable. It was centred on the child and their family – no matter how the child was receiving care and support, Kidstime added an extra layer of security. This was a safe environment where the children could openly and honestly express their concerns or worries. Or they could ask questions that they perhaps didn't feel they could ask members of their family. Children are very astute and often know when things are wrong with a family member such as a parent. But they lack the insight and experience to know how to ask about it. They often feel it is their fault and they should keep quiet rather than possibly upset the adults.

I remember as a child being terrified of my father. I also remember being told at approximately 14 years old that my father was mentally ill. It was a shock, and made me feel as though my childhood had been a lie. I had always thought that everything was my fault, but now I knew that my father's illness had played a huge part in his behaviour and that it wasn't my fault. That made me understand the need for communication with children. However here's the rub: when I was coping with my mental illness, even though I knew that communication with the kids was the best thing, I found myself avoiding the issue and just saying 'mummy doesn't feel well'. Then when their father was also diagnosed with mental illness, I found myself not explaining it again, other than to say 'daddy's not well'. It's difficult to open up and talk about mental illness with children. One is conscious of the fact that we don't wish to cause distress to our children by our explanation, and this tends to cause us to not explain our illness in an open enough manner. Without knowing it, we have swept it under the rug again.

Trying to compensate for having a mental illness is a double edged sword. As Chineye commented about her mother, 'Her way of expressing her love to us was by feeding us and always wanting to be around us'. I found this to be the case. I wanted the kids around all the time – I loved hearing them talk about their day and, apart from going to school, I didn't like them spending time outside of the home. Although this was my way of protecting them and doing a good job as a parent, unfortunately it meant I was very clingy and

Commentary on a young adult's chapter 83

very needy, which is the opposite of being supportive. However, as Chineye was lucky enough to find a supportive teacher in Primary School, I found the same in my children's Primary School. Support from those that surround our children on a daily basis is essential to help them realise their potential and to feel safe when they are away from home. It may be felt that this shouldn't be the function of a teacher. However, because children spend so much of their time in the school environment, teachers are well placed to notice if a child is experiencing difficulties. The information that Kidstime makes available, for example in the film, 'The Jass Story'[1], shows how children are affected and how support can make a huge difference.

As a mentally ill parent, visiting Kidstime with my children was an invaluable tool. I could relax knowing that my children were getting support in a fun environment, and that they could chat to other children who knew exactly what it was like to be the child of a mentally ill parent. The drama and other games played helped them articulate their frustrations, feelings and thoughts. In addition, it helped us parents to see things a bit more objectively. Having a mental illness makes one very defensive. We know that our illness has a negative impact on those around us, particularly our children, but the huge burden of guilt on our own shoulders makes us almost want to deny it.

It made me very upset to read Chineye's account of being fostered.

> My foster carer was generally okay, she ensured that we had food to eat and we got ready in time for school. She was placid but did not try to develop some kind of relationship with us. It was conspicuous that her job was to ensure we ate and had somewhere safe to sleep. She rarely spoke to us and there were a few occasions where she wasn't home when we came back from school and I would have to wait outside for hours for her to return.

This is a parent's nightmare, having their children taken into foster care, even if it is only for a short period of time. Often social services will attempt to place a child with a member of the extended family, but this isn't always possible. It is essential support for both children and their parents, but sometimes the care is the most basic as Chineye described. There is no emotional support for the children, no matter how essential it is at times for children to spend time away from their parents. I remember when my children were taken into foster care for a couple of weeks when I was particularly ill. There was a physical pain in the pit of my stomach; I had done something wrong as a parent and was causing so much pain for my children. I wish that I had been able to access Kidstime during the period immediately upon the children's return. I feel that I could have supported my children so much more with Kidstime's assistance. We did eventually join Kidstime once we had moved house to an area where it was available.

Chineye, quite rightly, comments that, 'Children also need to be clear on what services they have been referred to and be given a point of contact', and that, 'The young carers are also experts on their parents' illness. It is therefore important that the professionals involved communicate with the children and consider the young carers' opinions on their parents' illness as it might help them feel heard'. As I said near the beginning of this commentary, communication is essential to help children cope with the daily stresses of being a young carer. They are forced into situations where they have masses of responsibility at a very young age. They need the knowledge of *why* they are in that position, and *how* they can get support.

In conclusion, mentally ill parents are often loathe to discuss their illness with their children, but with the help of organisations like Kidstime, they can do so in a safe environment which gives valuable support to children who are young carers. Communication between different agencies such as social workers and health professionals is essential and *must* include the children in their discussions, rather than excluding them. Children of mentally ill parents need to be recognised as individuals who should have a say on the type of support that both they and their parent(s) receive.

Note

1 See Chapter 10 for link.

Chapter 7

Breaking out of the trap of constricting loyalty

Georgia Irwin-Ryan

My story – introduction

My name is Georgia and I want to share with you the experience I had of parental mental illness, and how the intervention of mental health care, social services and other agencies affected this experience. I hope to offer some insights into the impact of my parents' illnesses on myself, as well as some suggestions for professionals, parents and young people.

At the age of 10, I witnessed my mother have a meltdown, resulting in my parents wrestling throughout our small flat as my father attempted to stop my mother from leaving as she had said that she wanted to kill her own father – my grandfather. I was faced with a tough decision in that moment as my father shouted at me to call the police, something I couldn't do out of fear I would be betraying my mother. Calling the police meant I was wrestling with the decision of protecting my mum or protecting myself; I knew why my mum felt so angry towards my granddad, but it didn't change the fact in my mind that calling the police could mean I would never see my mum again. Eventually, my father managed to calm my mother enough for him to call the police himself, and they arrived shortly afterwards along with the ambulance service.

As the paramedics treated my mum in the living room, the police officers talked to my brother and I by the front door; they had arrived around the same time and I remember feeling on edge because I believed at the time the police only ever came to your house when someone was going to be arrested. They asked us about what happened, and I remember not telling the whole truth, scared to tell them that my mum had wanted to kill my granddad because I knew that she could be arrested for it. I was in a situation where telling the truth would leave me all alone; my dad had been hospitalised several times over the years and he had only having recently recovered from completely forgetting who we all were due to having Post Traumatic Stress Disorder (PTSD), so I knew he couldn't look after my brother and I on his own.

This was not the first time I had experienced scary behaviour from my parents; there were times when my dad would disappear and end up staying in a halfway house after being found in a nearby park, or close to a level crossing. Other times my mother had ended up in hospital due to her drinking problems in conjunction with the mental health issues she had already been dealing with. But this time felt different; I was feeling so frightened that my family would be pulled apart forever; there was an extreme knot in my stomach that wouldn't go away the whole time I watched the police and paramedics wandering around our small living room; I knew that there would be more consequences this time.

Shortly after our conversation with the police officer, a social worker came and asked my brother and myself again about what had happened once more. When we had finished going through it again, I remember being told that my parents were going to be in hospital for a while, and that my brother and I were going to be staying with another family for a while. In my mind I had imagined a classmate's family. I had no idea she meant we would be staying with complete strangers until we got into a police car and were driven to meet the mum of this new family.

Foster care: being faced with what I missed

The foster mother was kind, tactful; it seemed likely she was used to children coming in and out of her home who didn't want to talk about why they ended up there. However, we were given no indication as to when we would see our parents again. We were shown the bedroom we would sleep in, and although it was clean, warm and comfortable, I couldn't sleep. I thought I had lost my mum. Nobody seemed to really want to tell me what was going on. Whether they didn't think I would understand or that it was easier to just say my mum was ill, I will never know. The next morning we were expected to go to school as normal, taken in by the mother of the family we were staying with. I remember not wanting to go to school. I just wanted to know where my mum and dad were and how they were doing. We met the social worker a few times as she asked how we were settling in. I remember her saying my mother was in hospital to get better, but she never explained why she needed to get better or from what. Every time a social worker said this, I expected my mum to come home, back to normal, like she used to be when I was five or six. But this never happened.

A week passed before we were finally able to see our parents in a neutral setting where social workers observed. I remember my mum telling me that the only reason she was alive was for my brother and I, telling us that the week she had lost us was the worst week of her life. I remember the idea of my mum being dead flashing through my mind when she said that. I felt a much heavier burden to be loyal to her no matter what. The next day we were back home, with no real explanation of why my mother had tried to escape our flat and kill her father, nor an explanation as to why my father was so disconnected from us all.

I found myself upset that I had been shown what a normal family without constant fear or stress looked like, only to be thrown back into the tumultuous environment I had come from. For a week I had found myself in a tidy, calm environment with a clear, set routine; my foster mother combed my hair to get rid of the lice that had gone unnoticed and we had home cooked meals every night. Then I was back in a cramped flat with my parents who were still being severely affected by their respective mental illnesses. I was terrified of my parents but felt responsible for keeping them alive, desperate to receive the 'normal' type of love I could still remember from when I was very young, when we had home cooked meals and love was expressed without the pressure of my parent's mental illnesses looming over its meaning. So, I shut my mouth and forced myself to deal with the hand I had been dealt, assuring our social worker I was fine.

What was missing: an explanation

If anyone had told me that my mum behaved the way she did because of the way her brain handled information and thoughts, just that one simple sentence, I would have been able to understand her behaviour easier. If professionals hadn't given me the false hope that my mum would 'get better' as soon as she had finished a week or two in hospital, I wouldn't have found myself so devastated every time she came home and seemed just as bad as before she went away. I found myself expecting my mum and dad to wake up one day and be exactly the way they were when I was six years old. Being given the support and tools to face up to this helped me to come to terms with the idea that my parents would not be the same as they used to be, even when they had found the right treatment for their conditions. If even one adult had said anything to help me to cope with the stress of my home situation or told me it was okay to tell an adult when I was scared of the way my parents behaved, I wouldn't have struggled so much with my own demons on top of helping my parents to deal with their mental health conditions.

Throughout the years after that, I saw extreme behaviours not only from my mother but my father too. He was still struggling to come to terms with traumatic events he had experienced in his younger years. My brother was reliant on me to comfort him, playing games with him for hours on end, wrestling and having massive rows with him over the fact we had to clean the kitchen. I had to comfort my mother every time I saw her cry. My mother was angry with everyone, my dad, social services, frustrated with my brother and me. I had to quickly adapt to my mother's mind-set of trusting no-one, keeping secrets about my home life throughout primary and the beginning of secondary school. This helped me to concentrate on my school life in the short term; I didn't have to worry about my mother breaking down into tears under the scrutiny of social workers. I just tried to pretend I was the same as my peers, that my parents' mental health issues weren't as bad as they really were.

The fallout on my relationship with my mother

However, when I was aged 12, tension between my mum and I had grown due to the fact she was constantly fighting with my dad. I hadn't realised it yet, but my mother was taking her frustrations out on me whenever my dad called her names. One night I had enough when in the middle of a row, my mother threw a phone against the wall. Suddenly, I felt as though I was going to end up back in the old flat we had lived in the years before and I panicked; shoving my coat, shoes and grabbing my oyster card I left the house, slamming the door the same way I had seen my mum do whenever it all got too much. In the middle of the night I showed up at a friend's house and begged them to let me stay; when they asked me why all I could say was 'I'm scared of my mum'. My mum called the police, reporting me missing, they showed up at my friend's house at one in the morning to ask me if I would go home. I refused. They brought me my uniform and the next day at school we had a meeting to discuss what had happened and why I had run away. I remember my mum crying, saying she was scared that she would never see me again. By the end of the meeting all I could feel was guilt and helplessness that nothing was going to change; I had to just accept my mum's behaviour and ignore how it had made me feel that I was in a situation where I felt like nobody cared about me. They only cared about keeping up the appearance of me being in a family setting, no matter how broken and terrifying it was.

Adapting to a parent's world view as a way to keep contact

For years afterwards I found myself adapting to the way my mother viewed the world, mimicking her distrust in everyone as an outlet for my frustrations, believing that social services only came to the house to make us feel inferior as a family for not being able to function the way they wanted us to. Even when I finally began to be offered support that truly did help me through the charity Family Action, I found myself being reluctant to truly express how bad things at home truly were; I also found myself partially in denial – I had both of my parents when other people had neither, I should appreciate it, why didn't I? When I became involved with Kidstime, it was explained to me exactly what was going on with my parents, why they behaved like they did. I was shown a simple diagram of the brain and what was going on in comparison to mine. I finally understood why my parents had such extremes of behaviour; I also understood why they treated my brother and I the way they did. Through both Family Action and Kidstime I found myself feeling as though I was being surrounded by a community that understood, didn't want to judge and tried to help me understand just why the situation I was in was different.

Throughout the years I catered to my mother's view of the world, not challenging her in any way, only speaking about the things she wanted me to tell support workers, becoming more and more isolated due to the black and white mentality I had ended up with. I accepted that bad things happened to her and began to feel guilt if I couldn't protect her from insensitive doctors or harsh social workers. In one instance when I was about 12 or 13, I had to take responsibility for kicking a social worker out of the house. The social worker had started to blame my mother for the fact the house was not being looked after; cleaning had ended up being the duty of my brother and I because of my mother's history of back problems. My mum descended into a state of panic and I had to get the social worker out of the house. I asked her to go repeatedly, but she was ignoring me. It wasn't until I ended up raising my voice and telling her to get out because she was upsetting my mother even more that she finally left. That was one of the first times I really understood that I was the only thing protecting my mother from professionals who were overworked, underpaid and didn't have the energy to handle our situation with delicacy.

All in all, the impact of my adaptation to my mothers' views and experiencing several crises meant that I became extremely sceptical of most people in power. I found myself lying whenever I was offered support from mental health experts for my own anxieties and depression, playing how I felt down and not wanting to tell the whole truth about my home life.

A moral of the tale

Reflecting, if I had been more honest earlier, I could have found the right help quicker. It took several attempts at different talking therapies before I was able to address my mind-set honestly and candidly. That is the message I would pass on to other young people who have similar experiences.

Comment from Georgia's mother – Lou

It was a very difficult read, but I'm so proud that she has been able to be honest and is so articulate in her description of her experiences.

Chapter 8

Parental mental illness and extra difficulties for children when parents divorce

Gill Gorell Barnes

Introduction

In this chapter I will talk about some of the things that may happen to both parents when one of them who suffers from mental illness leaves, or is left by the other. Whether this separation has been planned, or happens without one parent accepting that it is going to happen, it changes the family and the way it runs. The ways in which each parent relates to each other, as well as to the children, take on new shapes. I have experienced this myself as a child, and later as a grown up worked with the complicated arrangements that often develop around looking after children following parental separation. My work has been in two settings, CAMHS (Child and Family Mental Health Services) as well as expert witness planning the future best interests of the child, in court proceedings. In the Children Act, 'the best interests of the child' are paramount in defining the legal basis for work in the Family Court, and in any planning that is made for future care and parental contact in troubled situations. Thinking about promoting the child's resilience is a continuous part of the work.

My story as a teenager

When I was a teenager my mother and father separated after many years of living unhappily together. My father suffered deep depressions and drank too much as a coping mechanism. Even as a child I knew this attempted solution did not work, and it usually led to extreme angry outbursts on my mother's part, to ongoing rows about money, and to further depression and withdrawal on the part of my father. In many ways I was relieved when they separated as I thought they might have happier lives apart from one another. For my mother this did happen, but for my father it did not; and I ended up feeling that I was the one who had to look after him, as many children do, and as testified by many of the young writers in this book. My mother encouraged my emotional involvement with him, as she thought it would 'cheer him up' to have me visit him often, but it did not cheer *me* up, and

I was often angry about the position she put me in, as well as about some of the very difficult situations I chose not to tell her about. Nonetheless, in the same way as the young people growing up with a parent with mental illness have written in this book, I did not question that I should look after him, although I later questioned some of the emotional jobs that I felt had been delegated to me. I continued to value the fact that he was my dad and wanted to see me, and over the six years I knew him after their separation and before his death, I loved him more as a friend who needed looking after, and did not expect any care from him in return.

When I work with families in which parents have separated, I am always alert to the different hopes and expectations that the children will have about their future relationship with their parent who no longer lives with them. Usually they take for granted that the parent they *live* with will go on being very much the same as they were before, although this is not always the case. Sometimes both parents change a lot. The question of how a mental illness itself is managed, whichever parent is directly affected, may also take on different forms; the absence of a partner leads the ill parent to need to find new ways to accommodate illness with a life he or she can live. A child can be drawn into this in ways that are not good for them.

In the examples of difficult situations that I give in this chapter, I will primarily highlight the childrens' experience. I believe it is important to continue to know about and be in touch with a parent who lives out of the home, even if s/he still suffers from mental illness and shows what you as a child see as 'weird' behaviours at times, as long as that parent can still love you as a person who is separate to them. If you are their child then they are still your mum or dad, and as long as your time with them is not harmful to you, their love can still be of value to you. As one dad said 'What's good for them about coming to see me? When they do, they experience love and I think that's good for everybody'.

As a child of a parent suffering mental illness, do you always experience love when you meet your parent?

However, there is often a gap between what a parent who is ill may wish to show their child and what actually takes place between them. If you are that child, there may be limits in the way you can have a good relationship when you are physically together, and there may be reasons why you will do better if there is another grown up with you when you visit your ill parent, or when they visit you. In some cases, as with Dawn in the final example in this chapter, a direct personal contact may not be in your best interests, as you may not feel resilient enough to manage the expectations put on you by your parent, for example sometimes over-extreme demands for love from you.

Indirect contact may then be safer until you feel ready, as an older person, to take the risk of being with that parent face to face.

Adapting to mental illness in a parent is hard enough when they live with you, as other chapters in the book describe, but when the ill parent lives away from home, and wants to stay in touch, adapting can be doubly difficult. This is because:

- The 'out of house' parent, who used to live with you, may have feelings of outrage and injustice about being separated from you, which can affect the kinds of texts they write, or phone calls they make
- You yourself will have lost touch with what was the familiar everyday mum or dad, and not be so attuned to managing their moods when they are unwell

For example one father I knew, who we will call Mark, was determined to have his children to stay overnight when they visited, and they *did* want to stay with him. However, sometimes he could not control his changing moods – which could include ranting and throwing things around – and the children became frightened because they could no longer predict how fast this change could happen, although they had been able to predict it, and were therefore not so frightened, when they saw him every day. Usually if he felt himself 'slipping' he could call on a close friend nearby to give support. However, his teenage son Ryan had lost touch with how to accurately gauge when his father was moving beyond his normal manageable emotional state, and tended to wait until Mark's mood had escalated too high, rather than involve the close friend or his mother. He knew that if he did call his mother, she would want to rush to collect them, whereas usually they wanted to stay and help dad calm down. The system of managing all this broke down when Ryan's younger sister Dionne became frightened at the way her dad was 'ranting', and at the same time rejecting her hugs and soothing words which usually calmed him. Instead he had pushed her away saying 'this is your fault', after which she texted her mother. Mark then had to give up having his children overnight, because the balance had swung too far in the direction of the children becoming his carers, rather than him being the dad they wanted to spend time with.

Trying to make arrangements that work better: developing resilience through having some control

During the 40 or so years I have worked with parents separated from their children, I have often helped them to draw up 'contracts' together on how visits will go in the future. However before a parent can engage properly with such an idea, he or she has to be ready to see their children's point of view. For example one father, Adie, said in front of his children 'Life without my children is a really horrible thing to think about' and his daughter replied 'I'm glad you feel like that because the way you feel is the way we feel about not having you as the father we want, and haven't had for a rather long time'. His two daughters then got down to drawing up a list of things they would *not* put up with when they were with him, which included shouting, hitting, ranting and 'stomping around', throwing things and swearing at them. They agreed to continue contact on condition that these behaviours were not repeated, which if they were would mean they would leave or call in a grown up, 'either mum or a friend'. Although this was an imposed 'contract', it was agreed and signed by all three of them and became a successful way of making a point to their 'out of house' father about safe and more age appropriate behaviour.

When risks are more extreme

Many children in the United Kingdom experience the divorce of their parents, but the court does not usually become involved in the arrangements for their care. It is sometimes not possible for the parents on their own to make safe arrangements for contact that hold together, even though the ill parent and their children may *both* want this. In these circumstances the court may become involved in making safe arrangements. The families described in this chapter involve children with mothers who are no longer living at home due to extreme behaviours generally associated with their own mental illness. However they want to stay in touch and be part of their children's lives in spite of the very difficult circumstances. On the other hand the fathers of the children often do *not* feel it is in the best interests of the children for the mothers to stay in touch. Children are often uncertain about what they want, and in fact are often as upset by all the rows about what will happen, as they are about losing one of their parents.

Elsewhere I have written in detail about what I ask parents to think about when they are making plans for sharing the care of their children in highly stressful and often angry situations.[1,2] At such times parents are often more pre-occupied with their own needs than with those of their children, with whom they feel intensely 'tangled up' and cannot think about clearly. As a result I ask parents to consider questions which will help me decide whether they can think about their children as having needs of their own. For example:

- Is each parent able to think about what might be best for their children given the circumstances they are in?
- Is each parent able to think about what the emotional needs of their children might be?
- Are they able to plan workable structures for their children to have time with each of them?

Where a parent has a serious *mental* illness it may be hard for them to think about their children's needs as separate from their own, and it may be necessary to repeatedly help them think about what their child may be thinking or feeling as distinct from their own thoughts and feelings. It has been very helpful to develop the child's resilience through engaging other family members when available, to help a parent work out plans in sensible ways that take into account the child's feelings, fears and anxieties. This may include having a familiar family member around during contact as part of a long term plan.

How long has a mental illness been going on?

Mental illness will often have already made looking after the children a more difficult shared task for parents, before the separation happens. Difficulties may start at the beginning of a child's life, if a mother suffers a mental illness, which first shows itself soon after the birth of a child such as depression or even psychosis (often referred to as puerperal psychosis). A mother may become invaded by terrifying thoughts and dangerous urges towards her baby as well as having delusions about what may be going on around her. When this happens, it may be a short lived illness from which the mother can recover fully, or it can recur or drag on, affecting the whole future story of a child's relationship with each parent. The trauma of the illness in the mother can then lay down patterns that minimise the direct contact between the mother and the baby, whilst increasing intimate contact between the father and his children. Those patterns may not be a logical response to the illness in the mother in the longer term, but will be affected by the beliefs and prejudices of all other family members involved and can become 'fixed', as though normal and necessary, even if actually they are not.

An ideal in family life is that parents can *share* a framework for bringing up their children and be responsive to one another in this process, as Alan Cooklin has outlined in the first chapter. A lot of research has shown how difficult it can become for children when their parents are *not* responsive to one another and continually disagree. Research also shows that when a father's attempts to look after his children are not supported by their mother, the continual disagreement and rowing become bad for children's everyday development and sense of well-being.[3] Unfortunately, a father's attempts to make up for a mother's illness by caring more intensively for the children are in fact *often not* supported by her.[4] This can be for many reasons; that she may feel he is taking her place, that it makes her feel more distanced from her children who are a source of love and support that she craves for *herself* (rather than that she looks after *them*) and because her illness itself may affect and even distort the way she thinks about her children and what they need on a daily basis. The children will naturally come to experience their father as the more stable and reliable parent, which can then be doubly hard for the mother to bear. An example of this follows from Tom and Jera, aged 12 and 10, the sons of Joanna and Peter.

'We can't be certain how mum will be when we visit her'

Joanna had suffered from a 'mysterious' illness, never named to them while their father had looked after her on and off for 15 years when she was unwell. When their parents eventually separated the children went to live with their father, which their mother opposed through an application to the Family Court. They were then faced with helping the Court decide how much they should spend with each of their parents. This had been difficult for them, since their parents separated, as their mother sometimes appeared very well and was able to hold down an important job, whereas on other occasions she was unable to function in the outside world at all. She had been able to hide this unevenness while she was living at home and their father managed the household, and they had been able to have a warm relationship with her. However, after the separation they did not see enough of her to feel confidently in touch with how she was functioning.

Tom and Jera described things that their mother said and did which made them scared about visiting her at home without another adult present. Joanna, although contesting this idea, had gone along with it, meeting them only in public places, until their father, Peter, became engaged to another woman. This led Joanna to apply to the Court for the children to return to live with her, as she could not bear the idea of another woman looking after *her* children. Tom and Jera still insisted they did not want to live with her.

Joanna's mood fluctuations had not so far been the subject of any diagnosis made available to the Court. This was partly because she was a legal professional herself, and her mood changes had remained almost 'invisible' in a work setting. Only Peter and the children seemed to be aware of them. Peter continued to say that he did not believe Joanna was able to manage the children on her own, particularly as she still did not admit she had ever been ill. However a year later, under pressure from Joanna's family, he risked the children seeing her in her own home, providing he could supervise the visit. As she refused this condition, he and the boys finally agreed to try the visit out as long as dad was *nearby* and they could phone him. Things went badly wrong. Joanna chose to lock the children in the house, including locking the windows, and removed their mobiles to prevent them ringing their dad (which she defined as 'interfering'). When Tom tried to unlock the window and climb out, saying he felt unsafe because she was 'acting weird', she wrestled with him to prevent him leaving. The reality of her fear of failing as a mother, and the determination to make contact in her own house, became more powerful in her mind than giving the children a warm experience of being comfortable to be with her. When this was discussed with her later, she was unable to take responsibility for any possible effects of her own actions on the children. Her eldest son said: 'I feel scared and out of control when these things happen, and I just want to stay with dad now'. So in this family the messages Joanna was getting from her own mind about proving she was a good parent were stronger than her ability to behave like one. As a result, contact required a more public setting for the children to feel safe and to be able to fulfil their part in her parental wish to show love to them. Contact had to remain in settings away from her house from then on.

Mother becoming ill and father taking charge

In each of the examples that follow it was the father who took on the primary responsibility for the care of their baby during the mother's illness following the birth. One father described his early experience this way

> Maria was really happy following Jake's birth. I sat with her in hospital, did everything for her and then at home I did everything for two weeks. The outside world didn't exist. As soon as I went back to work it started unravelling... I have never met anyone with such anger...she attacked me frequently, tore the buttons off my shirt, bit me.

Maria said about her own state 'I couldn't bear my conflicting emotions, on the one hand wanting him there, on the other wanting him out of my sight so I could be alone with Jake'.

How does it feel to be so vulnerable and out of control?

Maria described how her feelings towards her baby Jake could change. Sometimes she loved him and at other times she could feel very angry, and would be frightened that she couldn't control her own impulses and might hurt him. She wasn't sure how much her own mother could help her, because their relationship was very uneven. Some grandmothers can make their daughters feel that they are not good people, and that they themselves were not wanted or not really loved, and this is how she felt. Sometimes grandmothers themselves pass on by example the tendency to be violent as a response to stress, and have been unable to show, or teach, ways of containing and managing difficult and even dangerous feelings. We know now from many different pieces of research that any mother who has been at the receiving end of verbal abuse, laughed at or ridiculed for their sensitivity and even scorned or told they were odd or 'possessed' are less likely to manage their *own* babies and young toddlers well when the going gets tough. Many mothers with mental illness as adults had such earlier experiences of being described in negative ways. So if a husband or partner also makes critical statements, this can then play into these earlier experiences, and confirm self-images of themselves as bad people that have built up over time. This can then make them feel even less able to cope with their babies.

If a mother is later unable or not allowed to resume the direct care of her baby, and she continues to be seen by her partner as a possible or actual threat, the child's relationship with her won't have a chance to become secure and strong. In addition, the father may have become very vigilant, watchful and even fearful of the mother, on his own behalf, as well as wary about how she is with the children. This further gives a message *to* her that she is *not* a safe person to become attached to. Of course there can often be a realistic basis for the father's original fear and wariness. The children may have witnessed extreme behaviours in their mother such as harming herself, or harming their father, destroying loved objects, hurting pets or neglecting brothers and sisters. Weird behaviours can include refusing to feed the children, or involving them in rituals they recognise as odd compared to their friends. Many fathers in such situations may feel they have to physically separate from the mother for the protection of their children as well as themselves, although they may find the latter hard to admit.

Following the separation of their parents, children may receive, or just sense, complicated messages about the absent parent. These will be based partly on their own anxiety and concern, but also on their observations of their father's fears about their mother. As a result both parts of this complex mix of direct experience, and of having to watch the tense relationships between their parents, may remain a part of their frightening memory of their mother when they no longer live with her. This, in turn, may make it more difficult for them to feel safe to have contact with her in the future.

Using the Family Court to reinstate contact: 'do I want to know this mummy who keeps writing to me?'

The story of Euan aged five, his mother Oona, his father Colin and his stepmother Louise follows. When the focus of family stories after a separation, is on mental illness, and behaviour attributed to mental illness, then the more positive aspects of an ill parent, as well as good times that were had by the couple together, usually become suppressed or forgotten. This forgetting then often spreads to any good relationship a child may have enjoyed with that same mother, in the mind of the father, and therefore of the child as well. It is as though the positive images of the mother have been cut out, and the family has become closed against them. The way in which a family can close off a person or event which was disturbing – as though they had never existed – was named by Dennis Scott, an English psychiatrist, as 'closure' in relation to patients who had been kept in mental hospital for long periods.[5]

This pattern of 'forgetting' happened in the story of Oona and her son Euan, where descriptions of particular aspects of her illness behaviour had replaced the more whole person of 'mum' in the stories told about her. Her life was indeed characterised by impulsive actions, unstable moods and chaotic relationships linked to drug use, drinking and other risk-taking behaviour. These behaviours were recorded in different court papers at the time of Euan's birth and in his first year of life. She had made an application to the Court for contact and I was asked to advise the Court as an expert witness. When I first met her four years later, her warmth, her desire to develop her son's mind, her delight at enjoying his being in the world and her wish to be part of his identity were also clear, even if her way of attempting to be in his life had not been reliable or safe in earlier times.

The Court had to decide whether Oona meeting Euan, and becoming a part of his life again, would harm him as well as his secure step-family life, or whether a relationship with his biological mother would enrich his family life for the future and promote his own resilience as a child and young person. In order to try to achieve a safer image of her for Euan to think about, I also had to help his father, Colin, to deal with his own memories of life with her, which were not only traumatic for him, but which had been reignited by her recent tempestuous visits to the United Kingdom to try to get back in touch with her son. Colin had a powerful image in his mind of an 'evil web' he believed Oona had woven around his son as a baby, which included the use of witchcraft symbols, and rituals surrounding Euan which Oona had described as to 'keep him safe'. It had remained unclear whether this behaviour was part of a psychosis or just of extreme ideas expressed as part of a borderline personality disorder. Confusion about what, if any, diagnosis would make sense of Oona's behaviour resulted from the fact that her lawyers in Australia had successfully opposed the early hospital records from being presented to the English court, presumably as they thought that these might prejudice her application for contact with Euan.

Euan's early family story

Euan was born in Australia into a large family; he was looked after by many people, including Colin on the weekends and by his own mother, who breast fed him. Oona suffered from extreme mood swings for which she took both prescribed and non-prescribed drugs. At first Euan had lived in a disorganised emotional and physical environment on his own with Oona. His early removal to his grandparent's farm, and the network of care which that provided, probably protected him from some damage, but the reports of this period of his life remained unclear. Oona herself was unable to give any account of Euan's early months. At two years old Colin brought Euan to the United Kingdom to visit *his* own parents on *their* farm in Cornwall, and then did not return to Australia. He later met and became engaged to a local GP, Louisa. When the news of his imminent marriage reached Australia, Oona's family instituted court proceedings in the United Kingdom to try to resume contact with Euan. He was five years old when I was asked by his mother's solicitor in the United Kingdom to provide a report for the Court, by which time he had a baby half-sister, Bella.

Helping Euan make the bridges in his mind become stronger and develop family resilience

My first meeting with Euan was in his bedroom at home, where I found him playing with a model Australian goods truck on a huge road map laid out on the floor. When I asked him where the truck was going he told me it was thinking about making a long journey, but 'there was a lady there who might take me away'. He thought that I was something to do with this lady. We talked about what this might mean, and how we might go about making that lady part of Euan's family in a safe way. I suggested he might need to get to know all of his family in Australia a bit better before *he* could decide whether he would like to meet her. He showed interest in this adding 'I might like her if it was alright with dad'.

My first task was therefore to help Colin to be less threatened by Oona's wish to see her son, and not see it as destroying his second family. He also had to find a way to talk with Euan about his mother in ways that removed the threat of 'the lady' from his mind. At my request Oona's family sent photographs of Oona with Euan as a baby, doing well together. There were also happy photographs of Oona, Colin and Euan doing well together. These pieces of a different story of happiness between Colin and Oona in the past formed a basis for the new family story that I was able to build with Euan and Colin, in which Euan himself could see that he had belonged in another family earlier in his life. This had so far been unclear to him. In a later visit Colin produced a large photo album of his early life with Oona, and with her mother's family in Australia. Louisa joined in as he talked about family members with Euan, naming each of them as his grandpa, auntie, cousin, etc.

It was also important for Euan to discover that his mother's mind could work well alongside his, sharing ideas, stories and projects with her. Her interests had developed around studying the natural world; wild-life was also a passion of Euan's. I therefore encouraged Oona and her large extended family to exchange ideas about common wild-life interests, sending letters and picture books which were quite different from the earlier distressing letters, which had focused on emotion and possession; 'only I love you' or 'I am your rightful mother'. We gradually developed a strong extended family story, putting together family photo books, and narratives of grandparents and great grandparents. Colin became engaged in this 'two family' family project, now that the power of the earlier threats had diminished through the protection of the Family Court. He moved to accept that his life was a matter of common concern in 'the family in two continents', and Louisa bravely and determinedly helped both of them with all the homework involved. It took two years before we were ready for a family meeting with Euan's (Australian) granny and aunt who came over from Australia to see what contact might be possible in the future.

'We have to build bridges between the people in this room'

Euan's granny said of her daughter, 'I would like to see her re-establish some kind of bond, even though it may be that he is a teenager or a young man before he comes over'. Colin said with much emotion, 'this (meaning the meeting) could have happened a long time ago' and added that it was his belief that a point of safety had now been reached.

Why did it now become possible for Euan to think about meeting his mother in a positive way?

Following his father's declaration that he thought it was now safe to plan for a future that included Oona, Euan's longing to meet his mother became more open. His thoughts about his 'other family' had moved from being scared to being curious, and the flow of straightforward information about what lay overseas as a part of his future life became really exciting for him. Six months later, at a second extended family meeting, Oona joined in for the first time. The framework for this meeting was 'a very special day' set by Colin, as he put it to make it the best possible contact for Euan and Oona. He added that he and Louise were there to promote and support the contact as well as they could. As a result we proceeded to work using the framework of the extended 'two family family' - rather than two opposing families- which we had by now established and agreed.

> Euan, there are many families in the U.K. today where a child has two mothers, the mother whose tummy he was in, and who he was born to, and the mother he knows through his growing up in childhood. However, in your school you are the only child that you know of who has two mothers, so that makes you very special.

Euan joined in adding, 'I don't know anyone in my school that has a family like mine'. We all knew he had never been in the same room as both his mothers before, and he had not met his birth mother Oona since he was able to remember. This was indeed 'a big day' for both him and for her.

Oona and Euan shyly said 'hello' to each other, and Oona started chatting to him about wild-life in Australia; the neutral topic they had been writing to each other about. She showed him many photographs she had prepared for him. I invited Dionne, Oona's mother, to describe similarities between Oona at the age Euan was now and Euan himself, which she then shared in front of them both. Oona then became engaged with Colin in talking about Euan's schooling, and his achievements, and this developed into a wider discussion about Colin's and Oona's own abilities and interests as their son might share these. So that at this point they were thinking of him together as his parents from whom he may have learnt or gained skills. It was the first time he had experienced, and seen and heard, a co-operative exchange between his parents, and the room was filled with goodwill.

So why was this meeting good for Euan and how did it contribute to his future resilience?

- Euan became free of the fear that his mother – formerly seen as 'the mad lady in Australia' – might take him away and threaten his secure family life with his father and Louise
- Knowing his mother with whom he had many interests in common, directly as a warm presence, and experiencing her love
- Gaining some understanding of himself through discovering that 'she really likes the same things as me'
- Knowing he could enjoy **two** families, not that one had to replace the other, and that they could be with each other in the same room

This meeting provided the basic springboard from which further plans could be made for him, which included future visits from his wider family to the United Kingdom, as well as a planned visit from him to that family when he felt mature enough to do this in his teens.

A mother returning to a child in her adolescent years: the story of Dawn, aged 15, Marianne her mother, Johan her father and Mary her stepmother

Sorting out hazy and sometimes frightening memories of a parent, who has left when a child was very young, may become doubly difficult if that child also had very unhappy experiences of unprotected contact with that parent later on. When a parent who has suffered recurrent mental illness is trying to get back in touch with their teenage child after many years, there may be a long series of unhappy stories to be disentangled before a young person's goodwill can be reached. Because there were actual bad memories that Dawn had to contend with, it was less clear to her that it might benefit her to meet her mother, after a prolonged separation, when she was 15, than it had been for Euan at age five. She insisted that 'mum needed to get better first' – a similar response to that of Tom and Jera in the first example. When I first met Dawn she remained confused and angry by her mother's ongoing attempts to get back in touch with her through the Family Court. Marianne, her mother, was intensely involved with Dawn in her *own* mind in ways that did not take Dawn's separate development during the years away from her into account. I faced the question of whether it was going to be helpful for Dawn to be brought together with a mother who had not been part of her life for many years, and who continued to show frightening behaviours – behaviours which were similar to those that were present when the original separation took place. While Marianne was trying to re-establish contact with Dawn through the court, her father Johan and stepmother, Grete, were very fearful of future contact and the possible effects on Dawn as well as on their family life.

The story of Dawn's earlier life with her mother was described by her father. Soon after Dawn's birth Marianne had suffered an acute postnatal psychosis. Johan had tried hard for the first three years to keep Marianne and Dawn together, by working from home, and trying to protect the relationship between them. This was despite Marianne making repeated physical attacks on the home as well as on himself, including breaking up furniture and using knives and glass as weapons. However, after three years, and following an admission of several months to a psychiatric hospital, Marianne did not return home and the marriage ended. As she grew up, Dawn was often anxious, and much of this focused on not knowing any detail about her mother and their earlier relationship. The fact that she had lost her mother so early, together with the unstable and confusing relationship she had experienced in earlier intermittent contact visits, combined with the letters she often received from her mother *demanding* a relationship, made it difficult for Dawn to imagine anything positive for them together in the future. Dawn remembered her puzzlement as a little girl about the meaning of expressions on her mother's face at times when they were together, and showed me photos of her mother holding her close which showed her own uncertainty while being held. She reflected; 'what did my expression in those photos mean'?

In addition, although she was now aged 15, Dawn's mother continued to address her as though she was still the little child she had left, preferring to relate to the younger pictures of Dawn and herself than the more recent ones of Dawn sent to her. In this way, and by talking to Dawn as though they were almost in a kind of partnership together, she tried to keep alive the illusion of continuing closeness. For example, in her letters she would write things like

> a daughter needs a relationship with her mother. I was so happy to be pregnant with you, giving you nourishment, and now you need a different sort of nourishment from me, which your father doesn't want to let me give you. Write to me and open your heart

a way of writing which showed no recognition of what had happened between them over the years. Dawn finally found the courage to write to her mother and explain just a bit of what she had felt when with her mother which had made her hesitant about getting in touch. Her mother wrote back angrily 'how dare you write to your mother like this' ... then ignoring what Dawn had felt and only talking about her own feelings: '...it has caused me great pain to be treated by you like this.... that you don't consider your own mother worth love and respect'. It was this behaviour that had made Dawn decide to remain distant and wary. She would clearly need a different storyline if she were to be able to reassess her mother.

Accessing memories about the early years and considering their impact on family life now

I worked with Dawn and Johan to review the disturbing stories that had been 'held onto' in her mind. Dawn had held onto some of these stories from a very young age, and soon discovered through more open talking about them that there were a few which had a possible different meaning. For example, Dawn recalled an experience of contact when she was four and her mother had 'gone mad' and returned her to her father within an hour of her arrival. Like many of the young people who have given their own testimony in this book, Dawn assumed that this was because of bad things she had done, and still carried the guilt. To help her begin to 'rewrite' that guilt I helped Dawn to draw up a list of specific questions for her father to clarify, about the sort of events such as the one just described, which she remembered in a confused and indistinct way. He was asked to provide dates for such events, and his own memories and understanding of what had happened at the time. With some encouragement from me he was able to give a more detailed series of descriptions, which focused less on Marianne's frightening behaviours and more on Marianne's helplessness and recognition that she was unable to manage looking after her little daughter; 'one hour after I left her there I got a phone call saying "collect her or I will kill myself"'. Johan had actually understood Marianne's wish for no further contact at that time to be the result of many drawn out and failed attempts to sustain a physical relationship with her child, which she found she just could not cope with. However he still did not seem to want to explain anything to Dawn about Marianne's bipolar disorder, which had developed following the earlier puerperal psychosis. He explained this reluctance as 'this is something Dawn is already anxious about because she knows it has inheritable characteristics, and because I find it very hard to be neutral about it'.

I asked Alan Cooklin to provide an outline of bipolar disorder that young people could understand:

> Bipolar disorder means that a person has big swings in their moods or their feelings about themselves from feeling down or depressed to feeling 'high' or elated. Everyone can feel down sometimes and excited or happy at others, and some of us can change between these feelings very quickly. In bipolar disorder this is greatly exaggerated, as the swings can be very extreme and sometimes very fast. Also the 'high' or excited state is not exactly happy. In fact people with this disorder are usually very anxious as they become high, and when they are high they can feel 'driven' to do things like drinking a lot of alcohol, take drugs, spend lots of money, or become very sexually active with different people. When it is very severe, the person can become very depressed, so that they cannot do anything, and then so 'high' that they can believe strange things, see or hear things that are not there – then it would be called Bipolar Psychosis, or in past times called Manic Depressive psychosis.
>
> The illness can also increase some aspects of a person's already developed personality in ways, which can sometimes make things worse. People will say that Bipolar Disorder has a high 'Heritability'. However this can be a confusing word because it does not mean that you are likely to have the *illness* if your parents did. It means that many different genes can make you more vulnerable, and that a whole lot of different things which are very stressful – especially ones which happen repeatedly over a long time – can increase your risk. Treatment for bipolar disorder needs to be considered in two ways:
>
> 1 For the person to learn about their emotions and how to manage them in response to stress, as well as talking therapy about how to manage their lives, as well as the effects of the illness on their personality.

2 With medication to treat the depression when it is there, or the excitement when it is too much, and sometimes additional medicine to try to 'stabilise' the person's moods, so that they do not change so extremely.

Developing resilience through expanding the narrative about her mother

Being able to talk more openly about *normal* behaviours exaggerated by an illness, and addressing the uncomfortable and angry feelings they provoke in the person at the receiving end – in this case in both Johan and Dawn – allowed Dawn to rethink the way she saw and named earlier emotional exchanges between her mother and herself which had previously remained very indistinct in her mind and therefore more frightening. This knowledge and the greater clarity it brought to her mind helped her feel much stronger and more resilient in thinking about her mother. Her indirect experiences of her mother's illness in her teenage years, and discussing these together, allowed new thoughts to develop so that she could think about her mother as a whole person in a new light. As the story about her mother expanded, Dawn could realise that she did not now have to feel so helpless in response to her mother, and could now attempt to direct the process of having a relationship with her for herself. As she put it 'Even if I'm not *taking charge* then at least I'm not being a *helpless child* to be screamed at'. The fact that the earlier vague stories and images of her mother were replaced with more detailed descriptions of her contacts with her mother's illness allowed her, in turn, to validate that her anxiety and earlier fear had been real and justified. This allowed her to say 'So I didn't make it up' as well as 'so it wasn't my fault'. This enabled her to write a 'forgiving' letter to Marianne; 'I know you were ill and I now know it wasn't my fault...I take that very seriously. I would like to focus on building up a relationship in the future'. In turn Marianne was able to share sadness in her statement 'I tried to be the best mother I could...I *made the ultimate sacrifice and pain* by giving you up'. At the same time Johan was also able to discuss this 'sacrifice' with Dawn in terms that did not blame Marianne, it seemed for the first time.

Building up a story of the forgotten relationship

One way in which I often help families to develop alternative and richer stories about a parent who has become a feared stranger is by inviting family members from all parts of a divided family to provide earlier family photos. In the Court process I then keep these as part of the court papers, to remind the family, the judge, as well as myself of the good and bad times that preceded the current situation. This helps us to generate a set of more balanced

106   Gill Gorell Barnes

images that distinguish the past from the present family. For Dawn, the recognition that her mother was formerly a women of many abilities, not just a person only defined by illness, allowed a transformation of her own thinking about her. In subsequent years Dawn was able to relate to these different aspects of her mother in their letters to each other, as a result of which Marianne was able to respond more authentically to what Dawn was able to offer.

Promoting resilience for Dawn

The term resilience has been used in different chapters in this book to look at aspects of a child's environment that strengthens her or his capacity to manage stressful events and to adapt to these without damage to themselves. Dawn found that hearing the details of her mother's illness, now more openly discussed with her father, met a need she had long had for clearer information about why she and her mother were separated – similar to the ways in which several writers in this book were able to experience relief from explanations as a result of joining Kidstime groups.

Alan Cooklin[6] has suggested that the power of an explanation in helping to free children from a distorted attachment with a parent can be understood in the following way:

> a mental illness is usually experienced by the child as a form of emotional withdrawal or loss of closeness to which the child may respond by trying harder to get closer (to the parent): a parent not wishing to be intruded on may withdraw further and the child may then become more desperate to reach him or her so that the distortion of the (child's) attachment becomes more extreme.

We could add to this the awareness that if the attachment with the parent has no protective aspects, due to the parents own helplessness and vulnerability, the child may also then become more vulnerable to the distorted aspects of the ill parent's thinking, and become more confused themselves. Dawn's own confusion diminished as her more open conversations with her father and myself helped her to understand the unrealistic expectations her mother held of her, as shown in her letters. She could then re-examine her fears in the light of the new understanding she had achieved about the *unintentional* distortions in her mother's love for her. Over the following three years her own developing awareness also allowed more ongoing correspondence between them in which Dawn could take account of her mother's limitations and fragility, while also recognising her current strengths and more realistic love for her as a young adult daughter.

Some reflections on promoting resilience for all professionals who work alongside families where a parent and child are estranged

- *Finding an explanation for the effects of illness on a parent, that enables a child to think about it*, has been a recurrent theme in this book. Many of the young people writing in this book have testified how strongly they have held the beliefs both that they are responsible for a parent's illness and that they must fall in with their parent's *world view* because of this. Alan Cooklin[7] has written about ways in which children may need to be helped to separate their own minds from an ill parent's mind, before they can begin to develop their own separate ideas about the relationship. This needs to include constructing a good enough explanation for a child about their parent's behaviour in a wider context of understanding the process and progress of the mental illness itself.

- The success of work in bringing together an estranged mother and her child/ren now living with their father and a stepmother will depend first on showing a *solid respect for the second family that the child lives in.* That is where the child's safety and security has had to be based. This must include giving recognition to the dual fears and wishes of a new partner, both in role of wife, and as a stepmother who has taken part in the careful upbringing of a child within the context of a larger difficult early history. As described in this chapter, these early relationships together with the direct experience of an angry and sometimes still mentally unwell mother can powerfully invade a second family life with very damaging consequences.

- In relation to promoting contact with a biological mother of whom the overriding experience has been disruption and anxiety, a primary goal is to find the *spaces in the overall narrative about her that allow stories about the good even if ill mummy* to be elaborated, and lead to the possibilities for future relationship, rather than be seen only as threats to current relationships. Where there is indirect contact, finding things of common interest to share ideas about between an absent parent and their child takes some of the heat out of over emotional letter writing between them.

- *The role of a father who has been the primary carer,* but then shared his parenting with a new partner, incomer into the former family, also becomes even more complex when the earlier ill parent seeks to re-engage. Bringing together elements of the *two family* systems he has previously believed he should keep apart, when in many ways this separation of earlier *bad* and current *good* has become a part of his own life's core narrative, is hazardous. Protection of his children has formed a large part of his parenting, and it can be hard to know how to loosen this as the child gets older, particularly in the context of memories of upsetting and disturbing times becoming regenerated by a mother re-appearing as part of her child's life.

A father's warmth and closeness to his children then also has to become shared with a person, his former wife, for whom he may have formerly displayed no love or respect in front of his child. Love, as well as any tenderness or sympathy, has to be rediscovered, and *mined* from his store of emotions to allow his child a different kind of understanding about the wider family context and its changes over his or her lifetime. As a father begins to drop his defences and allows changes to the original storyline, it is important that the professional does not let him down, but shows him whatever limited support he can.

Leonard Fagin has also spoken about his experience of hearing mother's voice their anger about absent fathers, and how those fathers might have done more for the mother's themselves. This additional burden of anger may also have to be addressed when a mother returns into the family story. Just recognising out-loud how difficult all these threads are can begin to help. Offering phone back up and ongoing consultative chat also helps.

- A final recommendation I would make is *to always build in extended family or third party support for ongoing contact,* so that there is a mediating bridge between the different anxieties that are inevitably part of the contact arrangements. Loss of contact with siblings and with the wider family of aunts, uncles, cousins and potential loved ones, a supportive network, is too often a further loss when contact with a parent is lost, and this is insufficiently thought about in working to support families.[8]

Final reflection on the difficulty in the work

A professional worker such as a Social Worker, Court Welfare officer or expert adviser to the Court will have the job of assessing the pros and cons of re-establishing secure safe modes of contact between children and an ill parent. This can be hard, but it is the job that the Court asks them to do on behalf of the best interests of the children. Professionals are likely to want to restore a child/mother relationship in particular, and may incline towards believing that when a father expresses concerns about the children's safety, that this comes from a wish to *alienate* the children's mother from them, rather than from a genuine wish to protect them.

A parent may refuse to see themselves as ill, even in the face of evidence from other family members about illness behaviour, and demands for contact with their children are often compounded by an increasing sense of failure. A parent's ability to accept their own unpredictability and then work on building in third party security back-up arrangements or accept third party supervision during contact are essential aspects of keeping contact working. For me as a clinician, trying to make decisions about what contact between the unpredictable non-resident parent and the children should be recommended to the Court – *that is in the best interest of the child* – has been the most challenging aspect of the work.

References

1 Dowling, E. & Gorell Barnes, G. (1999) *Working with Children and Parents through Separation and Divorce.* London: Palgrave Macmillan.
2 Gorell Barnes, G. (2015) Narratives of attachment and processes of alienation in post-divorce parenting disputes. In A. Vetere & E. Dowling (Eds.), *Narrative Therapies with Children and their Families: A Practitioners Guide to Concepts and Approaches* (pp. 182–198). New York: Routledge.
3 Cummings, E.M. & Davies, P. (2002) Effects of marital conflict on children: recent advances and emerging themes in process oriented research. *Journal of Child Psychology and Psychiatry*, 43: 31–63.
4 Schoppe-Sullivan, S.J., Brown, G.L., Cannon, E.A., Mangelsdorf, S.C. & Sokolowski, M.S. (2008) Maternal gatekeeping, co-parenting quality and fathering behaviour in families with infants. *Journal of Family Psychology*, 22(3): 389–398.
5 Scott, D. & Starr, I. (1981) A 24-hour family orientated psychiatric and crisis service. *Journal of Family Therapy*, 3: 177–186.
6 Cooklin, A. (2010) Living upside down: being a young carer of a parent with mental illness. *Advances in Psychiatric Treatment*, 16(2): 141–146.
7 Cooklin, A. (2013) Children's resilience to parental mental illness: engaging the child's thinking. *Advances in Psychiatric Treatment*, 19: 229–240.
8 Blair, K. (2004) In a daughter's voice: a mental health nurse's experiences of being the daughter of a mother with schizophrenia. In V. Cowling (Ed.), *Children of Parents with Mental Illness 2: Personal and Clinical Perspectives* (pp. 85–98). Melbourne: ACER Press.

Chapter 9

Notes from the edge
Supporting parents with mental health problems

Leonard Fagin

Introduction

A pioneering study by Sir Michael Rutter[1,2] found that whilst children of parents with a mental illness experience difficulties in a number of dimensions, the presence of an adult who is available and can communicate what is happening to the child was a factor which encouraged resilience. But how do parents, relatives or professionals talk about this to their children? How can parents be supported in their continued roles to offer safe nurturance to their children when they are experiencing mental health problems?

In 2011 a report[3] by the Royal College of Psychiatrists summarised the dilemmas facing parents with a mental illness:

> Many of the experiences of parents with mental illness are similar to those of all parents in that they describe the relationship with their children, and fulfilling the parenting role as extremely important to them.[4] However, they are very aware of the negative impact of the illness upon their children, particularly disruption to everyday life, and have concerns about significant behaviour problems that may arise in their children.[5] They may also worry about the risk of genetic transmission of their mental illness to their children, and about children mimicking their behaviour.[6]

What do parents say in these circumstances and what are they asking for? Some examples:

- Being a parent should come before being a person with a mental illness. We need to feel supported to meet the needs of our children. How can we protect them from the effects of our mental illness? Whilst professionals may not think so, we as parents may know, and be sensitively tuned into, the needs of our children. But sometimes we are stuck about how to talk about our mental illness.

- Whilst service providers need to work out the best way of ensuring the health and safety of our child, we as parents need to be included in the decision making process, and they need to be willing to listen to and value a parent's point of view and feelings. Our ability as parents should be evaluated before removing children without question. The most profound loss for some parents with mental illness is the loss of their children if they are taken away. Professionals should also respect confidentiality with regard to sharing information with other family members, and be sensitive to the parents' cultural background.
- Professionals should give the parent with mental illness and their partner information about the effects of medication, possible side effects and the effects on the person's behaviour. Service providers should be educated to network services and link parents into the most useful ones. Professional support is needed for the partner when a parent is acutely ill and education is required to prepare for ongoing treatment, recuperation and recovery (see Editors note 1 below).
- Schools need to understand how mental illness might influence a child, and take this into account when the child is behaving badly.

> (Adapted from Vikki Cowling, one of the
> early researchers in this field[7]).

Editors note 1

For a discussion of the concept of recovery see editor's notes in Lara Brown's comments both on Alan Cooklin's chapter and on Ambeya Begum's and Georgia Irwin-Ryan's chapters.

This chapter will focus specifically on the needs of parents with a mental illness and how to begin to address these concerns.

Kidstime Workshops

It was these concerns – the negative impact of parental mental ill health on children, and the relative neglect from relevant agencies in taking adequate preventative action – *which prompted* Alan Cooklin and Peter Bishop to start Kidstime Workshops in Camden, North London in 2000.[8] In Hackney, East London, they have been operating since May 2009. They are multi-family monthly events for parents and children where one or both parents have mental health problems. The workshops' main aims are, by means of drama, play and educational opportunities, to explore and discuss in a simple, non-stigmatising way mental health concerns, broadly addressing the following issues:

- To help children and young people gain understandable explanations of their parents' mental illness and the behaviour of the ill parent associated with this
- To address the children's fears, confusion and lack of knowledge about mental illness and its treatment
- To help the parents who suffer from mental illness to discuss the illness and its impact with their children
- To help the parents to access or rediscover their pride, confidence and competencies as parents

Whilst not setting itself up as a specific therapeutic intervention, these workshops have been shown, in qualitative evaluative studies, to benefit families.[9,10] They have become popular and are now operating in various cities in the United Kingdom, as well as in Spain, Germany and Portugal, where similar evaluative studies are showing emerging evidence of their benefit.

The structure of the workshop follows a prescribed and well-worked out format, which allows some flexibility *according* to the season of the year, number of families and age of children who attend, the nature of mental health difficulties, as well as the expertise and creativity of the facilitators.

Referrals to Kidstime arise from a variety of resources: Children and Young Persons Social Services, Adult as well as Child and Adolescent Mental Health Services, Schools, Primary Care and Voluntary Agencies – such as Family Action and Young Carers Organizations – and families that have heard about us also refer themselves. We have been struck by the fact that these agencies often have a history of fractured communication between them: our experience is that Kidstime is often in a position to bridge that gap.

Parent groups form an essential part of the structure of Kidstime Workshops. Although the focus is definitely on children who grow up with parents who have experienced mental health difficulties, one of the main factors affecting children is the loss of parenting skills *by their parents* which often accompanies mental illness. Parents find that they are frequently so overwhelmed by their breakdowns that they struggle to keep their children in mind, and sadly, this often leads to concerns over their viability as parents, especially with young children. Many children are placed into alternative forms of care as a result of mental illness, either through the intervention of their family networks, Social Services or family courts.

These parent groups differ significantly from other groups dealing with mental health issues. The focus, by definition, is on aspects of parenting and how this has been affected by parental mental illness or emotional distress in all its aspects. Inevitably, parents will talk about how their experiences

Notes from the edge 113

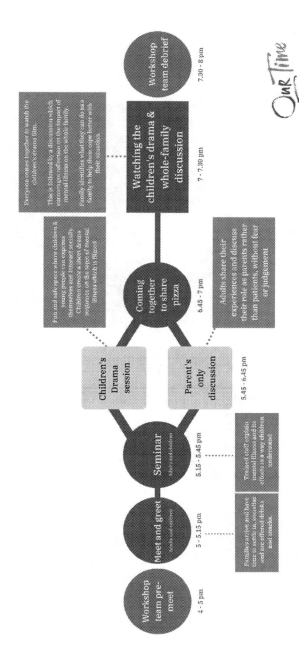

Structure of Kidstime Workshops.

of mental illness have affected their relationships with their children, an experience which most of them believe is unique to them, and one that has been difficult to articulate to themselves, let alone other parents or their children. There is a sense of guilt, anxiety, awkwardness and resistance in talking about these experiences, and the group often provides the first opportunity they have had to share it with other parents who are in similar circumstances. There is also an implicit assumption that talking about this is dangerous, because of the possible impact on their children.

Although there is literature addressing the issue of parental mental illness, and the effects this can have on their children,[11–13] there is a lack of detailed accounts of what parents say about their worries in relation to their parenting. The parent groups in Kidstime offered parents an opportunity to share some of their concerns with others. My experience of these groups is that given the opportunity, parents are open to discuss their concerns, and, perhaps as importantly, that in so doing they discover not only that they have not lost their parenting skills but also that they can offer insights and help to other parents in similar circumstances. Parents attending the Kidstime Workshops have all experienced mental health care and have received a variety of diagnoses. There is a tendency *by some professionals and others* to try and gloss over the names given to mental disorders, which parents and even their children are often aware of, and I found that parents are relieved when there is an opportunity to discuss these diagnostic issues openly as well as the treatments offered by mental health services. Gwen Adshead[14] has described how particularly parents with a diagnosis of personality disorder can have a devastating impact on the relationships between parents and their children:

> ... parental personality disorder represents a risk to child development, in terms of both transmission of genetic vulnerability and the environmental stress of living with a parent who has a personality disorder that negatively affects their parenting capacities. I argue that there are two compelling reasons to impose a duty on mental healthcare providers to offer services for adults with personality disorders that specifically focus on their parenting identity: first, because effective therapies for personality disorder are now available; and second, because there is a strong utilitarian and economic argument for improving parental mental health so as to reduce the economic and psychological burden of their off-springs' future psychiatric morbidity – an opinion which could apply to children faced with many kinds of mental illness.

I recorded and summarised what happened in the workshops we have been holding in Hackney since 2009, which are over 100 at the time of writing, and I have extracted below some of the impressions I was left with after each session of the parents' group. I will first list the main themes that were raised, and offer a few examples of how these were discussed. Names and some details have been changed to respect confidentiality. As will be gathered by the names I have chosen, families come from very diverse backgrounds, which reflect the ethnic mix of the population of Hackney, in East London.

Themes

Parent's anxieties about their children's worries and their attempts to comfort their parents: taking ownership of parent's anxieties and relieving children of responsibility to do something about them

There is ample evidence that children who are brought up by parents with a mental illness adopt prematurely caring roles.[15] Children as young as five express concerns over their parent's well-being, although this is articulated more in their actions and behaviour than in clear discussion. There often is an implicit contract of silence on these matters: parents do not want to discuss these issues with children so as not to burden them or because they believe children will not understand, and children do not want to ask questions in case this may upset their parents. The burden of these caring roles is taken on at considerable disadvantage to the children, either because they take them on when they are too young, which deflects them away from their age-related development – as one parent put it 'they lose their childhood' – or because the stigma, embarrassment and isolation affect their progress in other areas such as friendships with peers or academic achievements. Parents find great relief talking to other parents about how their mental health problems affect their ability to keep their children in mind. Occasionally these discussions bring to their own minds how as children, *they* had to endure similar difficulties with their mentally unwell parents.

> Ruth started off by saying that her daughter Rose would persistently try to comfort her, despite the fact that she had told her that she should not worry, that it was her job to be Mummy to her. Rose said she felt uncomfortable about her daughter's attentions. Ruth spoke about her anxiety, particularly when other people considered she had not been a good Mum to Rose. Ruth was concerned about how to communicate her moods and her periods of 'unwellness' to her daughter, whether she (Rose) could understand how she felt, the fact that when she was depressed she was less responsive to her, and how to address Rose's fears that she would become unwell again. Ruth was very worried about the possibility that Rose would inherit her depression.

Losing parental authority: difficulties in reassuming parental role after a period of mental illness

Parents find talking about their loss of confidence as parents very difficult and embarrassing, carrying a sense of failure which they struggle to acknowledge, and at times giving up hope that they can recover and become effective parents again. Sharing these difficulties with other parents allows them to reflect on how these roles can be realistically resumed or repaired, acknowledging at the same time the impact their breakdowns have on their children. The parents often sense that they are unable to set boundaries or discipline their children as a result, something that becomes even more manifest when their children become naturally challenging and rebellious as adolescents.

> Juana spoke about the difficulties she has as a mother having either to discipline or to be encouraging, loving and supportive, but also her urge to be alone when she is not feeling well. To my surprise, Jennifer – another parent – suggested that this was no different from what most parents have to contend with, and did not depend entirely on whether she had a mental health problem or not.

Being a single parent: the role of fathers, present and absent. Negative 'projections' (see Editors note 2) onto the well parent: family secrets

Many of the adults attending Kidstime are single parents, which adds to their experiences of loneliness and isolation, particularly when they have to assume total parental responsibilities over their children, without another adult support to them, and when mental health problems interfere. This is a subject which often spreads throughout all discussions in the group. In our experience, most parents attending Kidstime Workshops are mothers, either because they do not have partners, or because fathers are reluctant to attend. However, when both parents attend the group there is a qualitative change, reflecting the positive and balancing impact a parent who does not have a mental illness can have on their children. However, we have observed that when fathers (*who are not suffering mental illness*) do attend, they are often the recipient of negative comments from their children, despite the fact that they may be clearly holding the emotional fort and are very involved in childcare. It seemed that in those circumstances children have the confidence and reassurance to project and convey their worries through difficult and sometimes hostile behaviour onto the well parent with broadest shoulders, as if they were aware that the ill parent would not be able handle it. Often this hostility is manifested indirectly, with no immediate reference to parental mental ill health. It is as if the children are expressing their anger that the well parent cannot make the ill parent better, or even that they are responsible for the mental illness. During the course of these groups, underlying family dynamics and secrets emerge, which offer a foundation and an understanding of where the tensions are rooted, as well as a contextualisation of parental ill health.

Editors note 2

Seeing negative or 'unwanted' aspects of oneself in another person rather than in oneself.

Absent fathers also play a role in the fantasies of children with a mentally ill parent, as recipients of accusations of abandonment and responsibility for the mother's troubles. When the histories of parental splits are discussed, mental health problems are often pinpointed as the cause, and it is not unusual for the father to be overwhelmed and to take flight from a situation they feel they have no emotional resources to handle. On occasions the parenting role is taken over by an uncle, or an older son who might be thrust into the role of a substitute partner for the abandoned mother.

Suriya, Elver's eldest daughter, had even gone to the extent of saying that her mother should not speak to her father's side of the family, and has even challenged her father Sultan for not being there when he was needed. Elver again talked about how Suriya was imitating her headaches, showing her concern for her mother, and often entering into confrontations with Sultan, sometimes talking to him not as a daughter but as a berating equal, which annoyed the mother, especially when Sultan seemed to join into the 'ding dong' battle between them. My interpretation of this was that Suriya, who was oversensitive and over-involved with her mother, saw in her father the reasons for her mother's troubles – in that it is his family that rejects Elver – and targets him as the focus of her worries, although at a deeper level she loved and needed her father to contain her and to set boundaries. Sultan seemed to take this with some humour, although he acknowledged that sometimes his daughter's attacks irked him. This opened the discussion about what could and what could not be said to young children, but we eventually agreed that perhaps it was better to talk about things at a level the children could understand rather than leave things unmentioned and unspoken, as this could end up with kids making more of a situation than it actually deserved. We also discussed how both Sultan and Elver could point out that Sultan was there to protect his wife and the children, that this was his job. I was struck by the candidness and openness of both of them, and how easy it was to engage in their discourse and narrative. This allowed them to smile about their predicament as well.

Transgenerational influences: managing the responses from grandparents

Parents, and in particular single parents, are often reliant on grandparents to offer support when they become unwell, and they continue to play an active role with their grandchildren. The relationship between parents and grandparents is not always smooth, and can be fractious and painful at times, especially when 'old skeletons emerge from the closet'. This is particularly the case when grandparents' **own** limitations as parents are pointed out, or when parents have had to contend with grandparental mental ill health. We have had occasions when grandparents come to the workshops, either accompanying their children or when the parent is unwell or has been hospitalised and the children are keen to attend.

Esther – who has herself been diagnosed with schizo-affective and paranoid personality disorder – intervened at this stage, saying that sometimes people hurt those that they loved, and explained how in her situation she sometimes attacked those around her because she found her own internal struggles so distressing that she had to take it out on those close to her, partly hoping that they would then help her. She and her mother Estelle, who also joined the workshop, entered into an interchange about the difficulties setting boundaries for Mario (age 7). Mario could be responsive to either of them when he was alone with them, but tended to exploit splits between Esther and

Estelle to 'get his own way'. Another parent, Heather, a single mother of two who has been diagnosed with schizophrenia, was clearly distressed and wanted to speak. She said that she was overwhelmed with anxiety because she was terrified of her mother's reaction when she revealed that she was interested in starting a new relationship with a man she likes, but she expected her mother, who she described as strongly opinionated and undermining and someone she found it difficult to stand up to, to be critical of her choice. Heather was also scared that her mother would distance herself from her if she persisted in a relationship which her mother would say she could not cope with. At various points she became very distressed, despite the verbal and physical support she was getting from other parents in the group, who suggested ways in which she could communicate with her mother anticipating her response, stating that she was now an adult, mature and strong enough to make decisions for herself, that even if she did not want to lose contact with her mother, she did not want to find herself worrying about her mother when she already had enough on her plate. She was listening carefully to the responses that other parents and both myself and my co-facilitator offered, and she started writing them down on her forearm and hand.

Asking questions and giving explanations: talking about mental illness with children

Parents report that children ask questions about their parent's mental illness in a disguised manner, but that they struggle to find ways to explain it, or discuss other family secrets. It frequently indicates the parent's mixed feelings about being diagnosed as suffering from a mental illness. There is an apparent resistance in trying to understand how the illness in the parent could affect the children, or to get a measure of what the children make out of their experiences.

Parents often carry a history of mental illness in the family, and reflect that as children they were confused and baffled by what they witnessed in their parents, something that they are anxious to prevent in their own children. Frequently explanations to children about mental illness fall on the 'well parent', a task that these parents have to extemporise on, without much support from professional services. Obviously explanations also have to take into account the age of the children, and their ability to be receptive to descriptions which need to be adjusted according to their abilities. Sometimes parents are surprised to find out that their children already have some understanding of their mental illness, despite this not being a subject they have openly discussed. This understanding is sometimes lopsided and inaccurate, stemming from misconceptions children hear on the playground or on the television or social media.

In one workshop seminar, prior to the adult parent group, in an exercise to prompt discussion about the impact of mental health on children, we asked the parents to think of questions they would like to ask them about it. This proved to be helpful in that it anticipated questions the children would probably have liked to have answered about their parent's mental illness. They came up with the following questions:

1 Does she feel anxious, upset or frightened when I become unwell?
2 How does she feel when I have to go into hospital?
3 Do you worry about how long will I be unwell?
4 Do you wonder why it happens?
5 Do you think you will get the same problem?

Elver gave an illustrative example of how communication has to be timely and at a level which the kids could understand. When she had to explain to Orhan, her youngest son, that he could no longer sleep in the same room with his older sister, which he felt very upset about, Elver went on her knees, to get to the same level as Orhan, and calmly explained that boys and girls of a certain age had to sleep in different bedrooms, and Orhan accepted it, much to Elver's surprise, without any strong emotional reaction. I thought she was communicating how children's mental health questions could be responded to in the same manner. Heather told us about her admission to hospital after the birth of her second child, but that she had been 'psychotic' for three years before that, and had been given a diagnosis of schizophrenia. Only recently her son Luke had been discussing this, and she was able to tell him that she had been psychotic, and was surprised and relieved when Luke hugged her and seemed to understand and take it in his stride.

Problems with adolescents

Adolescence is often a time for identity search, rebellion and independence. In most families, at the best of times, adolescents present a challenge to parents, and this becomes all the more difficult when mental illness strikes. It also makes this transition into adulthood all the more difficult. On occasions, however, we have noticed that the normal course of adolescence is stalled, partly because these children have been thrust into caring roles, which give them a sense of imagined maturity and responsibility, and parents find that they end up relying on them in case of future breakdowns and possible hospitalisations.

Haniffatu, who has suffered from a Bipolar illness for many years spoke angrily about her daughter Babatunde who chose not to listen to her, not to share in household duties, preferring to do her own thing with her mates. Unfortunately she also seems to be doing badly at school.

Babatunde, is 14, barely is able to read, and all she wants to do is to learn to be a singer. Nazma, who has been diagnosed with schizophrenia, joined in to say that she was also having difficulties with her son, who is 15, and who initially said he would be coming to Kidstime and at the last minute decided not to. He also is breaking the rules, leaving home and coming back late whenever he has a disagreement with his mother, who sometimes feels helpless to contain him. He flings in her face the fact that his father is not around.

Isolation

Many people suffering from mental illness feel isolated, often self-imposed, and are aware that prejudice and discrimination make other people misunderstand the nature of their difficulties. Embarrassment about their condition also plays a part in this, and their assumptions are often conveyed, implicitly or explicitly, to their children. When they are able to share these feelings with other parents there is a sense of palpable relief to discover that their situation is not unique, and those parents that have managed to break through the entrapment that constrains them are keen to offer advice and support to others. These suggestions can have a positive impact on their children, who often also feel isolated and cut off from normal social encounters.

Parents palpably find these groups mutually supportive and gain from the advice and expertise of other parents' experiences, reducing the feeling of being alone with a problem, especially when sharing painful topics. This particularly applied to single parents.

Even parents who are not very articulate or rarely make contributions in groups appear to gain from their participation: one parent mentioned how the workshops had helped her 'because she could talk things over with Lenny' which surprised me as she was not always very forthcoming. Another parent said the workshop they attended helped her to meet new people and realize that she was not alone with her 'suffering'.

Not every parent can engage in parent groups. Many feel uncomfortable discussing their problems and issues with others, worried that opening up might make things worse for them or their children. Whilst certainly this is a feature when parents initially join a group, there is something contagious and appealing about witnessing other parents being candid about their experiences which often helps to smooth their resistance to being part of the group.

Hannifatu said that it was not possible to discuss mental health matters with friends because in her experience friends did not want to know, or took advantage by taking money from them, or thought that people who suffered from a mental illness were stupid or had memory problems and they completely misunderstood what mental illness was all about. This led Hannifatu to cut contacts with those that she described as not true friends. This was echoed by other parents in the group. Phuong did contribute quite actively, saying that so called friends preferred to remain distant, or that friends would be curious about what was happening to the person with a mental health problem but would not reciprocate by disclosing much of themselves.

Separations

Having a mental illness implies a risk that a parent may be temporarily, and sometimes permanently, separated from their children. This is a subject that parents rarely discuss with their children, an indication of how traumatic and stigmatizing an admission to hospital can be, especially if it is compulsory, and following an episode of acute relapse of their condition, which usually is witnessed by their children and not always explained. We have detected that it is often a silent worry for children; the possibility that their parents may become unwell again and that they would be taken away. Parents often struggle to discuss and appreciate how their admissions could have affected their children, let alone invite them to discuss and ask questions about them. The groups give space to discuss these experiences with other parents, and especially to share the difficulties of re-integration into the parental role post-discharge. In our experience, adult services often fail to incorporate this dimension into their care, sometimes are unaware of arrangements made to care for children during parents' admissions and even more rarely follow up meetings with the family to discuss the impact on children or parenting.

Separation from the parental partner also was regularly brought up by single parents, and the impact this had on their parenting and their abilities to manage on their own without support. They often had to contend with accusations from their children about who was responsible for the marital breakup, an issue that as mentioned earlier was often not discussed openly, leaving children to fantasize about the reasons and focus their resentment on the available parent. Added to this, the single parent would often unconsciously attribute problems with their children to characteristics they identified in them which reminded them of the abandoning parent, especially if the separation had been bitter.

> Nazma, who has been diagnosed with depression, and has a son, Mohammed and a daughter, Zahida, spoke about her recent worries and depression, prompted by her difficult relationship with her ex-husband. She was struggling with Zahida, because she blamed her mother for telling her father to leave, and she then proceeded to attack mother at every opportunity, calling her nasty names and constantly made demands to go and live with her father in Northampton. Nazma felt very alone with this pressure, believing that her ex-husband was poisoning her daughter's mind against her,

which sometimes overwhelmed her, to the point that suicide seemed to be an inviting option, something that she shared with her older son, Mohammed. He then became the receiver of this burden, assuming responsibilities to protect his mother, taking Nazma's and not his father's side. Nazma was aware that this was affecting Mohammed's education. However, he gave her comfort, assuring her that he was there for her. At one point someone said that he had become the substitute husband and that he was now the 'Man of the House'. Ruby, who also separated from her husband, suggested that Nazma should be glad that she got rid of her husband and should celebrate and make light of it.

Perceptions of prejudice: ambivalent, fearful relationships with Social Services and worries of children being removed from parental care

Parents often report that they feel misunderstood by different agencies, and use the group to ventilate their fears and frustrations, but also to balance their perceptions when they experience a helpful and supportive response from professionals. These concerns hover constantly in the background of discussions in parents' groups. There is a tendency to demonize Social Services for taking on unnecessary intrusive interventions with the children, and this demonization often stands in the way of parents reflecting in a balanced manner how their emotional or mental health difficulties may have affected their children. The enemy is projected outside, on to professionals, rather than accepting vulnerabilities, deficiencies or mistakes in parenting.

> Ruth spoke about her relationships with Social Services and her fears that her mental health problems would make her vulnerable to her children being taken away. Parents were critical of Social Services, stating that they focused on the wrong people when they made decisions about care.

Dashing of parental hopes and expectations

The advent of mental illness can not only severely dent hopes and fantasies for parents in their roles, but also their expectations for their children. Many parents feel that they have tried their best with their children, despite the odds imposed on them by their mental health, only to find that either their efforts go unacknowledged or their attempts cause more difficulties and arguments. This is especially seen when there is an expectation that the arrival of children will act as a panacea for their previous bad experiences, as an opportunity for healing old emotional wounds, or when there is a hope that they will not reproduce the mistakes they experienced at the hands of their parents. These disappointments are painful and not often articulated.

Effects of medication on parenting

Psychotropic medication for psychotic or depressive illnesses often results in side effects. These may add to the limitations imposed on parents by their condition and set barriers to them being in tune with their childrens' needs. Children often struggle to understand why parents have to take medication and are rarely told anything about the possible effects and problems associated with them. Often kids know that the parents need to take medication to remain well, and keep a watchful eye on whether their parent is taking them or not, assuming some responsibility to ensure adherence to their treatments. Children often ask questions, but are rarely given answers, either by parents or professionals. The groups give parents a chance to share their experiences about side effects, and discuss risks of continuation or discontinuation with the treatment plans, as well as how to respond to questions posed by their children. The presence of a clinician in these groups can help to clarify some misconceptions about medication, but the most telling part is when parents are able to identify similar problems with medication.

> All parents in the group said that their kids did talk about medication and that thanks to the workshops they felt more comfortable to address these issues with their kids, because they were not alone and it was 'normal'. However Phuong said that she did not discuss these issues with her children, and that her children did not know why she was taking this medication, which Ho (her husband) did not agree with, saying that his children did know why Mum has to take medication. He pointed out that his wife sometimes was not in control of her emotions and that his children noticed this. She made no comments about this.

Holidays do not always mean holidays

School offers respite to parents and some children when tensions at home get too demanding. Holidays, despite the assumptions behind them of a care-free time full of possibilities and enjoyment, can sometimes be difficult for families, and home can become a pressure-cooker of undiluted tensions, bringing to the surface issues that get diluted during school term. When parents, and especially single parents, return from their holidays they often feel exhausted and overwhelmed, and welcome an opportunity to discuss ideas on how to better manage the intense time they share with their children.

> As it was the summer the workshop spoke about impending school holidays. I introduced the idea of the possible extra pressures on parents over the holidays, and asked them all whether there were any worries. Elver and Sultan immediately launched into a description of how Elver

Notes from the edge   125

found difficulties in coping with the demands of her very active children, who follow her around the house wherever she goes. Sultan said that he noticed that his wife got very irritable and needed to withdraw, and he had to take over the care of the children. Both of them seemed to be saying that the children were unable to understand their pleas to leave Mum alone for a while, even if explanations were given, and when asked to stop, they would soon forget and start pursuing mother again.

Cultural differences

Many of the families attending the workshops come from diverse ethnic backgrounds, which not only have a bearing on how parenting is delivered but also on cultural biases regarding mental health issues. Parents will talk and compare their own upbringing in a different culture and the efforts they have to make to adapt when their children are exposed to different experiences from the ones that they had back in their country of origin. Many parents also offer references and experiences of discrimination because of their background, which mirrors the way they feel about other people's reactions to their mental health problems.

Finally, I would like to give Heather's voice an airing

At the start of the session we discussed developing an awareness of how our illness affects the children's emotions. We discussed the effects of medications and the depo in particular, mostly finding the effects of them negative. The depo made some of the mothers hands shake, interrupted the menstrual cycle and created a less responsive temperament. However personally I found moving to the depo beneficial in that it stopped my arms becoming 'wooden'.

There was a new mother in the group, I found her story very painful and hoped she felt supported. We discussed her practical difficulties. I thought, she didn't seem aware enough of how much help there was available to her. When Lenny had to leave the room to collect the pizza the group mainly discussed our relationships with men and their attitude to our illnesses, also touching on weight. The discussion was relaxed and spontaneous, we naturally formed a circle, and it felt very supportive. I noted that Phuong was very passive during the times when Lenny was out, as no one took the initiative in including her.

Personally I feel very supported when the group are sharing experiences and finding common ground, with the feeling of a group counselling scenario. I also feel that it is important for us to think about how we affect our children and to help them develop emotional awareness.

Conclusions

Parents who have experienced a mental illness derive comfort and support from groups where they can openly discuss the difficulties they are encountering in their roles as parents. The subjects parents want to share are varied and cover a wide spectrum. The facilitator of these groups adopts an enabling role to allow parents to share their experiences in a way that they would find difficult in other settings, because of embarrassment, stigma or isolation. The group is encouraged to address issues that relate to the impact on their children, rather than focusing on their individual experiences or symptoms of illness or their treatments by professionals.

Summary

In this chapter I give an account of the Parent Support groups which took place as part of the Kidstime Workshops since 2009. The workshops took place in a Children's Centre in a deprived London Borough, and families arrived to us following referrals from a number of agencies, including Social Services, mental health services, schools and even word of mouth. Parents shared with us their concerns over their children who were affected by their mental health problems, but which they rarely had an opportunity to discuss either with their partners, if they were in a current relationship, or with their children or with other parents who had similar experiences. In a safe setting, and given the chance, they were keen to ask questions they had never dared talk about. 'How will my children understand what I am going through?' 'How can I be there for them when I have so much going on my head?' 'Can I still be a good parent?' Parents not only reported a sense of relief to find out that they were not alone with their difficulties but also in so doing rediscovered their parenting skills and were also able to support and give advice to others.

By taking notes at the time of what transpired during each of these groups (nearly a 100 at the time of writing), I realized that there were recurrent themes which parents were struggling with. Parents found it difficult to resume parental roles after a period of mental illness, especially if they were single parents, which most of the participants in the groups were. Parents struggled to respond to questions their children posed to them. They worried that their children were taking premature caring roles when they were unable to function. Many felt isolated and embarrassed and stigmatised by their illnesses, which limited their social interactions, particularly with other parents. Parents were anxious that they could be temporarily or permanently separated from their children, and were apprehensive about disclosing their difficulties with professionals for this reason. Many of their hopes and expectations for themselves and their children were dashed. Medications often had side effects which rendered them less able to respond and be attuned to their childrens' needs.

References

1 Rutter, M. (1966) *Children of Sick Parents: An Environmental and Psychiatric Study.* London: Oxford University Press.

2 Rutter, M. (1985) Resilience in the face of adversity. Protective factors and resistance to psychiatric disorder. *The British Journal of Psychiatry*, 147 (6), 598–611.

3 Royal College of Psychiatrists. (2011) *Parents as Patients: Supporting the Needs of Patients who are Parents and their Children (College Report CR164).* London: Royal College of Psychiatrists.

4 Nicholson, J., Biebel, K., Katz-Levy, J., et al. (2004) The prevalence of parenthood in adults with mental illness: implications for state and federal policymakers, programs, and providers. In *Mental Health, United States* (eds. R.W. Manderscheid & M.J. Henderson), pp. 120–137. Rockville, MD: United States Department of Health and Human Services.

5 Stallard, P., Norman, P., Huline-Dickens, S., et al. (2004) The effects of parental mental illness upon children: a descriptive study of the views of parents and children. *Clinical Child Psychology and Psychiatry*, 9, 39–52.

6 Aldridge, J. & Becker, S. (2003) *Children Caring for Parents with Mental Illness: Perspectives of Young Carers, Parents and Professionals.* Bristol: Policy Press.

7 Cowling, V. (2004) The same as they treat everybody else. In *Parental Psychiatric Disorder: Distressed Parents and Their Families* (eds. M. Göpfert, J. Webster & M.V. Seeman). Cambridge: Cambridge University Press.

8 Cooklin, A., Bishop, P., Francis, D., Fagin, L. & Asen, E. (2012) *The Kidstime Workshops; A Multifamily Social Intervention for the Effects of Parental Mental Illness: Manual.* London: CAMHS Publications, Evidence Bases practice Unit.

9 Martin, A., Hoffman, J., Nolas, S.-M., et al. (2011) *Evaluation of the Kidstime Workshops (2010–2011).* London: Anna Freud Centre Report.

10 Wolpert, M., Hoffman, J., Martin, A., Fagin, L. & Cooklin, A. (2014) An exploration of the experience of attending the Kidstime programme for children with parents with enduring mental health issues: Parents' and young people's views. *Clinical Child Psychology and Psychiatry*, 20 (3), 406–418.

11 Gopfert, M., Webster, J. & Seeman, M. (eds.) (2004) *'Parental Psychiatric Disorder' – Distressed Parents and their Families*, 2nd edition. Cambridge: Cambridge University Press.

12 Cooklin, A. (2006) Children as carers of parents with mental illness. *Psychiatry*, 8, 32–35.

13 Dunn, B. (1993) Growing up with a psychotic mother. A retrospective study. *American Journal of Orthopsychiatry*, 63, 177–189.

14 Adshead, G. (2015) Parenting and Personality Disorder. *Clinical and Child Protection Implications Advances in Psychiatry*, 21(1), 15–22.

15 Cooklin, A. (2010) Living upside down: being a young carer of a parent with mental illness. *Advances in Psychiatric Treatment*, 16, 141–146.

Chapter 10

Storytelling & drama

Telling our stories, building resilience – Drama processes and techniques for empowerment

Deni Francis

Introduction

> I always wanted to act.
> As a child, as far back as I can remember.
> Why?
> It was fun. Exciting. I could have adventures that didn't cost money.
> Escapism.
> I could say whatever I wanted to say and behave any way I liked, free from fear of punishment.
> I could be whoever I wanted to be.
> I was in control of the story I wanted to tell.

For me, acting was an escape, and a doorway to self understanding and discovery. I am the oldest of seven children, and come from a background of domestic violence. At an early age I started to try and help change the situation. Being able to escape into my own world was a sanctuary, a safe space to process my thoughts and feelings and to make sense of things. When I was 17, a theatre company called actorshop came to my sixth form. It was my first taste of theatre in education and I experienced the transformational power of theatre. I realised that part of the reason that I loved the drama and acting skills I was learning was because I was using them to help myself to develop coping strategies, and to build my sense of self. In my work as a facilitator with groups (in business and in therapeutic drama settings), I harness the transformational power of drama techniques and storytelling to help and support others.

The Kidstime workshops and the use of drama

The Kidstime workshops were started in 2000, and this chapter will look at some of the drama processes and techniques that are used with the families. The aim is to help the children, through story and play, to develop self awareness and to build confidence and self esteem. It is also to help them to understand explanations of mental illness, to process their emotions and be able to express them, by developing their critical thinking and emotional literacy, and telling their stories.

Drama in Kidstime: six creative steps for empowerment and resilience

1 *The Framework*: safe space, boundaries, structure.
2 *The Tools*: drama processes and techniques, the journey of self discovery, skills for life
3 *Story*: creating & devising, genres, characters.
4 *Action: Rehearsing*: exploring options, catharsis, practice for life
5 *Performance*: filming, escapism.
6 *Relationship with Audience*: shifting the gaze, seeing self reflected.

Step 1: The Framework: the role of drama in creating a safe space; boundaries & structure, ground rules & games

In the rehearsal room, actors use their own emotional experiences to create living breathing characters. They talk about finding the emotional truth[1] of the character. To do this they need to be able to be vulnerable and take risks. For that to happen the rehearsal room needs to be a safe space.

In *Kidstime*, in the drama session, the children are being asked to explore their inner world. They are invited to explore their thoughts and feelings and to share them with others, to tell stories and create characters. This can be scary, and the workshop needs to be a safe space for them. This is created by a number of factors: the Kidstime workers, the structure and regularity of the workshop, the physical space itself, and clear and consistent boundaries within the workshop. It is this last factor, i.e. clear and consistent boundaries, that drama techniques can be useful for.

Ground rules

Setting ground rules, the contract at the beginning of the workshop gives everyone an opportunity to have a say in how they want to work together as a group.

The children are often pleasantly surprised when they realise that they have an equal say in deciding the rules, and it is not just the adults who get to make them up.

It starts the process of engaging the children's critical thinking as lively discussion ensues about rules: rules at school, at home, in society, which rules they think are fair and which rules not.

The top ground rules are:

1 Respect
2 Listen to each other's views

130   Deni Francis

3   One person speaking at a time
4   Being non-judgemental
5   No shouting/swearing/fighting/running
6   Confidentiality
7   Mobile phones

Deciding the rules together helps to make the workshop a safe space. The group understands what behaviours are expected. They know that their opinions will be invited and that they will be heard without being judged. Most of the ground rules are self explanatory and do not generate much discussion.

RESPECT

Take more time. Discussion around respect highlights that different people have different ideas about what respect means and what it looks like. It lays the groundwork for how the group will talk to each other and how they will conduct discussions as a group.

CONFIDENTIALITY

Unsurprisingly, prompts rich discussion. Both adults and children want re-assurance and clarity about how information will be shared with outside parties. The group often chooses to share experiences of confidentiality, and confidentiality breaches at this point. This starts to build trust in the group, essential for the space to be safe.

MOBILE PHONES

This discussion falls along inter-generational lines. The younger members of the group often do not understand why they can't just be on their phones. The group always ends up agreeing that all phones will be kept on silent and not be used during the time of the workshop. Exceptions are if someone has an emergency situation ongoing, and the Kidstime worker is responsible for ordering the pizza.

It offers a powerful example of how an issue can be discussed respectfully, with explanations given, and understanding and agreement reached.

In Kidstime, the ground rules are pretty much respected by the group and, as a result, the group has a sense of autonomy and largely self manages. That said, the Kidstime workers play an important role in modelling the behaviours and maintaining the ground rules within the workshop. It creates safety for the children to experience the Kidstime workers as trusted responsible adults, maintaining the boundaries so *they* don't have to.

Storytelling & drama   131

The act of playing games

One of the things that I have discovered in Kidstime is how important playing games is in creating boundaries and structure. Some children struggle to cope with managing their behaviour in the group. They find it difficult to work within and to respect boundaries. This may be because they are helping to manage their parents' mental illness, and boundaries at home are not consistent and/or are blurred.

Games are a fun way to learn about rules and working together. In the workshop the children want to have fun and play games so are happy to learn the rules and engage with them. If a game isn't played by the rules the game doesn't work. The children feel dissatisfied, and so following rules becomes a positive experience.

In the children's drama workshop, games are played before a story is created and filmed. The children like learning new games but they like to start with one of their favourite, familiar games. They know the rules-they know what to do. This seems to give them comfort and helps them to relax and feel safe. Apart from comfort and safety, games provide an opportunity for the children to learn to set rules themselves. They vie to explain the rules of their 'old favourites' games to new children who join the group.

Once a framework of safe space is in place, the group is free to play. The children can settle into the workshop with the comfort and safety of knowing that trusted adults are holding the space. They are free from responsibility, for their parents and/or younger siblings, for two hours. They are free to explore their own thoughts and feelings and to express them, or not, in whatever way they wish.

Step 2: Tools & skills: developing self awareness; understanding and emotional vocabulary: ways of expressing our thoughts & feelings

In Kidstime the children are encouraged to become comfortable with talking about mental illness with their parents and others, and to express how they are thinking and feeling. So first they need to be able to identify what they are thinking and feeling.

A – Identifying thoughts and emotions; developing self awareness

'Anyone Who': a good game to start the journey of self awareness. It involves movement so thinking is freed up, and it is low risk as it allows the child to be in control of what they share.

The game invites the group to share information about themselves, beginning with low risk statements of fact such as 'everyone who is wearing blue'. Once the group is warmed up, the drama worker can move the group on to

132   Deni Francis

sharing what they think and feel using statements of belief. This starts the child's thinking. What do they like and not like? What do they believe in? What do they share with others and what is unique to them?

How to play 'Anyone Who':

Everyone sits in a circle on a chair. One person stands in the middle. The aim of the game is for the person in the middle to sit on one of the chairs. They do this by making a statement beginning 'Anyone who...' and then saying something about themselves that is true, e.g. anyone who is wearing black, anyone who likes ice cream, anyone who likes school.

The rest of the group have to decide if the statement is true for them, and if it is they have to change seats. The person in the middle has to try and sit in one of the chairs. The person left without a chair is the new person in the middle and has to make an 'Anyone who...' statement and so the game goes on.

Rules

1   The statement must be true for the person saying it.
2   If someone leaves their chair they must commit to the action of leaving and find another chair.
3   Everyone to take care of themselves and each other, no pushing or shoving.

EMOTIONAL VOCABULARY: EXPRESSING THOUGHTS & FEELINGS

When the children in Kidstime are asked how they are feeling, they often do not really say. This could be because they don't *know*, or don't *want* to say, or don't know *how* to say. Once the children have begun to identify their thoughts and feelings, they need the language, the emotional vocabulary and the confidence to be able to express them. There are lots of games that build confidence and start conversations.

B – Emotion card charades, and how to play it

This is a game created for the Kidstime workshops to help the children and families to identify and name emotions. The game gets them to start talking, specifically and easily, about emotions in a fun way.

First you will need to make your own set of emotion cards which is very simple and satisfying to do. These are small hand torn pieces of card with the name of an emotion or feeling on each card. They could be made with a group in a workshop setting.

Put the group in pairs and give each person a couple of the emotion cards with strict instructions not to show their cards to their partner. Taking turns, each person mimes the emotion written on their card and their partner has to try and guess the emotion.

Pairs can swap cards and continue playing.

Common threads of discussion include how many different names there are for the same/similar feeling, which feelings they like and don't like, understanding their feelings, which feelings they choose to hide and which to reveal, how they show their feelings, coping with feelings and whether they know and understand what others are feeling, e.g. parents, children, friends.

The game moves from the non-verbal to the verbal, which means that it works across a huge age range. The experiential nature of the game means that feelings are felt in the body in the moment of playing. This allows emotional memory to be accessed which makes the discussions truthful and meaningful. It is a rich landscape to explore and the game helps to build an emotional vocabulary for the children as individuals and a shared language for the group.

CRITICAL THINKING

In Kidstime, critical thinking skills, including reasoning and logic, analysis and interpretation, reflection and evaluation, are being developed. Throughout the workshop, the workers ask questions and encourage opinions which are listened to and validated by workers and by other children and parents. There are also specific games and exercises that help.

These critical thinking skills can help the children to deal with difficult situations, and to manage emotions. They need to be able to identify how they are feeling, to evaluate the situation or the emotional state they are in and to consider their options and make a choice about what to think, feel or do. They also help the children to engage with and understand explanations of mental illness.

C – Developing critical thinking: agree-disagree game

Agree Disagree: an active debating game is fantastic for developing critical thinking. In the game the group are asked to think about a topic, to have an opinion, to express their opinion, to listen to others, to evaluate and to negotiate and debate.

Create an imaginary line by placing two chairs at each end of the room and one in the middle.

Designate one end of the room 'Agree' and the other end 'Disagree'.

Ask an either/or question or make a statement, e.g. chips are better than chocolate, Nike is better than Adidas, adults always know best.

Each person has to decide if they agree or disagree with the statement and place themselves on the line between the two chairs depending on the strength of their opinion. If they are ambivalent, they can move to the chair in the middle.

Once everyone has chosen a position the drama worker facilitates a discussion asking why people have chosen to stand where they are. Debate ensues. People can move if they are persuaded by a different viewpoint or choose to remain where they are.

The drama worker sets the tone, starting with light and low risk questions and statements, e.g. chips are better than chocolate. Once the game is established more weighty topics can be introduced, e.g. I never talk about my parent's mental illness at school, I always feel safe at home, it's good to talk about mental illness.

Step 3: Storytelling: creating & devising, genres and character

Devising and creating stories utilise the skills already introduced; developing self awareness, emotional literacy and critical thinking, and offer opportunities for practice. The next step is creating a story.

As humans we have always told stories. Before we developed language we told stories in other ways, with petroglyphs, cave paintings and dance. We made up stories to warn of danger, to make sense of the world and to pass on knowledge. With language began the rich oral storytelling tradition that still exists today. From indigenous tribal storytelling... to stories around the camp fire... to bedtime stories.

We carry our stories with us, through all of our senses, in our body memory and in our imagination:

Take a moment to think of a favourite story from your childhood. A story you were told or read for yourself. What can you remember? What images come into your mind? How do you feel? Focus on the images, the sensations, smell, taste, feelings.

I am currently reading one of my favourite childhood stories with my seven year old, as their bedtime story. 'The Enchanted Wood', by Enid Blyton. As I read out loud to them, the memories flood back. I can feel the excitement I felt as a child. I can hear the 'Wisha, wisha, wisha', sound of the whispering of the trees in 'The Enchanted Wood', see the slippery slip and feel the tingles of anticipation in my body as I climb the *faraway tree* to see which magical land is at the top today.

Creating and devising

In the Kidstime workshops, a story is created in the children's group and then filmed for the whole group to watch together at the end. The story emerges from the topic and discussion of the workshop, which deals with some aspect of mental illness, directly or indirectly. This is sometimes obvious in the stories the children bring and sometimes not. There is always a link although it may not be overt. If the children bring a story then it is

Storytelling & drama   135

important to them in some way. The ideas for stories shared by the children may be from their personal lived experiences. They need to feel safe to share them without worrying about revealing too much information, so the process used to create the stories needs to be protective. Creating composite stories is one way of doing this. Everyone's ideas are listened to, and then all the ideas are amalgamated into one story.

Once the story outline has been decided the roles are distributed. Some children want to be in front of the camera, as actors, or behind the camera as writer, director, camera operator or designer. Whether the children choose to be an actor in the story or take a role off camera, they are given a *clear role to play* in the creation of the story and filming. Assigning roles helps to create distance. For the actors this includes choosing a character name, rather than their real name or the name of someone they know.

The story is rehearsed for a very short time before it is filmed. It's rough and ready filming; one hand held camera, no editing. The process is more important than the end product. That said, the end product is always beautifully received by the group. More of that later.

Creating characters

Creating characters is fun, playful and cathartic. In the process of creating a character the children move from thought to action, from thinking to feeling. The children practice their critical thinking skills to make choices; how does my character think, feel and behave? They have to separate *their* thoughts and feelings from those of their character and as they do their understanding of themselves is increased.

Acting is a good discipline for practicing emotional self-management. The emotions of the character are played out in rehearsal and performance, and then left.

Genre

A story can be told in a myriad of ways. In Kidstime we have explored many genres including naturalism, fantasy, documentary, fairytale, surrealism, live television, sci-fi, kitchen sink drama and horror.

Creating stories creates powerful emotions which can be experienced and processed safely. An early Kidstime story dealt with the worry about a mum being unwell and needing her medication. The story was told in a naturalistic form. It showed Mum, played by an eight year old boy, lying on the sofa, unwell because she didn't have her medication. Her young son calls the doctor, and then goes to the chemist to get her prescription. The story ends with the Mum dying because she didn't get her medicine. The creation of this story allowed the child to talk about their fear of their Mum dying and for the clinical lead to reassure them that their Mum wouldn't die if they didn't take their medication. It also opened up discussion about the children's feelings of responsibility for their parents and their medication.

Using the genre of *fantasy*, we made a film about aliens coming to earth to learn about mental illness. The children drew representations of mental illness and created a character, called Mentoskins, who explained the effects of mental illness to the alien visitors.

Kidstime Question Time uses the *live TV* show genre, with 'experts' and a live studio audience. The children create 'expert' characters, e.g. the psychiatrist, the social worker, the mental health expert. Sometimes one of the Kidstime workers takes part in their real role. The show host poses questions to the experts about mental illness that come from the live studio audience played by the children. In addition to opening up discussion, the idea of who is the expert is raised. The children have a sense of being the expert of their own experience.

Step 4: The rehearsal process: catharsis, options, practice for life

As the children embody their characters, saying their lines and interacting with others, the rehearsal process moves them into their bodies and into their feelings. The children and young people can let go of the constraints and frustrations of everyday life and take risks. The drama facilitator needs to hold a strong boundary in this part of the creative process, partly so the children can safely push against it and take risks as their characters, and partly because there is not much time. Energy is high. This is their chance to say the things in their head that they don't dare say out loud in real life and to try out different behaviours.

Rehearsal is about practice and during rehearsal the children practice the story that is going to be filmed. Things change in rehearsal just as in life. In rehearsal it is ok to get it wrong. To be brave not perfect. A wonderful opportunity. Who gets it right first time? It can be a rehearsal for life or an escape from it.

Practice for life: exploring options

In rehearsal the children can escape into a fantasy world and play out their wildest dreams. Or they can take on roles and characters similar to themselves, and play out realistic alternative scenarios.

Some themes come up time and time again and power and status run throughout them: power struggles in families, between friends, at school and in wider society. The children can explore options and practice conversations and behaviours.

Recurring themes include mental illness and what is the nature of mental illness – children often choose to play doctors giving diagnoses to patients in various settings. Storylines exploring the differences between physical and mental illnesses are also common.

Storytelling & drama   137

Laughter therapy: one film tells a story about different 'treatments' for people with mental illness. The children created scenes showing three different types of therapy: talking therapy, medication and laughter therapy. The laughter therapy scene showed a helpline that people could call if they felt unwell. The helpline operator took the details and the caller was visited by a comedy double act who came to their home and told them jokes to make them laugh. This was the children's favourite treatment.

Bullying theme: the children create stories that deal with bullying at school and try out coping strategies. Some children choose to play teachers, some of which are supportive and some of which are not. The psyche of the bully is explored when a child chooses to play the bully, as the children try to understand the reasons that some children bully others.

After a Kidstime workshop seminar discussing stigma and prejudice towards people with mental illness, the children wanted to make a film about bullying. They came up with a story with three strands.

Strand 1 shows a boy being bullied in a corridor and having his dinner money taken. There is a close up on him looking upset. He tells a teacher but the teacher is too busy to listen and tells him to come back later. He doesn't.

Strand 2 shows two children laughing about cyber-bullying another child.

Strand 3 shows three children who have experienced being bullied who are unable to talk about their experiences. They hold up sheets of paper that they have written on the words they can't say; upset, scared, lonely.

After the film had been made the group shared their experiences of bullying. Everyone had a story. They talked about who they trusted enough to tell and shared ideas about what to do. When they showed the film and watched it with their parents, one of the children told their parent they were being bullied. They hadn't told them before because they didn't want to worry them. It was an emotional moment. The group was incredibly supportive, and the empathy and advice given brought the group closer together.

Dealing with professionals, and parent in hospital themes: the children often report that they do not feel listened to by professionals. They complain that they are shut out when a parent is admitted to hospital, and not given information or allowed to visit because they are children.

In one particularly moving film the story follows a young boy looking for his father who has a mental illness, and has disappeared.

In a documentary style, brandishing a flip chart marker as a microphone, the young boy faces obstacle after obstacle on his quest. He begins, hopefully, with a meeting with his father's friend who tells him that his father visited him late at night in distress. He learns that his father has been taken away by the police. The police refuse to give him any information but despite this the boy tracks him down at the hospital he has been admitted to. Our hero bribes the receptionist and gains entry but the psychiatrists at the hospital won't help him either. The film ends with the boy evading the psychiatrists and running down a corridor where he flings open a door and shouts 'aha'. The film echoes the trajectory of the hero's journey (found in many stories), and highlights the anger and frustration the children feel at the lack of information and respect for them from professionals.

Home and Parent unwell themes – parents being unwell, conflict with parents, conflict with siblings. The children playing both (other) children and parents in these scenes. There are also recurring themes of fear of the parent's illness, that they may themselves become unwell with a mental illness or that their parent may die.

School & Friendship themes: these can range from classic rebellion and anarchy in the classroom scenes to the impact of hiding a parent's mental illness from everyone at school. The children have rarely told their friends that their parent has a mental illness. If they have, it is only to very close friends. A common storyline involves a character confiding in a teacher or friend at school and their response.

Some of these themes were used to create the demonstration film the 'Jass Story',[2] a professional film made for the Kidstime workshops. In the film we follow the story of Jass, who lives with his mother who has a mental illness, and his younger sister. Jass is struggling to hold everything together. Things start to fall apart as he gets into trouble at school and resists his best friend's attempt to help. It is a powerful and poignant testament to the pressures on a young carer, and to their strength and resilience.

Whatever the theme, the most common emotions the children choose to play out are fear and anger, with a large dose of comedy which leads me to catharsis.

Catharsis: 'There is no greater agony than bearing an untold story inside you', – Maya Angelou[3]

Catharsis is defined by the Collins dictionary as getting rid of unhappy memories or strong emotions such as anger and sadness by expressing them in some way.

Acting is a means of catharsis. In Kidstime, the children enjoy creating their own narratives and playing out emotions as different characters. It is a release. They can express strong and powerful emotions: shout in rage, laugh, be powerful, scream in fear. They can play out imagined conflicts, be heroes and baddies, choose to confront, to appease, to create havoc, to be magical or to walk away.

Step 5: Filming, performance, escapism

In Kidstime there is a short period of time for the whole creating/devising/filming process. There is an hour at most. This, it turns out, can be helpful.

The aim is not to develop performance skills and have a polished finish. The emphasis is on process not product. The piece is filmed on a tiny hand held camera with no editing. There is no time for any lengthy rehearsal or for re-takes. The focus is on getting it done in the short amount of time available, with the promise of pizza for dinner when the film is finished. The time restriction gives an impetus and lowers the stakes, as there is less time for nerves to take over.

During the filming stage the drama worker needs to become the director and drive the process. Everyone needs to be assigned a role: actor, writer, camera operator, designer.

There is only 20–30 minutes to film the story. Once, a film was made in five minutes.

The children get the best of both worlds by their performance being filmed. There is no audience at this point which means a lack of self censor. Catharsis comes from the creation of characters and the rehearsal process, as well as in the performance for filming. When the audience watch the film later the children are able to share their gaze, and the whole group experience the powerful energy of the performer-audience relationship.

Acting is all about escaping to an imaginary world. During the performance/filming the children are in the imaginary world that they have been part of creating, a world in which for a short, intense period of time they are empowered and have complete control over what happens. They are free from responsibility and free to play.

Step 6: Audience, watching the film, reviewing

The magic: filming as a medium is exciting and engaging for the children. As they move away from the written word they are increasingly influenced by the moving image, both in terms of cinema and TV, and increasingly other forms of social media such as YouTube and Instagram.

The magic happens when the whole group; children and parents and workers, are watching the film together. The parents/carers are watching their children on screen. The children are watching their parents watching them. The parents are engaging with the story that the children are telling. The children are seeing themselves reflected, and their story is being told.

The children are able to communicate their thoughts and feelings through the story, to the parents, via the medium of film. Film is protective because the children are controlling the gaze. They are one step removed. They have decided what story to tell, in what form to tell it and what role to play in making the film. They are also in control of how they want to watch the film as an audience member. They can choose to watch the film or to watch others watch the film. They may choose to leave the room or hide under a table. Sometimes the group chooses to watch it again.

The group shares this experience and there is an emotional connection in the act of watching together as an audience. It is a magical moment. The story may be sad or funny or both. There may or may not be a happy ending. Whatever the emotional journey, there is shared pride and celebration and applause.

The medium of film provides distance for the audience who feel connected but separate. For the children watching themselves performing on screen they get the chance to step back from the emotions they were feeling during rehearsal and performance. This allows them to think about themselves in relation to those emotions, and their options, from the safety of their seats.

The discussion that follows the making and watching of the film also benefits from film being engaging and distancing. The group is less likely to take things personally or be defensive. The process of critiquing allows the group to say what they think and also to consider the thoughts of others, as separate viewpoints from their own.

Seeing ourselves reflected: we need to see to be

In the media, books, films, TV, theatre, there are few representations of people living with mental illness, and even fewer that are positive. It is even rarer to find stories of children who have a parent with a mental illness. An exception is 'The Illustrated Mum', by Jacqueline Wilson,[4] a story about a mum who has bipolar disorder.

In a recent Kidstime workshop, parents talked about how they felt that the only representations they saw on TV of people with mental illness were extreme and over dramatic. They wondered what it would be like to see people and families living with mental illness doing ordinary things, getting on with their lives without any big dramas, an idea for a future film.

In Kidstime the children struggle to think of stories that reflect their lived experience. By creating their own representations, and by telling their stories, they see themselves reflected. They exist. They are no longer invisible. Seeing positive images that reflect who they are and aspects of their lives is affirming and helps to build a healthy sense of self.

My normal, your normal

In an age with increasing pressure from social media to present a perfect self and lifestyle, it is important for the children to see themselves reflected in a positive way. The idea of normality, based on mainstream images, norms and values, can be detrimental to their self image and sense of self. Creating their stories and seeing themselves reflected is empowering and decreases feelings of shame and isolation. It builds their self confidence and self esteem, helping them to be proud of who they are.

> 'There's no such thing as normal. No-one in this room is normal and no-one in the world is normal'.
>
> Adrian, age 12
>
> 'We are all normal-in our own-way'.
>
> Liam, age 10

The stories they create and the films they make put them on screen and are affirming.

Conclusion

Everyone has a story to tell and their own way of telling it. Every story matters. Drama is a powerful medium. It engages on an emotional and physical level. This framework of six creative steps shows how the different drama processes and techniques flow together in Kidstime. There is a transformational process from when children arrive at a workshop to when they leave. They can shrug off the cloak of responsibility for a short time and play, laugh and connect, create stories and be their *own normal*. In the most simple sense, through the drama and storytelling, a space is created where children can learn and grow while having fun, being free to laugh and play and dream.

References

1 Stanislavsky, K. 1936 *An Actor Prepares*. London, Bloomsbury.
2 'Who Cares?' 2012 (demonstration film) Director: Mark Ayres. Script: Deni Francis, Chineye Njoku, Kirsty Tahta-Wraith and the Young People from the Camden and Islington Kidstime Workshop. Now recut and available as 'The Jass Story' on Our Time website: https://ourtime.org.uk/resource/jass-story/.
3 Angelou, M. 1969 *I Know Why the Caged Bird Sings*. London, Virago Modern Classics, p. 75.
4 Wilson, J. 1999 *The Illustrated Mum*. London, Doubleday.

Chapter 11

The journey from young carer to doctor

Reflections on how the two roles informed each other

Suhaib Debar

My ideas and experiences before medical school

What I thought a child of a parent with mental illness or young carer was

As a young child caring for a parent, I was initially unaware that I was a young carer and did not realise that I had more responsibilities and pressures than other kids of my age. Coming home from school did not always mean that I could unwind from school and have fun, as I had extra work to do at home – be it house chores or caring for my mother. The caring role included providing emotional support for my mother and looking after my three younger siblings to relieve some of her tasks in order to provide her time to unwind and alleviate the stresses of daily life. As this was a constant routine, it became ingrained in my life and I knew no better.

The role of providing care is *not only an active role but also* at such a young age it is a loss of opportunity. Young carers are burdened with social stigma, excess responsibility, loss of school time and the loss of 'childhood' and *normal* activities of kids of a similar age. In addition, as these years are pivotal in development this added responsibility and stress is detrimental to the young carer's health, predisposing them to an increased risk of mental health conditions of their own. Certainly when I was caring, more so through the lack of available time, missing football would mean that I would be quite sad and somewhat resentful that I could not join my friends in having fun.

The first sign that I discovered that made me realise that I had extra obligations at home was when I could not attend social gatherings due to my caring responsibilities. Over time, with the help of various charities I discovered that I was a young carer and there was support out there for people like myself and my family. These charities introduced me to other young carers, usually in a fun environment that allowed us to unwind from our caring roles whilst appreciating that we are not alone in our caring responsibilities. Furthermore, I enjoyed interacting with the professional staff of these charities as it was affirming to be listened to by adults and it was reassuring that we knew we had them as a support network.

What or who is a young carer?

I had never considered the definition until it was mentioned to me that I may in fact be one. Seemingly a young carer ought to be any young person that cares for a family member with a significant health problem or disability. This definition and role may be obvious if the person being cared for has a physical ailment, as the carer may need to provide obvious physical support to help with their limitations. It is straightforward to recognise a young carer in such a situation as this. However, it becomes more difficult when the cared for person has a mental health illness.

Mental health illnesses can be notoriously difficult to identify and the care that is required can be quite different to that of physical disabilities. As such the role of a young carer in these scenarios can be more difficult to appreciate. Care can come in various forms; it can be physical (e.g. hoisting someone in and out of bed if they lack the muscle power to do so) or emotional (providing comfort and reassurance when the cared for person is in a depressive episode). Whilst it may be obvious to identify a young carer caring for a person with a physical disability, the emotional aspect of care can easily go unnoticed and may appear invisible. Subsequently, the identification and number of young carers providing care for someone with a mental health illness are seriously underreported. Due to a lack of awareness, there are *hundreds of* young carers looking after someone with a mental health illness unaware that they are in fact a carer. This issue will further translate into official figures; the government has only acknowledged the existence of under 200,000 young carers (in the United Kingdom) to cover all illnesses – physical and mental. The Carer's Trust mounted a campaign in which they identified about 800,000 – again to cover all illnesses. In hindsight, the term young carer was never mentioned at my school, in a deprived area and in all probability containing plenty of young carers, unknown to the school. If the school had discussions about young carers and let them know that there is support out there, this could have been a great source of identification of young carers and provider of help.

What my understanding was of mental illness

During my childhood, many of the experiences and notions surrounding mental illness were largely negative. Especially in school people would use terms such as 'mental', 'crazy', 'bonkers' as a derogatory term, which contributes towards the taboo about mental ill health and mental illness. Not many TV shows at the time explained mental health and those that did such as East-Enders displayed mental illness in a negative way. As a result I also developed a negative attitude to mental illness as something shameful that I could not discuss. My mother's mental health issues are something that I never brought up in conversation and unknown to all my friends. In my early teenage years I started attending an organisation called Kidstime that ran workshops for the children of parents with mental illness. This two and a half hours session every month after school provided me with an enjoyable escape and an invaluable opportunity to learn more about both mental health and illness. I greatly enjoyed my time there interacting with the other carers and wonderful staff in a safe and friendly environment. The tasty pizza provided was an added bonus too. Through Kidstime, I developed an understanding of mental illnesses including their aetiology, presentation and management. It made me realise that mental ill health affects many people, anyone at any time, and does not mean that you are weak or 'crazy' as was my impression from what I had heard on the school playground. Through these sessions, I learned to become more tolerant of my mum's condition, as at times I did not understand why she could not just get out of it. It was a great place to discuss the difficulties of caring.

My experiences and how this shaped my ideas

My initial experience of caring for someone with mental illness was largely negative, due to the lack of understanding of what a mental illness is and the challenges of caring. I resented that I had extra pressures at home and did not have the free time that I wanted to pursue my hobbies. At times, the responsibility I had led me to experience stress and this I believe had a negative impact on my education and probably my own mood too. The experiences of Kidstime changed my outlook, towards a more positive viewpoint, through learning about mental health illnesses and the opportunity to openly discuss matters. This allowed me to cope better at home and gave me a peace of mind as the Kidstime platform allowed me to consider my situation and discuss any matters that were on my mind.

How these ideas evolved throughout medical school

By participating in Kidstime I was more comfortable with my caring role and more hopeful for the future. Kidstime revealed to me that I was not alone in my caring role and that there was support available for myself and my family. I believe it is extremely important for children to be heard, as caring can often be a lonely role, and being acknowledged and discussing matters openly makes the role less isolated. This reassurance and the opportunity to discuss related topics were relieving, and gave me the strength to continue with my caring responsibilities. I was able to focus better at school and perform well academically, eventually leading me to study Medicine at university. Studying Medicine gained me a better understanding of mental health illness and recognising the role of carers in society.

When during my own medical training I did my psychiatry placement, I was fascinated to learn about the various common conditions. I was interested to hear what I was taught about the causes and risk factors associated with mental health conditions. I discovered that immigrants had higher rates of certain disorders, and coming from a refugee family I found this particularly interesting, as some of my mother's mental health conditions resulted as the consequence of conflict in her home country. My greater understanding of mental illness equipped me with the knowledge on how to identify mental health problems better and the treatments available, including the great impact of talking therapies. This further made me realise the positive influence that Kidstime had on me and my family.

Throughout medical school we are taught the importance of treating patients holistically taking into account the patients' physical, emotional and social needs.

How my understanding of the role of a carer changed throughout medical school

I have met patients with complex social needs and have encountered other young carers. It is difficult to ascertain the number of young carers I encountered, as aforementioned it can be difficult to identify carers, particularly those looking after a loved one with a mental health illness. The difficulty is further compounded as often the consultations are very short and the young carers might not always become evident as they may be in school at the time. I was further surprised by how many carers are out there, young and old, that should be embraced for their selfless dedication. Most of the time you are unable to tell that the person is a young carer and consequently they may have no support systems in place. This may lead to difficulties for both the carer and the person receiving the care. For example, the stresses placed on a carer may lead to their own mental health and health problems.

This has made me reflect on the positive impact that Kidstime had on me. By providing similar support groups (*through the NHS*) learning to understand mental illness and providing a forum to speak to others in a similar situation could help alleviate the detrimental effects of being a full-time carer. I believe that healthcare professionals should actively be keeping an eye out for young carers and providing them with the support they need. However, this can be hard to achieve due to obvious constraints on the NHS and more so the lack of active attempts at identifying young carers – but nonetheless we should be better at identifying young carers and helping them. By providing support for young carers we can improve the health and prospects of these people, preventing the adverse consequences that can arise due to the consuming role of caring. This would be beneficial to all parties involved: the carer, the person being cared for and for the healthcare system.

My ideas currently

In order to raise awareness of young carers and how to support them, steps can be implemented to incorporate modules into the curriculum of healthcare degrees. Modules explaining the role of young carers, and how it can impact them and their families, will be useful in providing the healthcare professionals the insight and empathy that are needed to allow us to support them. An awareness of the various support that is available to help carers will allow us to better refer them on to these services. This is an important issue as there are many young carers that go unnoticed and healthcare professionals, such as GPs, may be the first or best port of contact that can provide them with support. By the nature of being a young carer, meaning looking after someone with a physical or mental ailment, they are bound to visit the healthcare setting. I remember from my childhood various doctor appointments that I attended with my mother and upon reflection I have realised I was never once asked how I am or how things are at home. There are many missed opportunities each day to identify young carers and help them. Patients that are parents with young children and a significant illness, be it physical or mental, should be recognised by the healthcare team. They should also be informed about, and directed towards available support for young carers. An appropriate and easy to access referral pathway that can be initiated by any healthcare professional in order to identify and provide support for young carers by a dedicated team dealing with these matters would be the ideal solution. Ultimately, we as healthcare professionals should be better at this and this can be achieved by incorporating teaching of young carers into the curriculum.

What I will take away and incorporate into my medical practice

Ultimately, through my experiences as a young carer and exposure to the world of healthcare, I believe there is a lot more that can be done to support young carers, specifically children and young people affected by mental illness in a parent. The healthcare profession should be better at supporting young carers and this can be achieved by suitable education. Similarly, schools should also receive this education to better identify young carers. Neither my school nor GP knew that I was a young carer, which represents a missed opportunity for many unidentified young carers out there to receive the support that they need and deserve. Fortunately, I had the help of a great organisation such as Kidstime, that provided many benefits to me and my family that allowed us to better cope with the situation by providing the necessary support. My journey from young carer to doctor has provided me with the necessary insight and experience to understand how better we can support young carers. During my practice as a doctor I will be aware of young carers, as they may present as a patient or accompanying a patient, and inform and direct them towards the various appropriate accessible supports. Every young carer deserves the support they need to fulfil their potential and lead a healthy life.

Chapter 12

Keeping it together
Championing young carers' rights and raising family and public awareness

Ambeya Begum

My name is Ambeya and I am 24 years old. I was born and raised as a Muslim girl in the United Kingdom with my two younger brothers, and my parents come from a Bangladeshi background. Shortly after writing this chapter, my mum passed away unexpectedly. The last few months before she passed away, I finally had the opportunity to build a relationship with her, something I was unable to do all the years she was ill. I never got the chance to tell her she was the inspiration for me writing this chapter, and sadly I was never able to give her a copy of the book. I wanted her to understand that her illness made us stronger – despite the distress and pain I felt – and that I sometimes saw it as a blessing. It is important for us all to understand that what we face in life are tests of patience, devotion and trust. We need to hold onto the belief that our souls are not burdened with more than they can handle. My mother was a constant source of inspiration to me, and although she is no longer here in person to give me strength, her legacy will give me strength I need to meet my goals. Many people knew of my mum but did not have the chance to really meet her and I hope this chapter will allow them to know her true self through my writing. I dedicate this chapter to my mum.

Being a young carer

In this chapter I intend to use my own experiences and my journey as a carer to parental mental illness, to resolve some of the miscommunications and judgments which exist and are a part of our lives. This is against the background of a lack of education on mental illness, *regardless of the fact that one in four people experience a mental health problem in their lifetime.*

I am a carer for a mother who suffers from schizoaffective disorder, a combination of both schizophrenia and bipolar disorder. Once upon a time, my experiences of being a young carer were detrimental. Having been a carer since the age of 8, me and my siblings were never given an explanation as to why my mother was the way she was, or what was wrong with her. We always questioned our upbringing. 'Why is she constantly being taken away? Was

148 Ambeya Begum

it our fault? Are we being punished?' This is what childhood was like for us. We were made to feel ashamed of how we felt and embarrassed for living the life we did – by family, by the environment and by Society. Often, we didn't recognise ourselves as carers and believed we were just helping out our parents like a 'normal' child. We didn't take credit for the physical and emotional support we gave and lived our lives providing an unpaid 'hidden' role. This was our reality – constantly attempting to hide behind a mask.

Putting ourselves in this position meant we were constantly fighting for something (peace and happiness) whilst fighting against something (the consequences of dealing with parental mental illness). This ongoing battle meant we had to deal with different extremes on a daily basis and growing up in such an environment sometimes made it impossible to feel physically and emotionally safe.

For most people in Society, the word 'mental illness' has connotations of fear, discomfort and danger. How is it that simply replacing the word 'physical' with 'mental' evokes such heartless responses and an overwhelming difference in the way we react? As with all types of prejudice, this stigma around mental illness is born out of ignorance, and we have to accept that this will be the case. Eventually, when I was 16, I had no personal choice but to accept that this reality was my reality and I took off the mask I had lived behind. This was one of the hardest things I ever had to do.

Living with a parent with a mental illness

Nothing prepares you for being a young carer affected by parental mental illness. I grew up in a home where no one ever explained to me what was going on. There is no such thing as a young carer's manual that can help and guide you in understanding how your life can instantly change when you come to grips with such illnesses. It was always one extreme to another and I always had to deal with each situation in a completely different way. For this reason, I never had the chance to build a relationship with my mother and I taught myself how to play the mother role in the family for me and my brothers. There were times where she could not be admitted into hospital and I had to take over the parent role and keep everyone safe, tolerating verbal abuse and extreme aggressive behaviour, including her uttering death threats or watching the house burn whilst we were still inside.

My childhood was confusing but it never stopped me from looking at the world positively, which I will go into later. I believed that after every struggle comes ease and that if I carried on believing and had patience, then I could have anything and be anything I wanted to be. There were many times where I did view the world as a dark place to be, where even we were not safe from harm. Pressures always existed within the family, and there was even a time when my dad lost the capability of managing her illness but I am grateful that he didn't leave us, because if he did, I don't think you'd be reading this chapter from me today.

What is it like dealing with parental mental illness

Let me paint you a picture of what would happen during my mother's episodes:

- She would speak in a language which we couldn't understand and have continuous conversations with herself, meaning we avoided speaking to her
- She would become physically stronger, meaning we avoided being around her
- She would miraculously know how to get around London on her own, meaning we avoided going out with her
- She would treat summer like winter and vice versa, so her dress style was thrown out the window, meaning we avoided being seen with her in public to save the embarrassment
- She would disturb the neighbours and cause disruption in the neighbourhood, meaning we would have to go out, resolve any feuds and force her to come back home
- She would go days without sleeping, meaning we had sleepless nights so we could make sure we were aware of what she was doing
- She would think taking medication was our way of trying to kill her and when we tried giving her medication, she would swear and call us all sorts of names, so we avoided giving anything and left this to be my dad's responsibility
- She would tell us she doesn't have any children and forget who we were, meaning we became emotionally detached. Even though we knew this was her illness and not her, we couldn't help ourselves at such a young age
- She would refuse eating but would increase drinking tea and coffee; this increased her hyperactivity and adrenaline but this was impossible to manage, so we left her to it

This is only a snippet of what it is like to live with someone with a severe mental illness. Now let me paint you a picture of what else happened during these periods:

The world around the family:

a As a child:
- Social services – we were on a child protection plan due to the severities of her illness. I have very mixed feelings about their services. We dreaded opening up to them as we were always fearful that disclosing information on our circumstance would lead to us being taken away. As a child, I could not talk about my mother's illness, with confidence, without my eyes being filled with tears – tears of both emotional pain and shame.

- In my community there was always a sense of embarrassment and shame for someone who was suffering from a mental illness. Until something happened which made it impossible to hide, we tried our best to keep our mother's psychotic episodes hidden and unspoken of. Knowing how quickly gossip spread, I kept quiet.
- People were worried that her illness was contagious and that if their children were around us, they would catch it. If people had simply known what the truth was, they would have understood what we were going through and rumours would not have been circulating.

b As a teen and young adult: my mother's compulsory admission and the build up to my own distress:

In 2014, I had to decide whether or not my mother should be sectioned under the Mental Health Act again, since the NHS couldn't afford to provide a bed for her anymore. It was the hardest decision of my life. I was in my final year of university within weeks of facing my exams and in the middle of revising at home. My dad was out shopping and my brothers were out with their friends. I was home alone with her and I couldn't cope with it anymore. I called 999 and asked for both the police and ambulance service. Once I made the decision, I remember breaking down. By this point, my dad had come home and I was so glad he was back. The police and ambulance came within minutes and within the space of half an hour, they were ready to take her. Of course, it was never going to be easy. She was pepper sprayed and dragged down the stairs. Our front door was wide open and her screaming and shouting overpowered the voices of the police.

She was forced into the ambulance and I felt so much guilt in my heart – the look in her eyes when she was taken away is a look that one can never forget. I carried this heavy burden and it had a major effect on me to the point where I blamed everything that had happened before that stage on me. *At that point, no one asked me how I was.* I always knew that talking helps but the time where I needed to talk the most I became silenced by all the emotional pain I had to put up with.

Over the year, I began to victimise myself and I saw myself as my own hypocrite and deceiving those around me. I had lost the ability to help myself. How could I possibly help others when I couldn't even help myself? This exact question led me into a black hole and I lost my personality and positive spirit. I believed it was my duty to remain strong and reliable for everyone in my life and that I couldn't let them see the messed up person that goes into hiding. I found it hard to open up to my friends and family about how I felt. Through dissociation, I blocked all my social media accounts and disconnected my phone line. I decided to detach myself from the outside world and thought that this would numb my emotional pain.

The diagnosis

Being diagnosed with severe depression and anxiety in December 2014 left me afraid that I had lost the capability of being a role model to others – losing the motivation and commitment to carry on. In early 2015, I was diagnosed with both PTSD and OCD and this became a way of life for the next year. Normally social, I stopped trying to make friends or get involved with the community. I felt disoriented, forgetting who I was. I was trapped in a mental space which I felt I had no control over. I became unconfident with myself and started overthinking everything. All the emotional strength and resilience that I had built over the years of being a young carer had created a mental roof over my head. Being diagnosed felt like a storm had passed and this roof had finally collapsed, making my road to recovery, whilst completing my Masters, even more difficult.

Being on the receiving end of stigma and discrimination caused self-doubt and I questioned my self-worth. I can look back now and gently laugh at the idea that I ever thought life could be perfect life. I was young and talented, but unbeknown to everyone in my community, I was suffering from an unbearable mental illness which I had now finally accepted. As months passed, I became a part of the Society where talking about mental health in the Asian community was a taboo subject and hardly spoken about. I questioned whether all those assumptions Society had on those suffering from a mental health condition were now aimed at me. I did feel like people thought that I should have got over it by now or that I was being over dramatic about the whole situation. Completely ashamed of myself, I accepted the misconception that recovery from a mental illness was impossible, so I decided not to seek professional help.

I had faced stigma and discrimination and didn't know how to handle it. This is where all the memories of previous stigma and negativity came flooding back. I personally couldn't ignore the whisperings, the murmurings, the remarks and the distancing from friends.

I can't help but think that if someone had looked a little deeper, perhaps someone who was aware of mental health issues and that signs and symptoms to look out for, a simple conversation could have changed my life. For those who know me for my stubbornness, I would still like to believe I am superwoman. Even till this day, I am convinced that had I received better information about my mother's illness, I would have not been so ashamed of seeking help for myself earlier. But at the same time, no one should have to wait for something bad to happen for them to realise they could have done something to prevent it. I had to do something about it.

Coping with trauma

I did decide to receive help eventually, and wish I had much sooner as things would have been very different. But, like I mentioned earlier, the biggest obstacle is accepting that we need help. Undergoing behavioural therapy marked the turning point in my regaining control of my life. Without the treatments and coping skills, PTSD can become a debilitating and often life-threatening condition. Once the therapy came to an end, I thought I would just be able to put this behind me and nobody would ever have to know that I had had a mental illness. I thought that was the end, that I was 'cured'. I know now that for me there is no cure, no final healing. But there are things I can do to ensure that I never have to suffer like I did before being diagnosed with PTSD. I'm no longer at the mercy of my disorder and I would not be here today had I not had the proper diagnosis and treatment – if I had decided not to accept, I am sure it would have been the most damaging decision of my life.

At this present time, the world is now a new place to me and not limited by the restrictive vision of stress and anxiety. It amazes me to think back to what my life was like a few years ago and how far in my mental recovery I came. It is so important to look beyond the illness and live outwardly congruent with your internal values.

It's never too late to seek help, but let's look at what might get in the way: social media and public conversations

Nowadays, we only look at how many pictures we can post or what is the next thing we should post but we don't look at the effect of social media on our mental health. Taking Facebook and Instagram as examples, they allow us to present our own filtered sense of reality, showing only what we want to show. This can lead to a person critically comparing their life with other people's lives and using others' posts as measures for successes and failures in their own life. The impact of this could be catastrophic feelings of low self-esteem, resulting in negative 'I am' statements such as 'I will never be able to be like that person', or 'I could never do that'.

Daily conversations and including ideas on mental illness

Outdated ideas can only change when we talk about them, and it is vital that we challenge unhelpful language and deceptive imagery that are formed when being surrounded by mental illness. This is so that those experiencing mental health problems will no longer feel isolated or discriminated against. So, if we continue to introduce the subject of mental illness into our normal daily conversations, we can allow the topic to be more accessible, in ways that are designed to be more helpful and non-judgemental – not only to those who are affected by it, but by others too. We can all be influenced by this and can aid in continuing to reduce the stigma. *Investing in young people's physical and mental health shouldn't just be a moral imperative, but will prevent problems occurring later in life which may need more intensive and expensive support.*

People suffering from mental illness are no longer labelled as 'crazy' or 'psycho', but they are not spoken about as real people either. By starting meaningful conversations, we can tackle these misconceptions in order to build a better Society for those who are still in hiding; it will take three steps: educate, empathise and challenge. I know there are so many other kids out there who could be in the same situation as me. They avoid asking for help or avoid expressing that they care for someone. They are incapable of confronting their fears and it hurts to know that they have to deal with it on their own, just like I had to do.

You who read this could be at the heart of our campaign to change people's attitudes and improve young people's understanding towards those with mental health problems. You all have the power to help young carers dealing with parental mental illness heal and to help Society feel. If you shift your understandings and encourage others to follow suit, you'll realise that.

The more people can understand, the more I believe people will start being less frightened, and the less frightened they are, the more willing they will be to support. This cycle can continue if Society allows it to.

Culture and the framing of mental illness in Asian cultures

To be honest, I am not sure why struggling with mental health is frowned upon and shoved under the carpet in Asian cultures. It is annoying and it is painful. No one wants to listen. No one wants to talk. And it is troubling hearing other Asians repeat similar stories of trying to bring the topic up and being told that it is just a sort of 'sadness that will go away'. It is not acknowledged that having a mental illness can be isolating, indescribable and overwhelming; sometimes all these emotions often appear at once. Nor will anyone tell you that mental illness is more than just feeling 'sad'. When it comes to mental health, many feel it should be a private matter, kept inside the home. People feel as if the South Asian community is not open-minded when it comes to mental ill health, especially the older generation.

Whilst I love my heritage, one of the reasons why I knew nothing about mental illnesses is down to my culture and community. The Western world has finally accepted mental illness as a serious issue. However, in my culture, mental health is dismissed as something made up, an over-dramatic illusion so you can be signed off work, or as an excuse. They believe it is a sign of weakness and succumb to the age-old culture of keeping mental illness a secret. They do not realise that this 'made-up' illness has taken away the potential for many to be the best version of themselves. What many do not talk about is how damaging certain attitudes dominant in our culture can be when we are struggling with our mental health: the constant judging over your appearance, intelligence or life choices, being compared to cousins or a family friend throughout your entire life, the fear of what other people might say, the nosiness, the lack of acceptance when you want to try something new, the ridicule of failure, the fact that a child or young person cannot be left 'to be' and develop a personality of their own.

Any Asian person, especially women, will tell you about the pressures of growing up in many Asian households – the high expectations, the keeping up of appearances, and the toxic 'model minority' stereotype that continually hums in the background of your life. There's an expectation to stand out for the 'right' reasons – meaning good grades, a fancy job, high salary, good social standing. In my family's minds, having a mental illness can prevent you from achieving those things. And if you're not achieving everything, then why are you even here? Asian women in particular feel the need to prove themselves.

It is for all these reasons that we need to take mental health seriously, and ensure the next generation is not subjected to the same behaviours as us: whether you initiate that difficult conversation or challenge an outdated attitude, whether you correct an elder when they dismiss mental illness and just want to talk about the exam marks. There is so much to be proud of from our heritage and culture but it is time we phase out the mind-set most of us grew up with and replace it with one of awareness and acceptance.

I decided to go against the Asian attitudes dominant in the culture and I count my blessings that my subsequent experiences have brought me back somewhat closer to my culture. This has been through offering others a sense of purpose to feel comfortable sharing their stories. I applaud how famous people have come forward to talk about their mental health problem openly but it's still rare to hear stories from ethnic minority groups. *I hope that together we can continue to raise dialogue within the Asian community and change cultural awareness towards mental illness.*

Religion

Based on personal experiences, mental illness was very much seen as a taboo subject in Islam. Growing up in a big Muslim community, there was hardly any talk about mental illness – it was as if the problem didn't exist. It made those suffering ashamed of the illness itself. It is a taboo subject in general, but specifically in Islam it is so difficult to speak to your family members and get them to understand. Family is an important part of mental recovery and when you feel like you cannot even speak to them, then the world seems even darker than it already is. In general, Muslim families disregard the issue of mental illness because of the lack of knowledge and understanding which leads to them thinking that it would bring shame on the family. Those that are mentally unwell seek support from their friends and family. But, when turning to the Muslim community, they are targeted by their ignorance, wrapped up by faith inspired advice. It was ironic how uneasy and difficult it was to find comfort amongst religious people when the religion itself is supposed to be the source of comfort. If mental well-being was proportional to religious observance, then religious people would not be struggling or suffering with their mental health. Religion does not protect those with a physical illness; so why would it protect you from a mental illness?

As mental illnesses are invisible, it is tempting to turn it towards the unseen world or talk about it superstitiously. However, mental illnesses are influenced by factors in the seen world and most methods of coping are managed here. A person who truly cares about their recovery or those of their family and friends would help them access methods of coping in the seen world. Suggesting that mentally ill people are possessed by Jinn and evil spirits because they are simply not 'religious enough' will most likely hurt their relationship with God and distance them from religion instead of bringing them closer.

As a young British Asian Muslim, I struggled with understanding how our religion played a role with mental illness. So many questions used to run through my mind:

1 What happens when my feeling of hurt and emptiness can't be cured by faith?
2 Does God hate me for not praying in my times of need?
3 What did I do to deserve this life?
4 Am I not a good Muslim?

My faith stopped providing the answers to my questions and it scared me. Instead, I told myself that if faith can't help me, then nothing will be able to. So, I stopped looking for help because I became afraid that any answer to my questions would deepen my guilt. I stopped calling to God when I was in a black hole and then slowly distanced from my faith. The habit of beginning the day in God's name and ending the day in God's name left me. Thoughts of religion and observance left me. Reading verses from the Quran or reading my supplications stopped crossing my mind. I stopped asking God to help me. How did I let myself fall so deep into my self-misery?

It felt like I was drowning. Were these obstacles I had encountered a test from God? I ended up losing count of the amount of times I had been told that the difficulties I endured were due to my weakness in faith. I struggled with my beliefs when I couldn't find anything else to hold onto. When you feel abandoned by God, the easiest thing to do is turn away – why was I the one going through so much turmoil and pain? This spiritual battle that I suffered added to the mental pain I suffered from my mother's illness.

In Islam, we rely on God to heal us. If we are depressed or ill, we pray to God to make us better. We pray and make invocations whenever possible. The term 'tawakkul' in Islam means completely trusting God, which is a fundamental part of the religion. If you are a spiritual and faithful person and rely on God to make you better, then there is nothing wrong with that at all. I think that believing in a higher power when feeling down is the most amazing thing to have in you. We are told in Islam to have 'sabr' (patience) with any afflictions, trials or tests from God and that with hardship comes ease. However, having patience does not necessarily mean to ignore the issue and not do anything about it. It is crucial to have trust in God but at the same to be active in trying to resolve the matter at hand. Combining proper treatment to get to the root of the illness will make the sufferer see things in a new light.

Returning to God

After a few years, when I came to realise that when there was nothing left and I was at rock bottom, I found that God was right there in the heart of my pain. He was there with me all along and my organised practices reformed my faith and developed my restored relationship with God. It was never easy. It is not something that one can wish away. It is a battle that only the strongest will win. God will always be there to turn to but, sometimes, we need to talk openly about our problems to someone who can help us practically as well as emotionally and create a support network of friends and family. There is nothing in the Quran and teachings of the Prophet (pbuh) that discourages treatment for illness, be it mental or physical illness. We as Muslims should encourage the mentally ill to seek treatment, not discourage them.

My life was saved and I instilled the belief that it is because I have so much more to give to the world. If I didn't regain my faith, I wouldn't have had anything to sustain me. There is so much more to do in convincing the community that talking about these issues is a sign of strength, rather than a stain on the family or cultural pride. We should be ashamed of our prejudices and closed-mindedness, not of our struggles with mental health. Even when people disappoint you, God never will. He is always there and He will always be there for you. If He has kept you breathing, He has a purpose for you. The power of faith and practically addressing mental health issues will aid in overcoming many of the problems we face. As a Muslim community, we should come together and address mental health and bring awareness to it on a larger scale. It will benefit so many individuals, not only mentally, but spiritually! One last thing we should all address, no matter what our culture, religion or personal beliefs – if someone had a broken leg, you wouldn't ask them to walk on it. Why say to someone with a broken mind, 'Just get over it'?

Keeping it together 157

Turning my darkest moments into sparks of hope: how Our Time helped me with my physical, mental and emotional journey

Every single one of you reading this book and getting this far through my chapter has something in common with me – we are all survivors in one way or another, whether it's related to mental health or overcoming your own barriers. We all want to change something that has had significant effect on us.

Some of the worst parts of being a young carer somehow turned into positives as the years went by. From the first time I stood up and spoke out in public during a school charity launch (aged 17) to becoming a young carer's champion and campaigner, I finally feel like I am being listened to and understood. I have found my voice and I am now using it to free myself from the traumatic experiences of the past. I am not letting these experiences define me, but I am encouraging them to continue making me the person I am today and I would like to encourage others to do the same. Being a young carer doesn't set us up for failure and it definitely doesn't make us feel like we are alone.

I began to see mental health as a continuous scale of change, using the power of people's voices. This has now become my coping mechanism. Before getting involved in charity work, I would often fear the opinions others would have of me and I used to dread even thinking about my mother's mental health deteriorating. After my mum was forced to leave us, I believed that this was now my moment to speak out on everything I couldn't say whilst growing up. Since then, I have gone on to raise money for children dealing with parental mental illness as my way of raising awareness.

Becoming the type of person that was not there for me

I sometimes look back and wonder why I started getting involved with work in parental mental illness and then I remind myself that I would like to become the type of person that was not there for me. I see people putting up posts on social media all the time, with one off comments on how they've struggled, and that's great, but they only receive short-lived moments of support that quickly fizzle and burn out. There is no lasting substance to them. Society doesn't intimidate me anymore, because I now understand how to deal with the stigma and how to control my emotions if it does ever affect me. It sometimes takes me a while to open up, and I do avoid showing others that I am struggling and need help; but I'm also showing people that I'm not afraid anymore. By speaking more directly about mental health issues, we can continue to change the outdated perceptions and prejudices that are associated with mental illness.

Being part of Our Time

Becoming an Our Time ambassador, trustee and beneficiary has given me the confidence to talk openly. I no longer feel the need to lie about or hide my experiences or worry that the conversations I would have would make others feel uncomfortable. Having attended the monthly Kidstime workshops as a volunteer, I got the chance to relive the childhood that I should have been given. The kids I help give me every reason to pick myself up again. If they can carry on life as normal, then I should be as well. They become fully equipped with the tools needed to be responsible young carers. If Kidstime (the groups were sponsored by The Kidstime Foundation, now renamed Our Time) had been available to me when I was younger, life would have been so much easier for me. I wouldn't have had to learn about my role as a carer or study mental illnesses like a subject through Google. I wouldn't have had to over excessively try to manage multi-tasking everything when someone else could have taken that mental pressure off me. But mainly, I could have been able to attend the monthly workshops with my mum and built a relationship which my brothers could have then followed. That's impossible now, because she can't even live with us properly anymore (written before she passed away).

Our Time has not only inspired me to create change but also given me the opportunities to actively create it. Sharing this enthusiasm for change with the rest of the Our Time team, and seeing the incredible work we have achieved and will achieve, makes me genuinely proud to be part of such a wonderful campaign. By seeing the power talking openly and confidently can have on people, I have become even more passionate to end the stigma surrounding mental health, raising awareness and ultimately saving lives. Mental health and well-being is challenging, not just for individuals and families, but also for communities and society in general. I endorse that Our Time conversations change lives – conversation is the first step for help and support.

Working on past hurts through therapeutic conversations

The lens through which we view the world, the way we come to understand people and things and many of the past hurts we carry can be traced back to our childhood. Confronting and working through past pain as young adults is in our best interest if we want to heal and release any hurt we've been carrying. For many people working on healing from within, it can make you realize truths about your past that you didn't understand before. It can teach you about why you think and act the way you do, why you may carry certain beliefs and stick to certain habits, why you may attract or gravitate towards certain people or why you have the fears and worries that you have.

One thing I know for certain is that inner work is hard. It's uncomfortable. It's emotionally and physically draining. It can be re-traumatizing because you are reliving moments and experiences you have buried and pushed aside. It is no wonder people often focus on changing external things (i.e. getting a haircut, buying a new outfit or trying to get fit) when looking for a change. However, nothing outside of you will fill the void(s) that exist within you. Buckling down and working on your soul is the only answer. As difficult as it can be at times, the more you reconnect with yourself you will come to better understand yourself.

A healing journey is also not always a linear path. You may revert back to old thought patterns and self-destructive habits. You may know what you need to do but stick to the familiar. A lot of this process is taking one step forward and two steps back. One day you may practice gratitude, pray, stick to your goals and feel at peace, but the next day you may feel incredibly low, unmotivated and revert back to old tendencies. Not being hard on yourself is important during this time. You cannot change by wishing to become this idealized version of yourself. In order to grow, you must first accept where you're at, accept your weaknesses and accept your brokenness. This is the first step to change. Then you can slowly begin to take the necessary steps to improve yourself.

What I know now that I didn't know at the start of this journey is that I am not fixed in time. The negative, self-limiting beliefs I've carried with me for years I can let go of. Past hurts, I can release. I can reinvent my life whenever I chose. I have more power than I recognize. I can transcend my worries, fears and doubts. I am more than my goals and dreams. Besides, when I'm constantly in a perpetual state of trying to do and be, to create and accomplish, to build the life of my dreams and to be successful it can make me become unhealthy and exhausted. Sometimes in the pursuit of our goals, we constantly look to the future and never live in the now. Never appreciate the process. I'm also learning the importance of having balance in my life, in everything that I do. Having a proper focus on what your true purpose can be will help you.

You've been through a lot and you've got some healing to do. Stop being so hard on yourself. You will not change and achieve everything all at once. Make small, incremental changes over time, as this is more likely to stick. Making big, drastic changes all at once will only leave you feeling overwhelmed and more likely to quit. Also, don't expect to change overnight.

Throughout my journey, I have learned that everything happens for a reason, whether we understand the reason or not. I wouldn't change any part of my life – this has all happened to me and it has made me who I am. My mother's illness has made me a stronger, more determined and empathetic person. But it's not these positive attributes that people would think of if they saw mental illnesses as part of family history. I will never fully escape the stigma from the outside world – but at least I know now that I don't have to keep running from myself. I'm not embarrassed about who I am, and I am not embarrassed about how I feel.

Start the conversations and keep talking: my message to other young carers

I've shared my story of how I made it through – I now feel a great sense of control and I am able to look at my life and start to write it the way I want it to be, gradually learning techniques of self-compassion and by giving myself a break for the things I cannot control. It's time to let those young carers who are suffering in silence, those running away, those too afraid to admit to even themselves that they are dealing with parental mental illness, that it is ok. A word doesn't define who we are; it doesn't make us any different to the people we were last week; it doesn't set us up for failure and it doesn't mean we are alone. The brain is complex, clever and often confusing but no matter how alone your thoughts make you feel, there is a world out there with so many others that understand.

No one always knows the right thing to do or say. Unless you've experienced struggles with your mental health, many of us aren't taught from a young age how to look after it so you may not be able to relate or understand. This means it is as important as ever to be talking about mental health and connecting with people is a huge part of that because mental health isn't a taboo subject. It's the demon many people fight with every day. It's something that needs so much more attention, care and time. Showing empathy towards the subject could make that a lot easier. Speaking openly will help break down those walls of stigma.

When a problem is deeply affecting a person, insisting that that problem is small can be very invalidating. Just because you, or someone you know, was able to cope well with a similar problem doesn't mean that everyone else will be able to. Writing off mental illness as a problem of ingratitude is also unhelpful. Mentally ill people are often grateful for the various blessings in their lives. They still feel depressed or anxious despite this gratitude. Moreover, many mentally ill people feel guilty for being mentally ill. Calling a mentally ill person ungrateful only strengthens their guilt.

Encourage the healthy relationships that a mentally ill person has. Mentally ill people are prone to socially isolating themselves when their mental health is low, even from people close to them. Suggesting that a mentally ill person should distance themselves from their existing healthy support systems is detrimental to their recovery. Do not take a person's mental illness as an opportunity to express disapproval of healthy relationships that you personally dislike.

To insist that someone is strong when they feel vulnerable can feel very invalidating. When someone is allowing themselves to express their vulnerability, grant them the safety to do so. Do not impose ideas of strength unto them. Challenge the stigma, explain that mental illness is an illness like any other and deserves the same amount of empathy and understanding as a physical illness. The more we discuss these things, the less we reinforce these damaging views to younger generations and the more we can give older generations a new way of thinking.

A personal journey to recovery

As a kid, I wasn't able to go away on long holidays or take a break from looking after my siblings. My mum leaving has given me the opportunities to explore the world now and link it to developing resilience through championing others. Through my fundraising, I have managed to successfully trek the Great Wall of China, complete a 3,000 ft skydive, volunteer in a South African orphanage where children had lost their parents to mental illness and trek the Sahara desert. Not only have I been given the title for being a NHS Young Carer's champion for my campaigning, I have been able to chair NHS mental health roundtable discussions and participate in medical research for Oxford University. Such events allowed me to present and host 'Making a Step Change' at City Hall (in London) and attend House of Commons events. My active participation in diving into the topic of parental mental illness has been recognised and over several years, I have been awarded for my ongoing commitment. Some examples include the London Mayor's Young Carers Award, Westminster Community Award, an Overcoming Barriers to Learning Award and an Outstanding Achievement Award.

Now that I have been able to write out my life, my emotions and my opinions into a chapter, I hope that my continued work has the capacity to educate, encourage and empower others who are going through something similar – I want to help create the change that these young people are wishing that some day will happen.

The importance of young carers' rights: listen everybody!

Ultimately, it will always seem like there is a long way to go before we arrive at having a knowledgeable and understanding society, a society which is unafraid, unashamed and upfront when dealing with mental illnesses. My main rationale is to always present a positive message about being a young carer and hope that everyone benefits from this message:

- Life is tough for parents with a mental illness – but it's also tough for their children. Children are innocent and should not be punished for their parents' problems.
- These children have to deal with the difficulties and heartaches on their own because they feel embarrassed to speak up.
- It is impossible to make this issue go away so it is our duty to raise awareness of it, so these children get the support they need to help them through.
- We need to help these vulnerable children and young people protect themselves from the negative effects of living with, and sometimes caring for, a parent with mental illness. I have met kids from the age of three who are caring for their parent. No child should be forced to become an adult from such a young age.
- These children have become isolated from a society where a mental illness is seen as a taboo or their caring responsibilities do not fit the attributes of a 'normal kid'.
- When children feel like there is no one to turn to for help, they can be left with no choice but to take over the parent role and keep everyone safe, sometimes tolerating verbal abuse and extreme and/or aggressive behaviour. This shouldn't be allowed by Society.
- Children who have a parent with a mental illness need the support and resources to better manage their roles at home, building resilience and confidence along the way in order to help them build a brighter future for themselves.

Being labelled as a young carer is an achievement: my message to children

I am a testimony to how you can use your experiences to help change and shape your future in the most positive way possible for yourself. My journey as a carer has come from emotional and mental abuse to a journey of compassion and purpose. However hard people made it for me, I have to always keep looking forward. I'm learning to manage it all – there is hope and there may be a silver lining to all of this. I have learned that one step at a time helps rather than big ones. I want to be able to better educate others and I want to help people to dig deep and find themselves again, to remember the person that they used to be and aspire to be the person that they can be. I want to help others make decisions in their life that are not unconsciously shaped by their past.

Although recovering from being raised by a mentally ill parent can be extremely difficult, it is possible. Many children grow up to be resilient adults who are able to rise above the pain that ensued during childhood. It is possible to positively redefine your identity even after enduring the trauma tied to living with a parent who is mentally ill. Expressing myself and letting go of the negativity which being a young carer brought has allowed me to feel empowered and feel the relief this can bring. So, my hope is that in the future the stigma of mental illness will not force young people to hide their strengths and talents for fear of what people might say or think, but rather be proud of who they are.

To young carer

I would like to take this as an opportunity to recognise all young carers who have to deal with parental mental illness on a daily basis and have to witness and live with the stressors of seeing loved ones suffer from such heart-breaking conditions. I wanted to share my story, so if you have read this and still wanted to give up, confused about your current stage in life or even if you were looking for something to inspire you to get up and achieve greatness, then this was for you. My story is simple, but my journey was hard.

Chapter 13

A parental commentary on Ambeya Begum's and Georgia Irwin-Ryan's chapters

Lara Brown

In Ambeya Begum's searingly honest and inspirational chapter about the reality of life as a young carer, for a mother who suffers from schizoaffective disorder, she initially outlines how she and her brothers were never given an *explanation* of her mother's illness. This is a theme that emerges again and again in the chapters, and was one of the cornerstones of the Kidstime approach: the importance of giving children a clear and easy-to-understand explanation of their parent's illness. An example is the idea of a 'filter' that is not working normally, offering children and young people a visual representation of the brain. 'Not knowing' and being in the dark fuel fear, uncertainty and shame. It is really critical for parents, particularly, to be aware of this, as the absence of an explanation – or the ability for the child to 'make sense of' what is happening – actually contributes to undermining emotional regulation and making them feel unsafe. However, many parents who are the sole parent who look after the children are not able to provide any explanation so that it falls on professionals to do this.

Alan Cooklin talks about how important it is for children and their parents to have a 'map' or 'model' of what is happening to the ill person's mind. Imagine how much fear a child such as Ambeya had when faced with this, and how settling a 'clear and visual explanation' can be.

Ambeya highlights the heartlessness and prejudice around mental illness, both in families and in communities, and shows not only that it is born out of ignorance but also how 'fixed' it can become. When she discusses how full of shame and embarrassment the children were in her own family, it shows that parents, and larger extended families, need to be careful not to allow the children to carry this shame – it isn't theirs and can be turned inwards into self-blame. Her massive caring role – carrying such a heavy load and having to be 'Superwoman' – which was both unrecognised and unpaid while she battled such extremes is profoundly shocking, precisely because it isn't generally talked about in society, and here is a young person presenting her stark reality.

But as a parent myself I know that using the word 'shocking' is not really helpful or fair to Ambeya is it? Because actually it contributes to the very feeling of being 'other' and 'hidden' that she talks about. The huge difficulty she describes of 'taking off the mask' at 16, and accepting her reality, should never be downplayed. However, I think we also need to emphasise, as parents, that it was also the beginning of a positive way forward to a more hopeful life. Ambeya's powerful story underlines how finding her voice as a young carer – through the support of Our Time – and her journey through the darkness of trauma and into the light has been truly liberating. I am struck not only by her courage to come through illness caused by the trauma of caring for her mentally ill mother, but also by her mission to translate that very painful experience into helping others. I hear what she says about not wanting to change any part of her life because it made her who she is today. That is really positive, and links to the point that parents need to be proud of children's achievements if they take on a caring role; acknowledgement is crucial here.

In Georgia Irwin-Ryan's earlier chapter we have the same theme of the lack of a simple explanation of what was happening with her mother's illness, which eroded understanding. Georgia's story shows how children and young people can take on a heavy 'burden to be loyal' which can hold them back and lead them to keeping secrets as also happened in Ambeya's family. What stays with me is the picture of being 'terrified of' parents but also 'responsible for keeping them alive'. Both Ambeya's and Georgia's accounts underline the way in which not one adult said anything to help cope with the stress or even to ask how they were. Ambeya's story gives the message that 'one conversation' with an empathic adult who was aware of mental health issues could have been life-changing. This is heart-rending precisely because this is something that parents and professionals could do something about, although I'm aware that children in these circumstances can also 'hold on and hold in'.

Editors note

Lara Brown finishes with two important recommendations – one for parents and one for professionals – made in such a very personal and compelling way that they have been left in full here, whilst the content also appears in abridged form in the 'Tips for parents and professionals'. Her notion of something or someone to be 'holding' a child during these frightening times is also very important. It already appears in several forms in different chapters: 'helping the parent to hold the child in mind' in Lenny Fagin's chapter, and the glaring absence of a holding person or even 'thing' described by many of the young adult authors. The way in which many writers have described Kidstime is as a 'holding network', and tips for professionals (see chapter 18) suggest that the creation of such a network – between family and friends if available, as well as professionals – may be a key factor in a child maintaining resilience.

In Georgia's case the idea of a child or young person being 'the only thing protecting her mother from social workers' shows not only how much responsibility can be taken on beyond their years but also how frightening that can be. Her story illustrates that guilt and helplessness can build up when people don't put the child first and allow them to talk about what's happening.

What might help them carry on with their own lives and develop their resilience?

- Being honest with them so they know the truth and can make sense of it and get on with their lives
- Making sure, if they have siblings, that they are able to understand and support each other
- Helping to boundary and 'hold' extreme emotions for them without patronising or 'babying'
- Making sure that they have some conception of recovery (see Editors note below) and what that might mean for them, if the illness is episodic and the parent has got much better. Then it is about letting go of something so they can move on

---

Editors note

Lara Brown's personal description of recovery is of a process of transition 'into a different place in which I am more connected and fully myself as a wife and mother, having hope and optimism for the future and feeling generally more empowered and that I have a voice again. It does NOT mean that I am going to fail to manage my condition/look out for trigger points and I fully recognise that I will be on lithium for the rest of my life'. For a more general description of the term see editor's note on recovery in Lara Brown's comments on Alan Cooklin's Chapter 1.

The need for a temporary substitute 'holding' person or environment

As a Mum, I can think of nothing worse than leaving children or young people in the dark to cope with things. Then there is no proper 'holding', leaving the child to imagine the worst and even begin to feel responsible. As a mother, one of my very important jobs is in talking to my girls and helping them 'make sense of' what's going on in their lives. This might range from how to deal with a playground slight to how to cope with a profound loss.

Acknowledging and naming emotions such as sadness and anger can help them learn to regulate them. But the reality is that when I was in hospital I wasn't there to do that.

I hope to have brought together some of the themes that might be useful to parents who have had experience of mental illness, as well as shared part of our journey as a family. Hopefully we can help our children by taking on board some of the hints that have come out of many years of experience with the Kidstime approach, to help them build confidence and resilience for the future.

Chapter 14

Not a framework, but a way to be

Reflections of a school nurse

Jessica Streeting

As a school nurse and practice teacher in the community, I have been struck by how often parental mental illness is at the root of many childhood problems.

The role of a school nurse is as diverse as the children and young people we care for. As a full time school nurse in one school, I had the luxury of being able to just 'be' around the children, in the dining room, out in the playground at break time and I could always be called on in our little room, for almost continual 'drop in' sessions. A young person might approach me to talk casually about their 'friend' who had an awkward or embarrassing problem (often, but not always their own issue) and could do this without having to book or plan their visit. Any school nurse reading this will recognise how enviable that is, as often we are spread very thinly, responsible for several secondary and primary schools and only able to pop into schools fleetingly or to address serious safeguarding issues. These days, with fewer qualified school nurses in the country and commissioning of the service under constant threat, it is harder than ever to be what children themselves said they needed from their school nursing service: visible, accessible and confidential.[1]

For me, the joy of discovering Kidstime Workshops (now part of Our Time – formerly The Kidstime Foundation) and the associated scholarship and methods of The Our Time, have been that they offer a gateway to understanding the very specific needs of children who have a parent with a mental illness. This understanding has been transformative to my practice and I have seen similar effects in others. There is a wonderful 'penny drop' moment when you realise that there is something constructive you can do to help here, that the situation is not hopeless and the children not helpless. For me this was because I realised that equipped with some core understanding – or a framework – **you**, a busy school nurse, an overstretched health visitor, a social worker run ragged by pressing need on every side, a GP with ten minutes to see a patient, a teacher with so many other children's needs to address – **you** – not some other 'expert' who will take an age to refer to, YOU can make that difference.

You might say: 'But I know nothing about mental illness. It's not my field'.

Not a framework, but a way to be 169

That doesn't matter. In fact, many who are highly trained in supporting the mental health needs of adults are not aware of the impact of that illness on the children. Similarly, those who are trained to support children with mental health problems do not automatically have greater insight into how a parent's mental health might impact on a child. It's not about that. It's a different thing. In this chapter I will try to explain just what 'it' is from my own perspective, *as I discovered it*, and hope to inspire you with the confidence and curiosity to know that you too can make a difference, not by changing, but by being yourself.

I first became involved with The Kidstime Foundation (now renamed Our Time), when piloting a project as a full time school nurse in one large, diverse, high-need London secondary school. This was a decade ago. The school was remarkable in many ways, not least because the head teacher *at that time* had a real understanding of the importance of public health in education. She led us all to support the children in our care. Our unofficial motto was: 'Don't leave your baggage at the door, bring it in, and let us help you'.

The essential concept of public health is prevention through early intervention. For example, by supporting a young person pastorally and practically, we can help prevent life events becoming overwhelming, enabling them to cope with school life and thrive academically and socially.

At this school, I was part of a large pastoral team, including youth workers, a social worker, two psychotherapists and a policeman. We shared a tiny office and supported one another, as well as the children.

I keep a learning journal – a simple diary really, but the interesting thing about keeping a work diary is that you write thoughts you had not quite even articulated, almost before you know they are important. One evening, shortly after I had started working in this extraordinary place, I found myself writing this:

'Home. Watching my own kids safe in front of the telly after supper, I wonder how little Paul (see Editors note 1 below) is. His mother has a mental illness that seems untreatable and the bullies on his estate are looming, press-ganging him into doing stuff he shouldn't, late at night, out on the streets. Paul is such an easy target. The big boys wont lay off him when they sense such vulnerability, when all he has to stand up for him are a 'nutty mum' (his words) and two little sisters, who he loves with fierce protection. How to ascertain his health needs? Is he in danger? I got nowhere today, but I think I asked the wrong questions....

Editors note 1

Names of children and parents are changed to protect anonymity. Names of workers are real.

170 Jessica Streeting

Soon after this, I became involved with the Young Carers' group at school and began to realise that there were ways to support the likes of Paul, ways to learn how to ask the right questions and practical ways to help support his mum at home, too.

Meeting weekly, in a small room behind the library, the carers' group had been running for several years, and consisted of children who had a caring responsibility for someone at home. Though some of the children had a parent or sibling with a physical illness, there were a significant number of children whose parent had a mental illness.

The Young Carers' group is a support group which was set up by two family therapists, employed by the school, who also worked as family liaison. The group was already well established when I came along.

At this point you may well be thinking: 'I can tell this was all over a decade ago…there is no money now for family therapists working with our young people….'

That thought may lead you to a downward trough of despondency about 'government cuts and the impossibility of supporting our young people these days', whether their parents have a mental illness or whatever problem they face. All that is true; we were infinitely better funded back then and we had what we now realise was the luxury of being able to work out together what worked best. But the hopeful truth – *or at least my discovery* – is that in order to support young people like Paul, we do not need to be experts in mental health ourselves. We just need to know and understand some key principles, and then do what we *already* do, and use more of the skills we already have.

My first Young Carers' group

The first week I attended the school's Young Carers' group, to introduce myself and to explain the role of the school nurse, I found the group of 12 young people and the two group leaders (Fran and Rosan) was in full swing with a captivating discussion about how we should discuss mental health and illness.

'I say my mum is mentally ill'

'But that sounds like she is always ill. How about saying she has a mental illness?'

'I just say "illness"'.

'I just say tired'.

'My dad is more than just *tired*'.

'Yeah, I know, but my mum is often in bed all day, so it's easier to just say that'.

They all agreed that they didn't like the phrase 'mental health problems' or worse 'mental health'.

'I mean, we all have mental *health*, don't we?'

'And people always whisper it, in that way, you know? "mental health"'.

'I just say mental! I mean when my mum turns up for parents' evenings it's pretty obvious she's not like other mums'.

They all laughed and helped themselves to biscuits and juice, provided by Fran and Rosan. This conversation had been the beginning of a plan hatched by the group to make a short film about the impact of mental illness on children and young people, which was being sponsored by the then Kidstime Foundation (see Editors note 2 below). The group had been asked by the charity to offer ideas for the drama in the film and were planning what should and shouldn't go into the plot. They all had strong views and much to offer. Fran and Rosan (the two family therapists) were guiding, but not leading the discussion. They *later* explained to me that in their carers' group they aimed to provide interventions to reduce social isolation for these children, who often felt alone with their home problems. Running this group had also made them realise that young people needed access to a neutral adult they could trust to listen, and act as an advocate. The children in this group trusted them because they were well known in school over a long time, as well as because the group leaders made it their business to make links with families of the group members. Trust was probably the most significant single thing. It was plain to see that the young people also trusted this group as somewhere to come in school, where they felt safe, understood and able to express themselves.

Editors note 2

This film (as noted originally called The Mental film, later The Jass Story as explained) is available for use by schools and families – as a discussion topic – from the Our Time website: https://ourtime.org.uk/resource/jass-story/.

I listened as they planned the plot, for what would become 'The Jass Story' and laughed with them, when they came up with their 'working title' for the film: 'We should call our group *and* the film The Mental Project'.

My mind ran back to other children, like Paul, who for whatever reason did not feel able to join the group yet, or become involved. Fran explained:

> In this school there are many children with high needs, and complex home lives. There are in every school, actually and probably always will be. The challenge is to make ourselves available in a way that the children find helpful, as they cope with their challenges and go about their days. Even in a school like this, with understanding leadership from the top, that can be hard

172 Jessica Streeting

Hard then, harder now, perhaps. She finished, sadly: 'And it's impossible to reach everyone. That's our main reason for making this film. In the hope that we can show it in assembly, for example, and more people will recognise themselves, come forward and enable us to support them'.

Rosan added:

> Yes, here we have been able to create an environment where it is possible for children who have a parent with a mental illness to come forward. There is so much stigma around mental illness. And of course lots of children don't recognise themselves as Young Carers. They are also often not recognised as such by their families or family friends....and if they do, they think they are the only one. You heard the children – it can be so hard to say your parent has a mental illness, but a broken leg or a heart condition, even cancer would be easier.

Shortly after this, I was asked to attend a safeguarding meeting for a young person whose family had been planning a forced marriage. Like many such professional meetings, this was led by a social worker, with representation from other stakeholders. Sitting in pride of place at the head of the table, I was pleasantly surprised to see the young person herself and next to her, as we introduced ourselves, a man who introduced himself as Dr Alan Cooklin, a consultant psychiatrist. It is unusual to meet doctors at professional meetings, but especially unusual to meet senior level psychiatrists. What was more, the young person, let's call her Amal, was chatting happily to the doctor as though they were old friends.

It transpired that Amal had for several years previously attended Kidstime Workshops in her London borough. I knew a little about the workshops then. I knew they existed to support families with the impact of parental mental illness and that you could be referred by a social worker or by someone at school, like, for example, Rosan and Fran. I knew that whole families attended and that the emphasis was on explaining mental illness in a supportive way, through fun and drama for the children, with time for the adults to talk with specialists.

At this meeting for Amal, I began to perceive how significant a group like Kidstime could be, in supporting someone with a complex home life. Amal's mother was not present, as she had been admitted to hospital with an acute psychotic episode. As Alan knew her and the whole family from the workshops, Amal had asked him to come and be an advocate for *both* her and her mum, knowing that we were to discuss the concern that plans were being made by stronger factions in the extended family to force a marriage for Amal in her country of origin.

What I noticed was that the impact of Alan's presence, as a senior professional, was more that it gave Amal the confidence to speak for herself than advocacy per se. We were all impressed by how articulate Amal felt able to be and there was no doubt in that meeting that her voice was heard.

She clearly explained to the assembled group that her mum suffered from a severe mental illness that made her periodically unable to care for Amal. At such times, her uncles would leap in and try to control everything, with Amal's mother powerless to act. Their latest plan had been to ship Amal back to their home country before she was 16, to force her into marriage with an older man she had never met. Amal's mother when healthy would be horrified at this idea and would literally defend Amal, like the fiercest tiger mother. Amal spoke proudly about her mother. But when her mother was unwell, all her power and might left her, leaving Amal undefended.

As I thought about it I began to see a pattern, linking back to Paul; when a parent has a mental illness, there can be periods when their child becomes horribly vulnerable in ways the parent would not countenance when well. The parent when unwell may not have the capacity to protect and care for their child, in Paul's case to defend him from exploitation by older gang members on his estate. The child who becomes hyper-vigilant about their parent's moods may be anxious not to compound their parent's worries and not share their own. So the roles of parent and child become reversed, *and* the child's own needs neglected. And when the parent is well again, it may be hard to revert to more appropriate parent-child norms, with the child always watchful for the next unwell episode and the parent resentful of a bossy child, behaving like a bossy parent.

Putting children's rights into practice

That day, a safeguarding plan was made that put Amal at the heart of things. She was not just in the mind of the professionals gathered together, but she was actually present *in her own right*. This reminded me of a seminal, but often overlooked principle from the United Nations Convention on the Rights of the Child:

> Children have a right to be listened to and their views taken into account on matters that affect them.[2]

After the meeting Amal proudly introduced me to Alan Cooklin. 'Jess, meet Alan. He founded Kidstime where me and mum and my brothers go every month. You should come along one day. We have pizza'.

In due course I attended a workshop, but initially I just remember Amal explaining to me the importance of the work of the charity: 'You see, when your parent has a mental illness, you need someone to *explain stuff*' Amal told me, as the three of us had hot chocolate in the school diner.

> I always knew my mum was different, but I felt ashamed of her, especially as it's not okay in my culture, where I'm from. People said she

was possessed. But in Kidstime, there are lots of families, so you know you're not alone and it all gets explained.

I wondered how on earth I would ever be able to explain mental illness. The kids who attended the workshops were lucky enough to have psychiatrists on hand...

Alan might have read my thoughts, because he said gently: 'It's not so hard, you know, but it is very important to provide a visual explanation of what is going on when a parent has a mental illness'.

I said: 'I wouldn't know where to start'.

Amal replied: 'You're a nurse, you teach your students, you are good at explaining things'.

'Maybe, but not something as complex as this! And to children of different ages and with there being so many forms of mental illness. I'm not mental health trained, you see'.

Alan took my email address and the next morning sent me a link to a clip of work with a group of children and young people, aged from 6 to 16. Watching this, I was hooked. He had used a simple method and simple language to explain the difference between the brain and the mind. All the children got it. They had fun with his questions; they tried to draw a brain in a head and were incredulous when it was explained that actually a brain was bigger than that.

'Bigger?'

'Even bigger!'

He then went on to explain to them that when you have a mental illness, it's as though the filter which usually helps us sieve out unwanted thoughts stops working and we become overwhelmed by our thoughts and our feelings.

Alan didn't use medical language, but neither did he patronise the children. He just simply explained and then the children asked lots of questions. They also found a flaw in his 'sieve' analogy, so at the end of the little film, a voice I later recognised as belonging to Chineye (a young person who had also been supported by Kidstime as a child) explained that there is not literally a sieve in our heads to filter out stuff. It all made sense and the fact that even a clever doctor was not afraid to have made a mistake in his explanation gave me the hope that I too might be able to work with children and young people in this way. Even if I didn't have all the answers, then at least I could start a conversation, and help the child feel less alone with their anxieties about their parent.

Like many school nurses, I had students in practice and my instinct was now to share what I had learnt with other school nurses who might be interested in supporting children who were suffering the impact of parental mental illness. Even in those early days for me, it felt like brilliant news that with only a little training and awareness, we might be able to make a difference. The school nurses felt much the same, though interestingly, it was common for even these specialised health professionals to feel they lacked the requisite skills.

My review of research in the field

Working with these professionals, and particularly with the children them-selves, had shown me what was most important, which as I became more interested led to my writing my Masters dissertation[3] on this topic. I found that there had been significant research into these children, particularly in Australia where they were grouped under the acronym COPMI (Children of a Parent with Mental Illness). I don't much like labels, but it can be im-portant to recognise distinct groups in order to support them. In the United Kingdom we recognise Young Carers as an entity, but do not make the distinction between those caring for, *or who may be greatly affected by*, a parent with a mental illness and those who have a care burden for some-one with a physical illness. We also do not count the numbers, so even to-day we only have estimates of how many children and young people this might affect in the United Kingdom (introductory chapter and Chapter 15). Our government to date still only officially recognises an estimate of under 200,000 Young Carers for all illnesses, whilst the Children's Commissioner for England has estimated that there are 3.7 million children living with a parent with either moderate or severe mental illness.

Key themes came through, the more I read. These were the same points that our school Young Carers had made. Put simply, research on COPMI concurs that they need;

1   to know they are not alone
2   have an advocate – neutral, relatively uninvolved person
3   a decent explanation of what is happening when their parent becomes ill

It struck me that *many* people who work in schools would be able to fulfil these roles. Though it was wonderful that our school had qualified fam-ily therapists in post and a strong pastoral team, it might be that a young person would more naturally turn to, for example their maths teacher to be an advocate. If they had formed a rapport through maths, and if maths was the subject that lifted them away from their worries about their unwell parent and let them be themselves for an hour each day, then their maths teacher might be just the person (see Chapter 5). But how well equipped would the average maths teacher feel to address parental mental illness, if I who was supposed to be a health professional initially felt such reticence? School nurses too have all the qualities and skills that young people say they need; they are naturally child-led, practical, approachable, compassionate, un-shockable and could be that all-important neutral adult for the child to talk to. But as I talked to other school nurses, I realised they shared my initial reticence to talk about mental illness with children, as well to be brave enough to try an explanation.

My first Kidstime Workshop

When I first visited a Kidstime Workshop I came away with my head reeling from fantastic impressions. What I saw was life changing stuff, miraculous really. For the small number of families who were referred and able to attend, it offered a place to be where the stigma of mental illness disappeared and families could learn together in a supportive, environment. Drama was central, and the drama leader, who led the children's group, explained to me that through acting and play the children's inhibitions fell away, and allowed important messages to be conveyed to us adults. At the same time the parents had time away in their own group while the children prepared their plays. Within half an hour of arriving, I had been roped into acting the corpse in a gory story about a terrible car crash. I don't think I was the only fatality; the scenario was carefully engineered carnage. The point was that here was a safe place where the worst could happen in imaginative play, then we would all get up, bow to applause, have pizza together and the world didn't end. Alongside all the hilarity there was huge pride from the parents, despite the sometimes potentially shocking content of some of the plays. There was an underlying awareness that life for these families could be very hard, that children could not always be sheltered, that sometimes the worst had already happened and, despite the solidarity of Kidstime, might happen again.

But we needed a way to bring this understanding and these principles 'to the masses', to reach the children and young people who were not able to be referred to a programme like this. School is where children spend much of their time, after all, and so it made sense to begin work trying to shift the perspective of those who work with children in schools to enable them to realise, as I had begun to, that they can make all the difference.

The Jass film and work in schools

The first weapon in our arsenal was our powerful film we have referred to as the Jass film. The young people at our Young Carers' group worked up an excellent plot which incorporated everything they felt relevant to their lives and experience. They all acted in it and invited other friends to join too. Jass was a fictitious Year 9 (age 14) boy who had been a promising, popular student, but was falling away from education. He was 'under the radar' – which meant that other far naughtier kids got noticed, while he wasn't drawing attention to himself. However for the close observer the signs were there that all was not well at home. He was often late to school because he had been looking after his mum and trying to get his little sister sorted out with

Not a framework, but a way to be   177

breakfast, and he was dreamy in school because he was preoccupied with worry about his mum home alone. In addition his homework was scrappy, with no time to concentrate on it. Eventually he got into a fight – quite uncharacteristic for him – because a group of kids were shouting rude insults about his mum. When asked why he had lost his temper, by an insensitive but well-meaning teacher, he could not begin to answer. Of course he couldn't. Where would he start? Jass, like so many other school kids, when asked if everything is okay at home, just shrugged and mooched off.

Jass had a good friend who tried to help him, but no adult advocate, which meant he had no confidence that any adult outside the family would understand his situation. Another aspect of having a parent with a mental illness is also well illustrated in this film; Jass' mother when unwell could not be consistently kind to Jass or keep him fully in mind as her child. As Jass tries in his 14 year old way to keep the home, look after his sister and make sure his mum eats, his mother turns on him, compounding his feelings of worthlessness and exasperation. This is not uncommon for these children. It is also common for them to feel that they have caused the illness and that everything is all their fault.

A powerful moment in the film is when the camera zooms in on the Jass' mother's face, showing how her emotions can rapidly shift from happy and normal to absent and ill. In this way, the film illustrates how children with a parent who has a mental illness can often be unsure from day to day how their parent will behave. Even on the good days, they are often on high alert for the next episode of illness and preoccupied with anxiety at school, which, in turn, makes it hard to concentrate on school work.

Not everyone had a speaking part in the Jass film. The Young Carers invited in other friends, including one boy who I only noticed later, standing silent and solemn behind his friends in the fight scene. His older sister had come forward and confided to our school social worker that life at home was increasingly hard as their mother was very unwell, with a severe mental illness. The boy – let's call him Ali – had not mentioned anything, not to us, not to his friends, but here he was choosing to take part in the film. A silent witness.

As the Jass film was so packed with relevant detail, I began to show it in my teaching, to groups of school nurse and health visitor students and when in schools, to staff training. Despite the amateur acting and low budget, the film was and remains an excellent way of demonstrating quickly some of the challenges for COPMI.

I also began to show the other film I mentioned, which explained mental illness, when working with children on a more one-to-one basis (see Editors note 3 below). For example, in a child protection conference once, I was asked to work with two small boys whose mother had stopped taking her anti-psychotic medicine when she became pregnant with a third baby. This had led to a dreadful summer for the family, who were refugees from Eritrea. Their father had only sketchy understanding of mental illness and had been away working, when the mother became convinced that the children's toys were possessed by the devil and made the boys throw them all out of the window. This was when a neighbour noticed something was awry and called the social services. A support plan was made for the family, but with my new insights, it occurred to me to ask if anyone had actually explained mental illness to the boys. I remember the Child Protection panel looking blankly back at me, but the boys' mother, who was by then stable sometime after the birth of her baby, asked me if I would kindly do so.

Editors note 3

This film (16 minutes) is available for schools, families and others from the Our Time website: https://ourtime.org.uk/resource/what-does-it-mean-to-have-a-parent-with-a-mental-illness/.

'I wouldn't know how to begin' she said, 'But they should know. They are clever children and it's not their fault'.

Armed with explanation from the Our Time (formerly Kidstime Foundation) website and clips from the Jass film on my laptop, I set about my explanation to the two boys in the little music room next to their primary school classroom. Their learning mentor, who they knew and loved, was also present. I was unprepared for the reaction from the boys, then aged eight and ten. It was as if an invisible weight lifted and they were rapt. They seemed to understand the explanation, which we reiterated, and we drew pictures together too, looking at other ways we might even explain it all more effectively than it had been in the clip.

'We could show our dad!' the younger boy said excitedly.

'We could show Mum too. It's about her'.

'And the baby when she's bigger'.

'Things feel better when you understand'.

The learning mentor also felt this way of explaining mental illness was a revelation and since has become a strong advocate for the Who Cares? work in schools. Happily, the explanations for younger children have now been incorporated into a new short animated film: 'Making Sense of Mental Illness' (see Editors note 4 below).

Editors note 4

This film is available for all on the Our Time website: https://ourtime.org.uk/resource/explaining-mental-illness-to-under-11s/.

Not a framework, but a way to be   179

Everyone's best instinct is that children should be protected from unpleasant events and some might feel that you can be too young to learn about all this. What should be remembered is that the child whose parent is suffering from a mental illness may be the first to realise when an episode is beginning, when, for example, the behaviour of a parent with bi-polar disorder is escalating, and becoming more manic.

One such in our school was Alice. She came to our attention when she completely stopped talking in school. Her friends knew her as chatty and easy-going at primary school, but in the transition to Year 7 at our school she became withdrawn, and over a period of two weeks gradually stopped speaking altogether. There might have been many reasons for this, but quite appropriately her form teacher raised his concerns with more specialised staff, after getting nowhere trying to talk with her. I was asked to join a meeting in the head of year's office, with Alice and her mum, Dawn. Dawn explained that she suffered from bi-polar and that recently she had been feeling very 'up and down'. It transpired that Alice had known the signs, but at home she and her mum had been having rows.

'The more unwell I get, the less good I am at recognising it, you see' Alice's mum said.

Alice suddenly burst out: 'Yes. You just won't admit it! I know you are ill when you start drawing huge circles on the walls and manically writing your diary in the dead of night, but you just don't see it'.

We all stared at Alice, delighted she was speaking. Alice's Mum replied: 'Was that why you stopped talking, love?'

Alice nodded, a silent and incredibly effective protest.

We were then able to make quite a practical plan with the help of Alice's mother's mental health nurse, Jacki.

'It's true' Jacki told me later. 'One of the first signs that Dawn is becoming unwell is that drawing on the walls in huge circles. Stupid of us not to realise that Alice would notice'.

But Alice had to be heard and then believed. It is astonishing how often children and young people are overlooked, when they are the first to notice all is not well.

Our plan was simple; a note was put on Dawn's notes, so that if Alice began to notice the warning signs again, she was to call the Duty number and inform them that support was needed.

'Will I be listened to?' asked Alice, reasonably.

I would like to say 'they all lived happily ever after', but it is seldom quite that way, though Alice was taken more seriously when she next contacted the mental health team, as well as by her own mum. School staff also held her in new esteem now they were aware what a pillar of strength she needed to be for her mum. Closing the loop for Alice involved linking her back to Fran, Rosan and the Young Carers' group at school, which we could do

180 Jessica Streeting

because such a group existed. The challenge is to ensure that all schools have an environment that is similarly supportive.

Since those early days, the work has expanded nationally, taking root more strongly in some schools than others. There is no magic formula, but as we try to reduce the stigma of mental illness in the whole-school environment and support individual children, we have through trial and error found ways that work best, with some tips along the way.

Tips for making our schools friendly to children experiencing mental illness in a parent

First, we need senior leadership on board with the principles developed by Our Time and others. In the schools where we have had most success, there will often be a senior leader who himself has experience of parental mental illness and wants to reach out to others. It can sometimes happen that this person does not even recognise themselves as a past young carer, until the signs are spelt out, perhaps when we are presenting at a teaching conference or increasingly by accessing our website through Twitter or other social media.

They might then invite us to do some work in their school, to present, for example at an Inset (teacher in-house continuing training) day or evening for staff. We are always very clear that this work should not be restricted to academic and pastoral staff – the best results happen when everyone is involved, because who are we to know which staff member a child will naturally trust and confide in? It could be a school nurse, teacher, support staff or the dinnertime assistant.

If pressed for time, as schools *always* are, then showing the Jass film or one of our more recent films, and then having an interactive discussion with a group of students, can offer a real insight into those key concepts and kindle curiosity in some members of the school community to drive further work.

The next steps will depend hugely on the individual school concerned and we have lots of supportive material which can help, from short pieces of work to whole-school year projects. It might just be that the school agrees to show the Jass film to everyone in one year group, with staff briefed so that if young people come forward afterwards, recognising themselves in the situations, there is a support structure ready for them.

As I said at the beginning of this chapter, it is now my firm belief that we make a difference to children, not by changing, but by being ourselves – our educated selves. The key priorities for COPMI are so important that I will restate them:

1   To know they are not alone
2   To have an advocate – neutral, relatively uninvolved person
3   To have a decent explanation of what is happening when their parent becomes ill

And it stands to reason that, equipped with some specific knowledge on the impact of parental mental illness, we can be there for children, be we school nurse, science teacher, deputy head or dinnertime assistant.

For me, the realisation that beginning to explain mental illness doesn't have to be farmed out to another more *qualified* person is the most exciting. With a little knowledge and training (and Our Time has plenty to share), this could be you, using your own skill base, your own metaphors or even better, once you have captured the child's imagination, theirs!

Some of us will have the skill-set, time and remit to create specific support, such as for example a Young Carers' group, as in our school. Others may not have this opportunity, but once we have some training and understanding, we begin to recognise the signs in children and young people who are suffering the impact of parental illness more swiftly. And by listening to the real experts, the children themselves, we can all do what we are trained to do best for those children. It is then that the magic starts to happen, differently every time.

Editors note

In this impassioned plea for all school staff – as well as those outside associated with their children or parents – to step outside their comfort zone and help children confront and understand what they are facing already, Jessica Streeting makes a number of key points. Because they are so crucial they are summarised again here:

1   That to make the kind of changes in a school which she advocates, it is essential to get the active backing of the head or senior management. Otherwise staff will be not only be anxious about whether they can 'do it right' for the children but also whether they are acting with the school's support.

2   That successive groups of young people have identified their own needs: an adult (not a therapist, but more an advocate) to talk to, an explanation which gives an understanding of what is happening to their ill parent, and some way – such as a Young Carers' group – of being able to share with others who have had similar experiences, so that they can discover that they are not the 'only ones'.

3   That the children and young people will themselves choose who they can trust, which may not be the most professionally qualified or specialist. Therefore it is important that all adults who may come into contact with these children – and all will as they represent at least one in five in every classroom – feel ready both to notice and to respond to these children, and know how to give, or point them towards, the resources highlighted in her chapter.

> 4 That a little understanding and discussion can go a very long way to helping a child build their own resilience.
> 5 That staff need not be so fearful of entering discussion about the sensitive topic of mental illness. The children are dealing with it, and trying to make sense of it anyway.

References

1 Department of Health. (2012) Getting it right for children, young people and families. Maximising the contribution of the school nursing team: Vision and Call to Action, DoH report.
2 United Nations Convention on the Rights of the Child. (1989) United Nations Human Rights, Office of the High Commissioner.
3 Streeting, J. (2014) What are the educational needs of school nurses to equip them to lead integrated care for children whose parents have mental illness? Unpublished Dissertation for MA in Practice Education, School of Health and Social Care, London South Bank University.

Chapter 15

School-based support for young people affected by parental mental illness

Anita Frier

Introduction

Stoke Damerel Community College is a co-educational, comprehensive school of 1,350 students serving an inner-city area of Plymouth. Students come from a wide and diverse range of socio-economic groups. Out of the 43 neighbourhoods in Plymouth ranked in the indices of multiple deprivation, the school serves the top four out of five neighbourhoods. Inequalities of health are of particular concern. The public health report for Plymouth City Council in 2016[1] stated that the life span in Devonport is 5.5 years less than in more affluent areas of the city. The Director of Public Health's annual report[2] showed that Stonehouse, Devonport and Stoke had significantly higher rates of poor mental health, self-harm and suicide. 11,000 residents are affected by mental health issues (40% young people), 47% of which are from the area the school serves. All of this impacts considerably on young people's physical and mental health. In addition Plymouth City Council's 'Plymouth Report' in 2017[3] demonstrated that 11,700 Plymouth residents aged 18–64 years in 2015 were estimated to have more than one mental health problem. The number of referrals to the Child and Adolescent Mental Health Services (CAMHS) in Plymouth in 2015/2016 was 1,207. This is a 10% increase from the 1,099 referrals reported in 2014/2015. Mental health service providers report that they have not only noticed an increase in the number of referrals but also an increase in the complexity of children and young people's needs and in the issues that need attention. Over the last three years hospital admissions of young people (aged 10–24 years) for self-harm have increased in Plymouth (from 425.5 per 100,000 population to 473.6 per 100,000), and the latest data for Plymouth are significantly higher than the average for England.[4]

Addressing mental health in school

Tackling the issues surrounding mental health within the school setting has required a multi-faceted approach which permeates throughout the ether of the school culture. It would be impossible to tackle the issues surrounding parental mental health in isolation without embedding knowledge, support

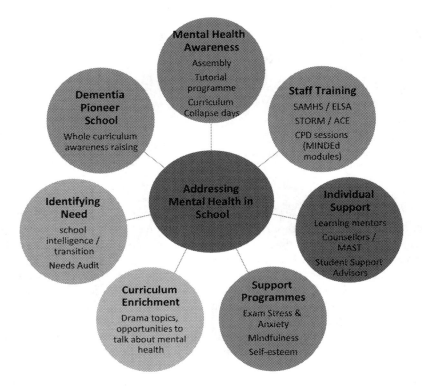

Figure 15.1 Demonstrates the key areas the school addresses.

and training into all areas of the college and all stakeholders – which includes staff and students, and parents (Figure 15.1).

Dementia Pioneer School

In July 2014 Stoke Damerel Community College was recognised by The Alzheimer's Society for its cross-curricular teaching and learning in a Dementia Project. The college won the very first Dementia Friendly Schools Award for its work. Staff took to the idea of delivering aspects of dementia education through their own subject areas in a cross-curricular approach. A project lead was appointed from within the existing staff who supported staff and helped to showcase the work of the college at events and via a microsite of the college website.

Subject contributions included:

- Year 9 and Year 10 students (14–15 year olds) producing campaign videos for The Alzheimer's Society as part of their media coursework

School-based support for young people   185

- Sixth form art students making posters to raise awareness of their locality as dementia-friendly
- PE students in Year 7 (11–12 year olds) playing bowls with people from a local Age Concern centre and later having monthly croquet sessions with residents of a care home specialising in dementia care
- Health and social care students making memory boards alongside people living with dementia
- Year 8 students (12–13 year olds) in English working with a storyteller with a focus on creating stories collectively 'in the here and now', and then training the students to run similar sessions with people living with dementia

The positive outcomes of this project included students and staff gaining an excellent understanding of dementia, not just through study but via partnership, working with people living with dementia, their carers and outside agencies, students gaining confidence in their own ability and their own voice, presenting their work to others at conferences, within universities and even parliament. In addition the college strengthened its standing in the community, welcoming in others, which made not only the college but also its locality more 'dementia friendly'. Furthermore, working on dementia education was not a distraction from the curriculum but rather a mechanism to deliver aspects of the curriculum in an engaging, dynamic way.

Several years on, and the college still holds dementia croquet sessions every six weeks with our Year 7 and 8 students engaging in playing croquet with residents of local care homes – the benefits to both groups are profound. The students receive training from our health coordinator and the Creasey Brothers (founders of 'Jiminy Wicket' who set up the dementia croquet scheme after their father was diagnosed with dementia).

Students love talking with the residents, listening to stories from their childhood, breaking down intergenerational barriers and it always involves drinking tea and eating cake. It helps the students to understand and empathise with elderly relatives and they have a greater understanding about how to help elderly residents in their community. What they enjoy the most is seeing the elderly residents laugh and smile.

Raising awareness – curriculum enrichment

The topic of mental illness is weaved into the curriculum through subjects such as English and drama. Our GCSE drama students created some wonderful drama pieces on living with someone with mental health problems as part of the scenes for the Who Cares? Programme of study (see page 196). We use many opportunities to educate students on the issues that may affect them or their family or friends. The school holds 'curriculum collapse' mornings which cover areas of SMSC (Spiritual, Moral, Social and Cultural) and which includes the delivery of the Who Cares? Programme, as well as mindfulness and physical and health enrichment opportunities. In addition all students follow a PSHE (Personal, Social, Health and Economic) programme of study which includes modules on: resilience, 'About Me', healthy lifestyles, healthy body and mind, keeping safe in the digital world, sexting, physical and mental health, How am I Changing? understanding self and others.

Every year we hold assemblies for each year group on mental health awareness, which showcases role models representing people who have suffered with their own problems. One of our assemblies focuses specifically on Young Carers – what is a young carer? How do you know if you or a friend is a young carer? What support is available in school? This assembly is led by our older young carers and our Young Carer Champion. We have found that students take more notice of their peers and are more likely to go along if they recognise or know one of the groups. It is important to repeat these assemblies, or at least the theme, every year as students may identify themselves at different times. For example, younger students may not have caring responsibilities early on, and therefore not recognise their situation.

The college creates a caring culture and empathy for difference at every opportunity – raising money for the food bank, giving clothing to the Domestic Abuse refuge, producing shoe boxes for local families in need. There are often stands in 'The Street' (our open communal area) with a 'thought tree' during mental health awareness week. In December, our five metre Christmas tree is decorated with heart and star messages where students are encouraged to write their thoughts and feelings. It helps us, as one community of students and teachers to empathise with others, remember that there are others that need support, and that everyone's lives are not all the same. We make it OK to discuss how we feel – students, parents, staff!

Staff training

It is imperative to ensure that all staff receive regular training about mental health issues. When I say all staff, I mean everyone who works within our school community – teachers, support staff, administrative staff, maintenance, reception, resources team and community support workers. Mental health awareness is everyone's business. All teachers have a responsibility for finding out what is going on in children's lives. So how do we support teachers to feel confident to do this and how do we overcome barriers to discussing parent's mental health? Whilst I consider this to be universal training, some teams of staff have more bespoke training on offer to support their professional development. For example two staff members have completed a 'child and adolescent mental health Services – CAMHS' degree on day release. We also have staff that are trained to deliver to others, i.e. our Director of Student Services teaches on a CAMHS degree, and a senior leader delivers mindfulness training to staff.

The table below shows the training that has been completed by staff over the last few years:

All staff	Living with someone with a mental illness (Dr Alan Cooklin & Jessica Streeting)
	Auditing Emotional Need (Plymouth Excellence Cluster)
	Time to Talk – Mental Health Awareness
	Carousel of workshops: self-harm, mindfulness, attachment training, young carers, supporting parents, Who Cares? Project, building a positive society: strategies to end sexualisation and stereotypes in the media, self-esteem
	Adverse Childhood Experiences (Dr Warren Larkin)
Sixth form teachers & tutors	Let's discuss suicide (workshop for staff and sixth form students and peer mediators with Dr Alan Cooklin)
Pastoral teams & welfare team	Mindfulness to staff
	Mindfulness training to deliver to students
	Person-centred planning
	Supporting students with autism
	PACE training
	Mental Health Toolbox two day training.
	Self-harm awareness
	Compassionate friendly and bereavement training
	LGBT and Transgender Training
	Internet Safety Training
	Eating Disorder Awareness
	Kooth training[5] to support young people (online counselling)
	Child Sexual Exploitation awareness
	Domestic violence support and awareness
	Sleep and anxiety training workshops
	Managing emotions
	Emotional Logic Training
	Criminal exploitation awareness – County Lines
	Family Group Conference and mediation awareness
Student peer support	Peer mediator training
	Young Carer mentors

Student support

It would be no surprise to note that with our context, our pastoral support team is quite extensive. And yes, also very expensive – but without question absolutely necessary (and worth their weight in gold!). Our school has a reputation within Plymouth for its excellent pastoral care and inclusivity, and is envied by other school pastoral workers! Our student welfare team is led by Director of Student Welfare, who has a BA honours in Childhood and Youth Studies, who also teaches on the CAMHS Degree course. She is also the Deputy Designated Safeguarding Officer, working alongside our

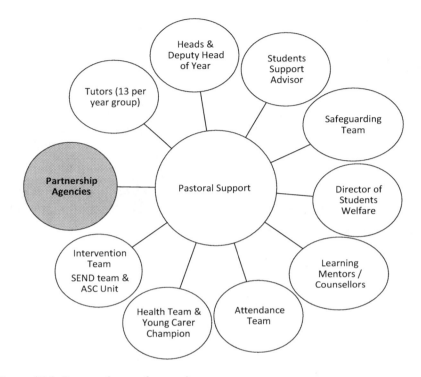

Figure 15.2 Range of team for student support.

attendance outreach team, and oversees the work and programmes of the year group Student Support Advisors. Our diagram above captures some of the teams that work with students (Figure 15.2).

Pupils who have significant emotional difficulties will be referred for individual or group support. The referrals are made by the pastoral team in consultation with the welfare team. The type of support will be agreed in line with the nature of the student's needs, which will be evident following the Behaviour Attendance Emotional Audit (BAE Audit – an innovative approach developed by the local Plymouth Excellence Cluster educational support service) need of each term.

Emotional category (Figure 15.3)

So, who are these staff? What is their role? What training have they had?

Every year group has a *Learning Manager* (*Head of Year*) and *Assistant Learning Manager* who are responsible for the strategic direction of the year team, pastoral support, behaviour and attendance. They are the direct

School-based support for young people 189

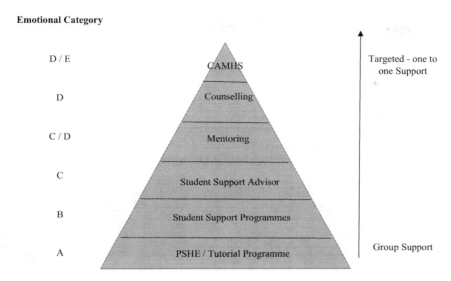

Figure 15.3 Range of targeted support dependant on emotional category of student.

link with parents, notice patterns of behaviour, and are a first point of call for students, staff, as well as parents. This is not unusual for schools, but in addition, each year group has a *Student Support Advisor*. Their role is one of the most crucial to students. They are there to offer support and advice to students, acting as their advocate – they deal with ANY student issues – friends, partner, teacher, parent relationship issues – they are the go between from lost pencil cases, homework issues to more serious issues – home issues, family breakdowns, stress and anxiety, domestic violence, sexual health matters, bereavement, homelessness or anything else. All Student Support Advisors have either completed the ELSA training (Emotional Literacy Support Assistant)[6] or SAMHs (School-Based Adolescent Mental Health) programme,[7] and deliver one-to-one cognitive behaviour therapy or group support programmes. They are available every break and lunchtime in the canteen providing a 'friendly ear'. They also run support programmes to groups of students on a variety of topics such as self-esteem, sexual health, drugs and alcohol issues, social skills and healthy eating.

Our *attendance team* includes our *attendance outreach worker* – she makes home visits, supports students and parents to identify barriers to attending school, and puts in place in school the support needed. She is on the door every morning monitoring patterns of attendance and greeting students. She knows all of our Young Carers who are sometimes slightly late for school due to their caring responsibilities. In general we are relentless on attendance – detention for those not in registration by 8.40 am. However, any Young Carer – who we define as any young person who cares, unpaid, for a person who has any type of physical or mental illness, physical and/or mental disability or misuses substances such as alcohol or drugs – is given a blue sticker in their planner that exempts them from detention. Our attendance team offers early support to parents, provides opportunities for learning about parenting and children's development, as well as signposting access to parenting groups and specialised support.

Our *intervention team* is an integrated team that works on student barriers to learning – academic, SEND (Special Educational Needs and Disability) and pastoral barriers. This includes our *Behaviour Manager*, who uses his time in the unit to talk to the students about their barriers to learning, and also works with parents to support students in being successful. He works with them on a 'person-centred plan' which is shared with staff. His background work has included a role as a Parent Support Advisor and Youth Work.

The *safeguarding team* is self-explanatory with the Designated Safeguarding Lead and Deputy Designated Safeguarding Lead, but our team also includes our *Human Resources Manager*. She supports our staff well-being, signposts staff for external support/counselling and is trained in Mental Health First Aid. Our First Aider regularly meets with the safeguarding team, and keeps a watchful eye on students' emotional health and well-being.

Our *Director of Student Welfare* has a degree in Childhood and Youth Studies, and is also Deputy Safeguarding Lead (DSL), leads and supervises the welfare team within the college in order to support, safeguard and impact on the welfare of students and families. She links with outside support agencies such as CAMHS, the youth service, police and other community organisations that support students and their parents, coordinating referrals to projects and counselling services. The Director also oversees the work of *our employed school-based learning mentors and counsellors*, who work with students on a one-to-one basis, to help them overcome barriers to learning, to raise their aspirations and promote effective participation in all aspects of college life. There are a variety of counselling services available within the college, depending on need, age and preferred style of delivery, including Relate, face to face counselling, Plymouth Options (over 16's self-referral only) and online counselling (called 'Kooth' mentioned earlier).

Students may be referred for CAMHS support where their emotional needs and behaviours displayed indicate that a targeted level of response is needed. These referrals may come as a result of early help intervention, GP consultation or school/parental concern. The school is able to access

School-based support for young people 191

a triangular consultation – between the child, the parent and the school – through the designated CAHMs worker that visits the school weekly to 'triage' – or first line response – cases and help to identify the level of support needed.

Extensive *multi-agency partnership* arrangements have been developed with a range of support agencies. These include the Educational Welfare Service, Educational Psychology Service, Careers South West, School Nursing Service, CAMHS and the Youth Service. In addition we work with a range of voluntary organisations including, but not exclusively, Hamoaze House, Harbour, The Zone, Plymouth Options, Social Services and mental health support services. These complement the work of support staff within school. The relationships developed with these agencies mean that we are able to offer effective support to meet the needs of most students. However we have learnt that physical presence can also be important, for students, staff and for agencies to really work together. Because of this we have co-located the School Nursing Service in offices at the school next to our Welfare Centre. This not only overcomes physical barriers for our students accessing the service but also allows us to tap into their expertise, and ensure a more coherent inter-professional response to the needs expressed by our young people. This also recognises the value of a comprehensive approach in which a team of health professionals, from intensive programs targeting support to those universal school health and well-being programs, is integrated into the school service. The presence of these services at school provides a level of access not typically available, because teams are able to consult regularly, ensuring that the whole team can keep their knowledge up to date and respond appropriately when needed. Our Director of Student Welfare is the conduit between the school and the agencies and health services. As the main point of contact she can assess and prioritise the support needed, and has excellent knowledge of the support services and thresholds that they work to.

There are several settings where we bring our extensive teams together, including multi-agencies – 'Team Around the Child' (see Editors note 1 below) meetings, and multi-agency support meetings. The diagram below shows how these meetings are structured and who attends these meetings.

Editors note 1

An in-house model developed within the school.

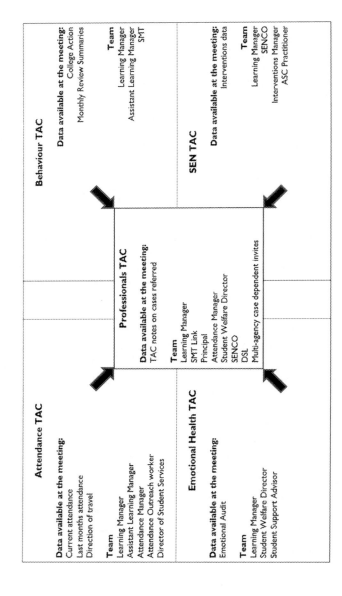

Figure 15.4 Team around the Child (TAC) meeting structure.

School-based support for young people 193

Team around the Child (TAC) meeting structure (Figure 15.4)

Identifying health and well-being needs/identifying young carers

---

Editors note 2

In the introduction we have discussed the different use of and meanings of the terms Child of a Parent with Mental Illness (or COPMI) and Young Carer. Young Carer defines a young person who supplies care of some kind for a parent or sibling in the family. They have some recognition in UK statutes, although what if any actual support they receive is up to each local authority. In addition, because they are defined in terms of actual hours of caring, the estimate of their numbers in the United Kingdom is still less than 200,000, whilst we know that over 3.7 million children live with a parent with mental illness.[8] Also, as explained in the introduction, support for young carers, when it is available, focuses on the burden of being a carer: loss of school and fun time, stigma, bullying and low self-esteem. On the other hand as identified in Chapter 1, children affected by mental illness in a parent also need help to manage their own thinking in relation to the thoughts and feelings of the ill parent, to challenge their tendency to feel responsible or to blame, their fear that they will 'catch' the illness, or that they must share the ill parent's view of the world.

All school systems are different, but some understanding of how to identify the affected students, and gather the intelligence and share it, is vital. Most affected young people do not identify themselves as young carers as they consider their experiences are the norm or try to hide the situation for fear of stigma and bullying. Within school, we may have been aware of students who are young carers but may not be aware of the subgroup who are caring for parents with mental illness. Taking a universal, whole school approach makes it easier for the affected children to come forward and not feel singled out. The following are some indicators that may suggest a student is managing or coping with a mental illness in the family:

- Lateness or absenteeism
- Appearing tired or anxious
- Appearing vacant or distracted
- Disengaged from learning
- Stalled or drop in grades
- Poor behaviour
- Changes in mood
- Working well in class but homework not completed

Figure 15.5 Identifying needs of Young Carers.

- Unkempt appearance
- Social isolation
- Parents not attending review days or parent evenings
- Children making excuses for parents

The BAE Audit of need is one source used to identify emotional need, and also identify those students that are young carers. There are several other ways that we gather our 'intelligence' – primary to secondary transition information, identification from multi-agency meetings, referrals from the pastoral teams, identification from parents themselves, external agencies (social care, Barnardo's) or through students disclosing to other members of staff. In addition our assemblies and tutorial programme raise awareness of what a young carer is, so students can have a clear understanding of whether they are a young carer or not, leading to some identification coming through self-referral (Figure 15.5).

Schools are expected to include information on young carers in a register by the welfare team – how they have been referred, whether they care for an adult or child, mental health issue or physical health/disability and whether they are eligible for the pupil premium (see Editors note 3 below).

Editors note 3

A financial allowance available to schools in relation to each student who is assessed as having a particular degree of social and/or financial deprivation or poverty.

Within our college we have identified 135 young carers (10% of the school). Fifty-one per cent of these care for someone with a mental health issue. There will be others that we either don't yet know about, or who do not recognise themselves as young carers. Is it likely that the ones 'we don't yet know about' are more likely to be related to mental illness. The aspects of the work of the college to raise awareness of caring, and the removal of the stigma attached to caring for someone with a mental illness, will support students to self-refer or seek support or guidance from peers.

Support for young carers

One of the most helpful support systems in school is the establishment of a young carers' group, which enables young people to gain support from and connect with their peers, allowing the experiences of others to inform and help with issues they themselves may be facing and creating a sense of belonging and counteracting the sense of feeling 'totally alone'. The 'Shining Stars' – as the group have named themselves – meet in an area provided by the college, designed by the young carers themselves, that allows them to have a space to meet and take part in activities. It includes soft seating, a rug, wall art, music and relaxation resources, which provides a calm, relaxing space where students feel they can express themselves and share commonality and support. During their meetings the group spend time taking part in a wide range of activities that offer relaxation and time away from the caring role. They include carers of parents, siblings or other members of the family, and those that support someone with physical disabilities, as well as mental illness. The self-identification of students allows us to have sensitive discussions with students or parents about the activities of the 'Shining Stars' Young Carers' group, which meets fortnightly and also offers students the opportunity to take part in therapeutic social activities, and to talk freely in a supportive atmosphere to promote positive well-being. The students are very proud of their role within the college, and their group, and can be identified by their 'Shining Stars' lapel badge. The assemblies raise awareness of the group activities, including the role of peer mentors, and attract students who are young carers to join the group.

They are the experts!

In addition to the fortnightly meetings, the older young carer students are trained as peer mentors so that they can peer support younger students or students that are new to caring. The training for this programme includes safeguarding procedures as well as mentoring techniques.

Activities the Shining Stars students take part in include:

- Mindfulness session
- Aromatherapy session

- Pamper Day & peer massage
- Cream Tea afternoon
- Movie night
- Pizza night
- Picnic & stroll on the moor
- Ice skating at Christmas
- Arts and crafts sessions
- Sports and fitness session
- Music creation sessions
- Health and well-being session
- Homework club
- Peer mentoring
- Art workshop and exhibition
- Creating the 'Shining Stars' garden

Each year the students attend the young carer festival run by the Carers Trust. Students stay in tents and get the opportunity to spend the weekend with other young carers from across the country.

Our Young Carer Group is led by the *Young Carer Champion* and the *Students Support Advisors*. They are well placed to identify and promote the group and activities.

Who cares project

It is important within the college to educate all students on mental health issues and also to help them understand what their friends and peers may experience as Young Carers, especially if they are living with someone with a mental illness. In 2015, Alan Cooklin approached us to develop a module of work in parental mental health and its impact on students. This includes a tutorial programme, how to set up a Young Carer group, training for buddies and a programme for a mental health awareness day.

Stoke Damerel Community College developed and piloted the materials for the Who Cares? Project. We have now been running the project for nearly six years, and every year it has a positive impact on the school, the students and the staff. Creating the project involved a team of four staff working on different elements. Our Year 9 GCSE drama students contributed to the next development of the original 'Jass Story' about a boy living with a mother with mental illness, and having to care for her and his little sister, which was filmed with students from another academy. Our students then wrote, acted in and were filmed making two films about two sisters living with a parent with mental illness, which were integral to the modules: one from the vantage point of an elder sister who wants to go away to university and has to leave the care of their mother to the younger sister, and from the perspective of the younger sister. In fact, one member of the cast is now one of our Maths teachers! The students understanding and confidence to talk about mental health during the creation of the script and film will be of lifelong benefit. During the project, more than one student was able to identify themselves as a young carer. For others they felt able to recognise their own mental health issues and to seek help and support. This had an impact on the whole school – one female student went on to work with MIND, another student worked with her Drama class, devising and leading a series of workshops. This culminated in a performance which was seen by the whole college population in assemblies with over 1,000 young people.

Every year now, our Year 8 students follow the six week 'Who Cares? Project' led by their tutors.

The aim of the online package is to:

- Help children who have a mental illness to better understand, and know how to cope with mental illness in a parent or sibling
- Help teachers to know which children might be affected in this way, and how to help them provide a general learning tool about mental illness for schools

The package is based on a mixture of films of different young peoples' and teachers' ideas and experiences, and some dramatised films, using actors, and online learning programmes.

The intention is that, through increased staff and pupil awareness, better support can be established to minimise the impact on young people's emotional development, learning and achievement.

How to do it – tips for adventurous schools

When starting the 'Who Cares?' Programme, it is essential to have a school culture that supports it. This means thinking about how to create a safe environment for everyone, briefing staff fully and considering the support mechanisms you already have in place. Select a senior staff member to champion the work and ensure it is sustained. They may wish to put together a team of staff to support delivery and raise awareness throughout the school. This could include:

- a Senior Leader
- Young Carer Champion – teacher (e.g. PSHE coordinator, SMSC lead)
- Member of safeguarding team
- Student welfare/pastoral lead

It is recommended that one member of staff acts as the main point of contact for staff and students in school, and links with existing support structures. The Young Carers Council provides various courses for champion training.

Before the project is delivered the tutor team undergoes two training sessions – first to understand the module components, to discuss the boundaries and rules for delivery, and to provide an opportunity for them to ask questions regarding the modules and air their worries and concerns regarding the delivery.

The second training session is led by our PSHE teacher (PSHE education) on the Stigma module which staff can find the most challenging. Whilst many tutors feel very comfortable delivering the modules, there are always some concerns that arise that we address. Some of these concerns and solutions are outlined below.

WHAT IF I DO NOT FEEL COMFORTABLE DELIVERING ALL OR SOME OF THE MODULES?

There are always two adults in the room, the tutor and an experienced staff member (welfare team, PSHE teachers and mentors). We encourage the tutor to deliver the programme for several reasons. First, they have the relationship with the students and know each student well, so can pick up sensitivities and watch for signs of anxiety and behaviour that may be out of character. The tutors are experienced 'teachers' and are confident delivering to a whole tutor group as practitioners. The most important factor is that if the students experience their tutor talking about mental health, they will be more likely to discuss any future concerns with them, knowing that they are open and interested in discussing their views and feelings.

WHAT IF I GET ASKED A QUESTION I CANNOT ANSWER? I AM NOT AN EXPERT IN MENTAL HEALTH, WHAT IF I SAY THE WRONG THING?

Each tutor group is provided with a 'question box' – decorated decoupage treasure chest boxes. At the end of the session students are given a post-it note to write down any concerns or questions they have following the session. All students must write one so that no one feels it is only them with a question. They then place it in the box at the end of the session. If tutors have questions asked of them during the session that they cannot answer, it is perfectly acceptable to tell students that you do not know the answers, and that they will find out by the next session – the tutor also writes those questions and adds it to the box. The questions are read and collated at the end of the session and answered by one of our counsellors, who writes the answers to any questions. The next session always starts with going through the questions and answers.

WHAT HAPPENS IF A STUDENT GETS UPSET?

There are always two staff present in case a student gets upset; they can then leave the room with one staff member. The sessions take place in classrooms located in one corridor and the Head of Year is situated on that corridor so that they are on hand to assist and support.

School-based support for young people   199

There are times when a student can get a little silly or say something inappropriate; this is usually through embarrassment or displays someone struggling with the content, and they use this as a defence mechanism. Again, having that additional staffing helps in these situations.

WHAT ARE THE RULES AND BOUNDARIES?

Before the first session students have an assembly to introduce the project. Then with their tutor they go through the class rules – do's and don'ts such as only one person speaks at a time, respect each other's views, talk in the third person so as not to disclose information about yourself, what to do if you are upset (see Figure 15.6 below).

As you might expect, we do find that following the modules students disclose about their home life as they relate to the characters in the videos, or that they know of a friend that has had those experiences. Students are informed who they can talk to, and who are the members of the safeguarding team.

WHAT DO WE TELL PARENTS ABOUT THE PROGRAMME?

Before the students start the programme all parents are informed via a letter about the programme, dates of delivery and an overview of the content. They have an opportunity to opt-out of the project or contact the school

Do	Don't
Listen	Feel you need to solve the problem
Take any child protection concerns to the appointed person	Force the young person to talk
Signpost to YC Support/YC Champion	Assume it's all negative
Agree protocols with the class on information sharing, discussing personal experiences, taking time out etc.	Share confidential information without consent
	Share your own story
Ask young person what support they would like	Feel worried about saying the wrong thing
	Be afraid to use terms like mental illnesss; after all they live with the illness

Figure 15.6 'Dos and don'ts' for Young Carers.

if they wish to know more about the programme – they never have in my experience. On the contrary, parents are very happy that we have this programme and will be discussing mental health with their child. In fact, it is these times again when parents inform us of concerns in the home regarding mental illness.

WHAT IS THE BEST WAY TO DELIVER THE PROGRAMME GIVEN ITS SENSITIVE CONTENT?

The programme has been trialled in a few ways over the years. The end of Year 8 tends to be the optimum time in their schooling to deliver the project; they have a level of maturity to discuss the content and they may be starting to have more of an awareness of possible caring responsibilities from themselves or in friends or family. The six modules work best when split into individual sessions fitted within a three to six week window. I would advise no more than two sessions a week to allow time for reflection.

WHAT IF I, THE TUTOR, FIND THE CONTENT UPSETTING?

The content of each module is discussed with tutors in advance. They decide if they wish to be the main 'facilitator' for the sessions, for some of the sessions, or that they are happy to be present but do not feel comfortable delivering the units. If this is the case, the experienced support staff will step in. If one in five teachers has experienced some level of parental mental illness then many of them will be affected. This can mean that a particular member of staff may feel too emotionally vulnerable to deliver the programme, or – depending on the degree to which he or she has been able to come to terms with the effects on him/her self – it may motivate the teacher to want to help young people now in a similar situation.

Implementation of the project

PREPARATION

The following steps will support delivery of 'Who Cares?':

1   Use a whole school approach including senior staff
2   Prepare staff by holding an awareness-raising training session
3   Devise your own 'Dos and Don'ts' list
4   Prepare students by raising awareness of mental health in general
5   Offer access routes for support to students, e.g. designated space, assemblies
6   Offer access to supervision or support for staff
7   Think about how to create an alliance between the family and the school in the best interests of the child

School-based support for young people 201

PREPARE STUDENTS

Ensure students are aware that everyone has mental health issues which can fluctuate during our lives. Use the information from the training session and resources to address parental mental illness using a whole school approach.

SUPPORT STRUCTURE FOR STUDENTS

Identify support structures for students that come forward. The programme may raise questions and concerns for some students who identify with the issues raised or know someone who is affected.

Students may choose to confide in any member of staff within school, so it's important for staff to know what to do once they become aware of the family situation. The issue may be directed towards the Young Carer Champion or pastoral care lead, who may signpost the student to internal support groups such as a peer-to-peer support programme or Young Carers' group, or to external support such as Barnardo's Young Carer Support or Our Time 'KidsTime Workshops', which offer support to the whole family to help them cope with the illness.

SUPERVISION AND SUPPORT TO STAFF

We recommend support for staff is available:

- To reflect on the feelings the work has raised, sometimes relating to their own childhood and upbringing
- To reflect on their experience with a student and how they were affected
- To discuss concerns or questions relating to young people and get perspectives and advice from colleagues
- Improve knowledge and skill through thinking together about both perspectives (staff member and student)
- Feel safe and contained in the context of the helping relationship

---

BOX 15.1

Here are some possible models for in-school supervision or support for 'Who Cares?'

If counsellors or therapists are employed in the school, allocate 1.5 hours per month for supervision.

A member of staff can be identified to provide supervision (e.g. SENCO). This staff member is given external supervision for 1.5 hours per month.

Supervisors can be found through the British Association of Counselling and Psychotherapy (BACP) or the United Kingdom Council for Psychotherapy (UKCP).

Group supervision can be facilitated by a trained staff member or external resource.

Peer supervision can be facilitated by a staff member with guidance from a professional counsellor.

Short supervision training courses are available for non-therapeutic staff to develop their skills to provide supervision to their colleagues (e.g. Young Carer Champion).

PARENT SUPPORT

It is often difficult for teachers and school staff to connect positively and cooperatively with families where there is mental illness. Developing a closer alliance with the family is most easily done through processes that support all families, rather than singling out those with particular problems. As most families experience pressures and difficulties during the child's school life, this normalises the situation and prevents stigmatising the children of parents with a mental illness. A letter to parents at the beginning of the school year highlighting the 'Who Cares?' Programme and encouraging those parents to come forward to work together to support the children is ideal. It is important that parents have a point of contact, e.g. parents' support advisor.

SYNOPSIS OF EACH MODULE

The modules follow the story of a girl called Alice and her older sister Emily, who at different times are both carers for their mother who suffers from a mental illness. It particularly catalogues Alice's journey through teenage years, her interaction with friends, as well as Emily's dilemma of considering going away to university, considering the impact it will have on her younger sister.

BOX 15.2

The six modules are as follows:

What is mental health?

To introduce the topic of mental health
To understand what a mental illness is – a good explanation on what is happening

Stigma

To explore how people stigmatize others and why?
To understand the impact of the stigma of mental health illness on someone.

Living with someone with a mental illness

To have an understanding of what it is like to live with someone with a mental illness.
To consider how it impacts on young people's lives.

Mental health and young people

Explore how young people are affected by mental health

Mental health and the media

To analyse contemporary media texts regarding their representation of mental illness
To raise awareness of how false representations are constructed in the media and in social media
To raise awareness of mental health and mental illness and recognise signs of ill health.

Reflections

To review life's rollercoaster of highs and lows.
To identify ways of coping with living with a mental illness.

From the evaluation of this project it is clear that it has had a huge impact on both students and staff within the school. The evaluation showed that students enjoyed taking part in the project, learning about a topic that is not widely spoken about in society and it helped resolve some misconceptions that they had about mental illness. Students identified they were scared or apprehensive at the beginning of the project. However as the sessions progressed and discussions developed the students soon felt relieved as they realised others were feeling the same. At the end of the project many students commented on how the project allowed them to understand other people's needs and how it is acceptable to talk about mental health. Other students identified they had a negative attitude towards mental health at the beginning of the project. However by the end they realised their perceptions and attitude towards mental health had changed.

Other feedback identified that students felt they were able to show a clear understanding of why they were taking part in the project and many were left feeling confident to talk about parental mental ill health and mental health more widely. A selection of students also acknowledged how they felt able to offer support to friends and family who may be suffering from a mental illness as a result of taking part in the project.

There were many staff involved in the planning and delivery of the modules. Staff who delivered these were provided with support to prepare for the sessions to ensure they felt comfortable and confident to talk about the topics being covered. Feedback from the staff was very positive. Staff commented on how confident they felt in delivering the sessions, and how the sessions allowed them to build up a more open relationship with the students they were working with. As a result of the project staff felt they could sensitively support students and have conversations around parental mental health and mental health more widely.

Since the Who Cares? Project has been introduced within the school there has been an increase in the number of students attending our Young Carers' group who have a parent or a sibling with a mental illness. Being involved in the Who Cares? Project and the Young Carers' group has allowed students to recognise they are not alone in their caring role, and realise there are many other students within the school who are carrying out similar roles at home every day.

The benefit for the school of this project is that through the vehicle of Who Cares? and our working relationship with the Our Time (formerly The Kidstime Foundation) we have become a mental health aware school. It has become embedded in our culture and something we – staff and students – are very proud of. We look forward to continuing the work of the Who Cares? Project within the school and continue to observe students engaging in the project and removing the stigma based around mental ill health.

References

1 Plymouth City Council (2016) Life Expectancy Report 2001–2003 to 2012–2014, Report of the Director of Public Health.
2 Plymouth City Council (2016) The Changing Causes of Poverty and Health Inequalities in Plymouth: A Public Health Perspective, Director of Public Health Annual Report 2015/2016.
3 Plymouth City Council (2017) Plymouth Report.
4 Plymouth City Council (2017) Joint Strategic Needs Assessment Report.
5 Kooth (2004) Mental Health and Wellbeing Platform for Children and Young People.
6 ELSA (Emotional Literacy Support Assistant) Support (2019) Emotional Literacy Support Platform.
7 Young Minds (2019) Adolescent Mental Health Training Platform.
8 Children's Commissioner for England (2018) Childhood Vulnerability in England 2018, Office of the Children's Commissioner for England, London.

Chapter 16

London calling – experiences with the Kidstime model in Germany

Klaus Henner Spierling

The impetus for Kidstime in Germany

Kidstime workshops began in Germany in February 2015 following an in-house training session run by Alan Cooklin and Deni Francis. Our reason for taking this initiative was the lack of programmes for children of parents with a mental illness available in rural parts of the country, especially those addressing whole families programmes which when available were concentrated in bigger cities such as Hamburg or Berlin, and almost exclusively addressed either children or parents, but rarely both together.

We initiated the first Kidstime workshops in a clinic in Northern Germany, the Agaplesion Diakonieklinikum Rotenburg (which we will refer to as ADR), situated between the cities of Bremen and Hamburg. The region of Rotenburg is mostly composed of a number of small villages of up to 2,000 inhabitants, spread over a predominantly agricultural area. The city of Rotenburg itself has a population of 20,000, significantly larger than any of the surrounding towns and villages. Based on aggregated studies this means that there are likely to be between 5,000 and 6,000 children in the region living with one or more parents with mental illness.

Creating the team

The ADR provides services for adults with mental health problems as well as for children who experience mental and/or physical health problems, including behavioural and school problems. Working in both the school and the clinic context we recognised the burden of feelings of isolation and confusion experienced by the children living with a parent with mental illness, as well as the role of young carer many had to adopt. We also recognised that the children of parents attending the adult psychiatry clinics were commonly neglected both by the clinic and by other services.

Convincing those commissioning services of the need to fund this intervention was a key initial hurdle, as well as an ongoing problem. The health system in Germany is based on a curative paradigm, thus giving little support to preventive programs. For example, to qualify for treatment requires a diagnosis, the focus of which seemed quite contrary to the ideas on which Kidstime was based – namely to support the healing and resilience of the children as a preventative measure, for the benefit of their future mental health. Also having a parent with mental illness is certainly a risk factor for children, but does not mean that they are ill or need treatment. On the other hand, social services, such as the Jugendamt which gives support to families and young persons in need, were reluctant to intervene in any field which was defined as medical. This pattern of agencies defining problems of children as the responsibility of the 'other' services is quite typical in Germany, leading to many children's needs being neglected by the statutory services. Fortunately, in this case, the social services did agree finally to support the project, which both helped us through the first year and helped create a model which could be adopted by other regions.

The groups in Rotenberg were mostly of a single ethnicity, in marked contrast to those later developed in bigger cities. A small number of parents from Albania or Bulgaria did attend, but this was still rather rare. About 80% of the parents with a psychiatric diagnosis were female, mostly with depressive or anxiety disorders. There have so far been hardly any referrals of refugee families, which we know are a considerable number, and many of whom we know suffer from post-traumatic stress, so that we are now seeking ways to reach them.

Setting up the Kidstime workshop team had quite an impact both on the team members as well as on the clinic itself. The teams in the different departments of the clinic were used to working each in their separate ways; whereas forming the Kidstime team meant bringing together a multi-professional team (e.g. psychologists, social workers, nurses, paediatricians) from both the adult psychiatry and the community paediatric centre, who all showed an interest in starting Kidstime together. This process had the added advantage of initiating cooperation between different fields in the clinic.

Hurdles and how we learnt to jump them

While establishing Kidstime workshops in the clinic opened up a fruitful new way of working for both families and workers, many problems and hazards still had to be negotiated. Some team members were used to a rather hierarchical attitude to both adults and children, 'as patients'. An essential element of the Kidstime model is that families experience the family workers as 'on the level', more as colleagues or friends than as subjects. Family members often expressed surprise at this approach with words such as 'you are so normal'. The less hierarchical model allowed the children to be both seen and heard, at the same time as allowing their parents to experience themselves without feelings of blame or shame, both of which are elements which we consider are key elements in building resilience within the family. However this stance towards the families did not come naturally to all of the team members, particularly those from adult psychiatry, where the structures promote hierarchical roles, which, in turn, can lead to patronising behaviour towards adults and children. Therefore as we – the initiators and later trainers of the new Kidstime groups – were clear that these attitudes did not fit to with the Kidstime workshop model, we had to confront conflicts within the teams. Much of this was resolved through supervision and team reflection, although the process is still ongoing.

There were also obstacles facing the families, particularly resulting from rigidity in referral pathways.

Currently there are four different referral routes to Kidstime:

a   Children coming to the social (community) paediatric centre commonly because of somatic complaints, school problems, behavioural problems or developmental problems
b   As the families of adult patients in psychiatric treatment
c   From other referrers such as schools or social services
d   As self-referrers

Regardless of the referral route we try to have a whole family interview to reach a mutual decision about coming to Kidstime.

Commonly the families face different issues depending on the referral route:

a   *Reticence from the parents themselves*
    Many parents with mental illness, who present their children to the social paediatric centre, are either not aware of their own mental health issues and how they interact with the child, or alternatively they try to hide these from the children. They may sometimes see it as shameful to talk about their own mental health – particularly as they came to discuss their children's health, so that the child is seen as the 'problem bearer'. While many parents have already received some form of mental health treatment, which we have found had rarely been explained to the children, our initial family meeting is often a first occasion when parental mental health issues have been made explicit. Although they frequently see their mental illness as a source of shame, parents often also feel relieved after a short while when the issue is addressed in a reasonable and non-judgemental manner. Creating a trusting connection to the family is very helpful if this can be established in the diagnostic process with the child and the family before engaging with the Kidstime groups. This is often facilitated by the initial family interview.
b   *Reticence from professionals treating the parents*
    Parents who have already been engaged in psychiatric treatment are more frequently open to the idea of Kidstime. Parents in this group rarely try to keep the issue away from their children or express sceptical

ideas, because the impacts of their mental illness often seem self-evident to these parents. As a result little explanation concerning the possible use of the program is needed for this group. Most parents show interest in overcoming social isolation and get support from talking within the family about mental health and illness. At the same time it has remained difficult to elicit such support within the institution – despite the positive results and feedbacks from the families. One possible reason for this reticence seems to be that opening paths to access and use of Kidstime is regarded as bringing about more work for the professionals, even those not actively involved in Kidstime or in the referral. There is often an underlying narrative of 'What else are we supposed to do? We can hardly manage our daily work with the adults!' – thus disregarding the children, as well as the fact that adult patients may gain much relief and be more stable when they feel better about their children and families. This is a point often made by the parents themselves. Another source of reticence is based on the perception by adult psychiatrists that Kidstime is a competing form of treatment. Therapists and psychiatrists, who are more familiar with a more hierarchical approach to treatment, tend to decide whether taking part in Kidstime is useful as part of therapy at a given point of time, instead of letting the family members decide. In some cases this leads colleagues to keep information on Kidstime away from the families. This tendency has demanded that we enhance our efforts to improve inter-disciplinary communication within the clinic. These efforts, together with many positive feedbacks from patients, families and professionals, have led to changes in this attitude, but at the same time it has shown how the Kidstime model has represented a challenge to the accepted assumptions of the institution.

c   *Limited information or understanding given to families by the referrer*
Families referred to Kidstime by outside professionals are often given scanty or poor information which can lead them to be suspicious or sceptical of the referral. This happens particularly if the referral is not their own choice, but has been accepted by them under pressure or out of loyalty to their particular mental health professional. However, most of these families have become motivated to engage once they have been given more adequate information and answers to their questions. An important factor seems to be when they receive the impression that they are personally welcome.

d   *Families wanting to invite others*
Some families in Kidstime ask if their neighbours/colleagues/friends may come to Kidstime as they think these others may profit too and like the programme. It is then important to find out whether the topic of mental health issues is relevant enough to these families. There are many examples of when these families do fit perfectly into the group, as well as a smaller number who remain just 'neighbours'.

It is very rare that the team decides not to invite families to Kidstime who show interest in taking part. In rare cases where there are post-divorce legal battles, particularly if mental illness is being used in a conflict over custody, then open discussion of mental illness may be seen as hazardous by the affected parent. In these cases we have been careful to ensure that the legal process is settled first, in order to avoid a further increase in the stress levels on the children and family.

Rolling out the Kidstime model throughout Germany

Setting up groups in other parts of the country is now an ongoing process, begun about two years ago. There are by now more than ten Kidstime workshops in different regions of Germany, with more emerging. Funding has remained a challenge that has had to be resolved in different ways in different areas. This has meant that there are some German teams in different parts of the country that are trained and keen to start, but still seeking funding.

Some reflections on progress

The problems of referral have been much more easily resolved when the Kidstime team is involved in a network or clinic where there is access to the families. The Rotenburg clinic offers help for the adults and for the children in different departments, so the whole clinic has benefitted from bringing these different parts of the clinic together, leading to better understanding not only within and between families but also amongst the professionals.

Concurrent evaluation of the impact of Kidstime was essential. We attracted much interest from Universities, so that several bachelor and master theses could be presented in 2017, and the program gained recognition in winning the 'Niedersächsishce Gesundheitspreis' and 'Hanse Merkur Innovationspreis', both prizes for innovative work in health contexts. This, in turn, helped us to convince local authorities to continue to support Kidstime or to establish their own local Kidstime workshops. Even more convincing were the voices of the participating families. For example one mother stated she felt more stable and trusting in herself since joining Kidstime, children expressed experiencing joy, togetherness and better understanding – sometimes on camera or broadcast for the first time. All of this helped our efforts to establish Kidstime as a necessary and effective part of mental health practice.

In the rural region of Rotenburg it is often difficult for the families to come to the workshops because there are distances of more than 50 km to be covered, and there are very few buses or other forms of public transport. Thus lack of driving licences, a broken car, or lack of money to pay for the fuel are obstacles that have had to be overcome, often with difficulty. Setting up a new Kidstime workshop is often facilitated by having an opening event, inviting press and referrers. This has also helped to engage new families as well as local sponsors who may contribute to the funding. We were often surprised about how co-funding opened up in this way. One example was a local dentist who supported Kidstime with the money he made from gold implants which he extracted from the teeth of his patients when these needed replacement, the extracted gold from which led to a significant donation.

At the moment, there are three most important challenges we have to meet:

> Open up more regional Kidstime groups to make the workshops available for more families
>
> Intensify cooperation with local authorities and schools, which was also a key recommendation of a University student's thesis
>
> Intensify contact between the different local Kidstime workshops both to ensure fidelity to the model and to profit from each other's experiences

To do so we formed an organisation, the 'Kidstime Deutschland e. V'. We hope to continue with the work we began at the same time as keeping close contact to Our Time – our parent charitable organisation – as well as other Kidstime workshops on a trans-national level. We hope that this approach will contribute to the international awareness of the needs of children of parents with mental illness (COPMI) to achieve long term support for interventions such as Kidstime in Germany and elsewhere.

Chapter 17

Kidstime experience in Spain

Miguel Cárdenas

Setting up groups

The Kidstime project in Spain started in 2014, after training by the UK team from the (then) Kidstime Foundation. It was based on a joint collaboration of professionals in Child and Adolescent Mental Health Services (CAMHS) (Fundació Orienta and Hospital San Juan de Dios) and Adult Mental Health Services (Parc Sanitari Sant Joan de Déu and Hospital Benito Menni), initially in the towns of Sant Boi and Castelldefels, both in the metropolitan area of Barcelona.

These towns have an approximate population of 140,000 in the Barcelona region. Their economy is based on agriculture as well as local commerce and industry. Sant Boi has a long tradition of attention to mental health, since one of the first psychiatric hospitals in Spain was established there in the mid-nineteenth century.

The Kidstime program was the first project in which those earlier institutions have worked together. Also there were no previous community projects for families affected by parental mental illness.

Challenges

Adult Mental Health Services and CAMHS used to work separately; therefore, identifying and intervening in the impact of parental mental illness on the affected child population was a difficult task. In particular it was difficult for staff in adult psychiatry to perceive an adult with a diagnosis as a father or mother having dependent children.

Although it is a community project, it has been fully financed by the Health System, with little participation by Social Services. This has created a further challenge as it has meant that families with serious mental health problems have not had social service support.

Another difficulty was to get professionals in adult mental health to refer families, as they believed the intervention might activate a crisis in them or would worsen the clinical picture. As a result most families were initially recruited from parents with mental health problems who came via referral of their children to the CAMHS. Those referred were mostly from the local population, with a minority of immigrants from Latin America and Morocco. Seventy percent were women with depressive disorders, OCD or Borderline personality disorder. More recently referral has been from adult or CAMHS or from primary care doctors.

Working in Kidstime was a new experience both for the families and the professionals, particularly the shift from the usual relationships found in the health services, modelled on the doctor-patient relationship, to a more personal approach, both looking at and communicating differently, which involved breaking down both the professional barriers and the resistance in patients and families to being more open about the experiences and difficulties. Early on this also meant that the professionals had to leave behind their comfort zone and confront the implicit hierarchies operating in the hospital system.

Another challenge was in part the result of the success of the approach in engaging children. Sometimes this meant that children opened up with many questions about mental health, but their interest was cut off after a few sessions by the refusal of some parents to continue attendance.

Not surprisingly in such an 'open' intervention we have also had to confront and respond to unexpected situations such as couple conflicts and rarely violence.

Reflections

Our experience of the Kidstime workshops is that they provide a transitional space for families and professionals, where the professional plays a role which is different to the common experiences of both patients and professionals, in that it creates an atmosphere of trust and equality, using drama and art as a resource. This then becomes a space to talk about mental health problems and their impact on family life, emphasising the impact on children, the struggles of families, and finding ways to deal with the issues associated with parental mental illness.

From the two initial Kidstime workshops, the number of workshops has expanded to 13 active workshops in Catalonia, (Barcelona and Girona). New projects are also beginning in other parts of Spain.

Funding has continued to be provided by the Health System, although also supported by some private contributions. We have continued to train new teams, and the ideas underpinning the workshops have now begun to arouse more general interest in the mental health field in the region.

Our preliminary research has indicated some significant improvement:

* In the parents' ability to express affection and emotions to their children
* Less stigma associated with mental disorder

The process that families have experienced has allowed them to create their own voice, giving testimony for both parents and their children, related to the experience of living with a mental health problem in the family, with the restorative effect of sharing the experience with the community, and breaking the barriers of stigma.

We have found out that:

- Families who are actively participating have built stronger bonds inside the family, through understanding mental health problems
- They feel being part of a safe space, lacking in stigma
- Kidstime allows them to understand and talk about mental health problems through play and drama
- Professionals have been able to work from a different perspective than usual, being able to achieve a closer relationship to the families
- Working together across different agencies and disciplines has also given all the professionals a better insight into what is happening in families

What the future holds?

- Opening more workshops in order to allow more families to access them
- Increasing networking with social agencies and schools
- Empowering of families living with mental health problems
- Creating a comprehensive research model

This work and the ideas were developed together with Marta Coromina, psychiatrist, Irene Ardevol, psychologist, Fernando Lacasa, psychologist and Teresa Ribalta, psychologist at Fundación Orienta, Parc Sanitari Sant Joan de Deu –Sant Boi, CASM Benito Menni-Hermanas Hospitalarias, Hospital Sant Joan de Deu, Barcelona.

Chapter 18

Some combined tips for parents, children and the professionals who work with them

Some tips for parents

Obviously, when a parent suffers from any level of mental illness, it can make the job of being a parent more difficult. This, in turn, can make the parent feel as though they are failing, then guilty and anxious, then ultimately feel worse themselves. However, as we have been discussing, most children are resilient as well as sensitive to their parent's needs, even if they do not always show it. So quite small things – if you can manage at least some of them – can both reassure your child and help them to cope.

1 *Try to find out as much as you can about your illness and share what you have learnt with your child.* Do not try to hide it or pretend it is not happening. Instead, show that you are trying to take charge of it by thinking about it and discussing it openly. Parents naturally try to protect their children from upsetting things, but actually it's best to explain as much as possible to children in a simple way. Often children sense problems, and research shows that they cope much better when they can understand how difficulties happen.
2 *Explain that a mental illness always has many causes, from inheritance to family and daily life.* Tell your child that their experience will be different from yours and that they do not have to develop the same illness.
3 *Explain to your child that she or he is not responsible either for your illness or your emotional state.* Like all parents you will get ratty sometimes, but the illness may lead to this being shown in very extree ways. It does not mean that your child is responsible for those extreme states, and he or she needs to know that.
4 *When you need to withdraw a bit in order to protect yourself, try and agree a code or some simple way of letting your child know that is what is happening and why.* Some parents use 'my feelings' filter is not working today' so the child knows the parent will withdraw until they feel more in control.
5 *Try not to overload your child with too many details of your emotional life.* When you are feeling overwhelmed, it is enough to simply explain that you might need to withdraw.

Some combined tips   215

6   *During better periods remember to show interest and curiosity,* about what is happening at school or in other activities your child cares about. However don't 'interrogate', and try not to be offended if your child does not want to talk much. He or she may have had to hold many things in for some time, and that habit can take time to loosen.

7   *Try not to become too afraid of your child's feelings.* Some of these feelings will be the normal issues that children and young people experience. Try to explain to your child that you realise you will not be emotionally available to them in your bad times. However, also explain that in good times you would like to hear what they think, feel and are doing, and that you will actually let them know when you are feeling you can be receptive.

8   *Try to recognise, encourage and praise your child's achievements,* inside and outside the home. Remember s/he may have had to take on extra responsibilities to cope with managing things at home during the bad times, but you may still have to remind him/her that s/he can lean on you in the good times.

9   *If you feel guilty – and many parents do –* do not try too hard to compensate with food or 'closeness'. You will feel less guilty if you can show your child that you recognise *his/her* love, and that s/he may need time on their own to get their own thoughts in order.

10 *Try to encourage your child to think* for him/herself, and to make it clear that s/he does not have to share your way of seeing things.

11 *Try to find a time to talk to your child* when you are feeling better and calmer and it feels like your child would accept a conversation, but without pressure on either of you. Then these are some of the questions you might invite your child to discuss:
    * Do you feel anxious, upset or frightened when I become unwell?
    * How does it feel when I have to go into hospital?
    * Do you worry about how long I will be unwell?
    * Do you wonder why it happens?

12 *Although you may feel anxious starting such a conversation,* it may help you to know that this kind of conversation can actively help your child. It shows that you are thinking about and caring about him/her as a separate person, despite your illness. Also, you can reassure your child that s/he does *not* have to develop the same problem, and that talking about it 'like this' is part of a way to protect him/her. Specifically:
    * Be honest with them so they know the truth and can make sense of it and get on with their lives
    * If they have siblings, encourage them to support each other
    * Try to explain recovery (see Editors note below), or ask a professional you trust to do that; what that might mean for them, if the illness is episodic and you - their parent - have got much better

216 Some combined tips

13 *Try to find other parents to talk to who have had similar experiences –* there are many of them, but often they do not know each other and all can feel isolated. Ask around if there is a parent's support group such as provided by the KidsTime Workshop.

14 *Try to encourage relatives and friends* you like not to be scared away or worry about interfering, by suggesting practical things they can do to help. This could include such invaluable things as inviting a child for a sleepover, or bringing a home-cooked meal if you, their parent has just been taken into hospital. If you can, tell them not to be frightened to talk about it as an illness.

> **Editors note**
>
> For definitions of recovery see notes in Lara Brown's comments on Alan Cooklin's and Ambeya Begum's chapters.

Some tips for children and young people

1 *It is never your responsibility* to make your parent well and you could not have made him or her ill.

   Although that is really obvious, we know that many children will feel responsible for both the illness and its 'cure', and sometimes parents may unintentionally encourage that idea.

2 *If you do feel responsible*, you may find it hard to trust anyone who tells you that you are not.

   It is really important for you to try to find someone you *can* trust to talk to. It could be a particular teacher or other member of school staff, a school nurse or a doctor, or it could be a family friend, an uncle or aunt or a grandparent. The really important thing is that you must not feel you have to hide what is happening out of loyalty. That will be bad for you, and in the long term it will not help your ill parent.

3 *Make sure you get a good and full explanation* which satisfies your curiosity and keep asking until you really do understand. In fact 'be a pain' until you find someone who can make sense of it for you.

4 *Try to keep or make a group of friends,* and *do* join in school and other activities such as cubs, scouts, brownies or guides, music or film clubs, sports. It does not help your parent to see you harmed, and it will make him or her feel more guilty, even if he or she cannot admit it.

5 *Enjoy and develop what you are good at,* whether in school or outside, whether it is a school subject, sport, music, art, or even your ability to care for your parent or to campaign for the rights of children in your situation. Young people who have campaigned for the rights of children of parents with mental illness or young carers, have often found their own strength and self-respect through that (see chapters 12 and 15).

Some combined tips 217

6 *Hold on to your own thoughts* and how you see things and try *not* to adapt your mind set to suit the 'illness'. That will not help your ill parent.

7 *If you have brothers or sisters,* talk to each other and try to plan together how to support each other.

8 *Ask an adult you trust in school* (this could include a school nurse, young mentor, or any other member of staff, or the leader a *young carer's* or similar support group - if there is one). If you or your parents have a social worker, ask him/her to find out for you. Talking to other young people who have had to cope with similar problems can be a best form of help.

9 *Be honest with yourself* – that is do not try to convince yourself that all is fine when it is not. If you can find someone to ask for help, then ask – and if something is offered try it. Don't let your self effacement or mistrust stop people who might care, from talking to you. It is your human right to be helped not left to care for a parent's illness on your own.

10 *During the good times – when your ill parent is better –* try to let him or her show some care for you, if s/he can. For example, you could try making a list of things your parent could do with you. It does not have to undermine you, and if it does then you may have to pull back. However there is more to your parent than his/her diagnosis, and allow yourself to experience and enjoy the other side to your parent when she/he is available.

11 *If you can find a professional you can trust* (for example one of the kinds we have mentioned earlier) try to get explanations to clear up any muddle you may have about:

- Your confusion and worry or fear about what is happening or has happened to your parent or parents
- How to understand extreme states of emotion in an adult, and at what point these are no longer normal emotions
- What defines an illness in your parent's mind and how it works to change the way he or she thinks, feels, and behaves.
- How to develop and keep your own mind going independently of your ill parent's way of seeing things
- To help you confirm that the things you see and feel are normal and can make sense
- To help you think about any tendency you have to take too much responsibility for what is happening at home, or for your parent's mental state
- To face the limits of what you can do at your age and recognise and deal with any frustrations resulting from facing this
- To help you think how to make contacts with other people of your age as well as adults, and keep in touch with them when times are bad
- To help you develop a life and activities outside of home, and outside of worrying about parents and illness

Specific tips for professionals which may be particularly relevant to families in which there is mental illness

1 *No one professional group* has responsibility for, or expertise in, helping these children and a small investment of time by any one of them can reap great rewards for the child.

2 *Whichever professional role you are in* – teacher, nurse, social worker, doctor or other – take the opportunity to talk openly with the child/ children in the family. Do not be afraid that you do not see yourself as a 'child' expert. As Jess Streeting has shown in her chapter, you probably know more than you think, and her chapter gives hints how to use it.

3 *Whenever you can*, do take the opportunity to help a child you have contact with, or the child of your patient, to access the simple resources described earlier – particularly explanation and discussion.

4 *Try to become aware of, and connect to, all the other different professionals* who may be, or even should be, interacting with the lives of the children and parents.

5 *Be aware that it is very important that these professionals work together* in a cooperative framework. If necessary you may need to make efforts to bring them together. Bringing families and different professional together may be the small thing which makes a key difference. If they do meet together make sure that the children – and their views – are included in planning.

6 *When you meet a family, do not be intimidated by the illness* from asking questions, and listen to the answers with curiosity which can formulate other questions. Always ask if they have children, how many children and the age of each child. Ask how the children have responded to the illness and what if any support they have had.

7 *Always fix another appointment before you leave a home visit*, as it can show that you know they need to be kept in your mind.

8 *Try to bring families and resources together*, not feel bound by your particular role. Remember that often children of parents with mental illness are commonly seen as the responsibility of some 'other' agency. If you are from adult mental health, referral of the child to a young carer's service or the family to KidsTime may be crucial. If you are a child's social worker, it may make all the difference to the child if the parent is referred to a parent's support group, or the family to KidsTime.

9 *Use each encounter with families.* You, or a service you recommend, may be the one that makes a crucial difference.

10 *Suggest to both parents and children simple things which can build the resilience of both.* Make a note of what small things either of them said helped a bit and help them build on it. Encourage them to use whatever resources are available, and to talk to each other, read together and play together.

Some combined tips 219

11 *While medication may be very important for some mental illnesses*, it is the whole family approach, and a 'holistic' stance which may decide if it is effective.

12 *Whichever professional role you come from, try to make sure that each child has an adult* who will keep them in mind and be an advocate. As Chineye Njoku described in her chapter, it was her English teacher who just stepped in and helped her face what was happening to her. Others have described school nurses, or young carers or KidsTime workers as playing a key supportive role.

13 *Try to ensure that each affected child has a 'holding' person* or environment, or discuss with other professionals, family and friends how this can be achieved. (See Lara Brown's explanation in her comments on Ambeya Begum's and Georgia Irwin-Ryan's chapters)

14 *Finally, remember that these young people are also experts* on their parents' illness. Therefore – whichever role you are in – communicate with the children, consider seriously their opinions on their parents' illness. It may give you invaluable information to help the parent as well as ensure that the young people feel heard.

Training resources

As explained in the introduction training in the United Kingdom may focus on the impacts of parental mental illness, but frequently focuses on generic young carers, with varying attention to the specific needs of children of parents with mental illness.

Young Minds offers a dedicated course: https://youngminds.org.uk/find-a-course/parental-mental-health-training/.

The Anna Freud National Centre for Children and Families offers a course for working with families of very young children: https://www.annafreud.org/training/training-and-conferences-overview/training-at-the-anna-freud-national-centre-for-children-and-families/itsiey-specialist-parental-mental-illness/.

Our Time offers a two-day training for KidsTime Workshop Teams, and a one-day awareness raising workshop for professionals in health, social care and education, as well as short sessions and INSET sessions for teachers and school staff: https://ourtime.org.uk/training/.

The Association for Child and Adolescent Mental Health offers a range of courses, including one-day courses: https://www.acamh.org/event/pmi-nov/.

The NSPCC and 'Think Family' in Northern Ireland offer models of intervention and advice, although specific courses are not currently advertised: https://www.nspcc.org.uk/preventing-abuse/child-protection-system/parental-mental-health/ http://www.ci-ni.org.uk/think-family; http://www.cypsp.org/wp-content/uploads/2015/02/Think_-Family_Checklist_Leaflet.pdf. They use Adrian Falcov's 'Family Model' which can be accessed online: https://thefamilymodel.com/.

The charity MIND offers specific advice to parents only: https://www.mind.org.uk/information-support/tips-for-everyday-living/parenting-with-a-mental-health-problem/#.XbSa1-hKjIW.

220 Some combined tips

Courses for young carers include: https://www.childrenssociety.org.uk/youngcarer/training-and-consultancy; https://carers.org/about-us/about-young-carers https://www.cylix.co.uk/courses/young-carer-aware.

In Australia the COPMI network (now renamed Emerging Minds) offers a range of good quality courses: http://www.copmi.net.au/.

One of the most comprehensive services has been developed in Finland, which also offers online access: https://www.tandfonline.com/doi/abs/10.1080/14623730.2006.9721744.

The Social Care Institute for Excellence in the United Kingdom has an online course, although this does not appear to have been updated for 8 years: https://www.scie.org.uk/e-learning/parental-mental-health-families. Its report, http://www.cypsp.org/wp-content/uploads/2014/02/SCIE-Guidance.pdf, does offer many reading resources, mostly about young carers (p. 39).

Virtual College offers a commercially available online package on parental mental health, but its content is not advertised: https://www.virtual-college.co.uk/courses/safeguarding-courses/parental-mental-health.

Index

Note: **Bold** page numbers refer to tables; *italic* page numbers refer to figures and page numbers followed by "n" denote endnotes.

achievements as carer 64–65, 162–163
action/rehearsal process 136–138
Act of Parliament 2
adolescent problem 120–121
Adshead, G. 114
Adult Mental Health Services 211
adverse childhood experience (ACE) 40–41, 46
advocacy 74–76
Agaplesion Diakonieklinikum Rotenburg (ADR) 205
Alzheimer's Society 184
anxiety 67–68, 74, 151
appraise 3, 38
Asian cultures 153–154
attachment bond 47
attachment relationships 8, 44, 47, 106
awareness of young carer 145–146

Begum, A. 41, 111, 147, 164, 165, 216
behavioural therapy 152
Behaviour Attendance Emotional Audit (BAE Audit) 188, 194
behaviour: extreme 96–97; illness 98, 108; ill person 21–22; problems of children 110
Bipolar disorder 43, 53, 104–105
Bishop, P. 111
Blyton, E.: 'The Enchanted Wood' 134
Brown, L. 41, 111, 165, 167, 216
bullying theme 137

Care Act 4
carer: achievements as 64–65, 162–163; rights of young carers 162, 173–175;

strengths and capabilities of 67; *see also* young carer
catharsis 138
Child and Adolescent Mental Health Services (CAMHS) 183, 186, 190, 211
Child and Family Mental Health Services (CAMHS) 90
Children Act 90
Children and Adolescents affected by PaRental mental Illness (CAPRI) 2
children of parents with a mental illness (COPMI) 2, 175, 180; advocacy 74–76; anxiety 74; children as experts 84; cognitive development of children 76; communication 81, 82, 84; cultural difference on mental illness 69–70; depression 71; environment for development 76–77; explanation for mental illness 74; foster care 70; genetics 76–77; impact of parental mental illness 70–72; Kidstime workshop 72–73; play 72, 76; resilience 77–78; responsibility 74, 77; sense of belonging 73; social workers 72; support for 81, 83
Children of Sick Parents (Michael Rutter) 3
child's sense of loneliness 3
cognitive development of children 76
communication 81, 82, 84
community project 211
complex family situations 1
confusion and stigma 51
contact: direct personal 91; indirect 92, 107; safe arrangements for 93–94

222 Index

contact reinstatement 97–99
contracts 92–93
conversations 4–5, 160–161, 165
Cooklin, A. 43, 45–47, 82, 94, 104, 106, 107, 111, 164, 167, 172, 173, 196, 205
coping with mentally ill parent 81
coping with trauma 151–152
couple 9–10
critical thinking 133
cultural traditions 10–11
culture 69–70, 79–80
culture and community 153–154
current environmental stressors 30
current family and environmental pattern 30
curriculum enrichment 185–186

dealing with parental mental illness 149–150
Debar, S. 5, 41
Dementia Friendly Schools Award 184
Dementia Pioneer School 184–185
depression 71, 90, 151
Deputy Safeguarding Lead (DSL) 190
developmental family and environmental pattern 29–30
developmental strengths and deficits 29
dilemmas with mental illness 110
direct personal contact 91
disease 21, 22
distress 1, 24–25, 57, 58
drama for empowerment: action/ rehearsal process 136–138; aim 128–129; bullying theme 137; catharsis 138; critical thinking 133; emotional vocabulary 132–133; framework 129–131; ground rules 129–130; home/ parent unwell themes 138; hospital themes 137–138; laughter therapy 137; performance 138–139; playing games 131; practice for life 136–138; relationship with audience 139–140; representations 140; school and friendship themes 138; self awareness 131–132; storytelling 134–136; tools and skills 131–134; transformational power 128
dynamic support network 57–58

economic misfortunes 11
effects of medication on parenting 124
emotional category of student: attendance team 189–190; Director

of Student Welfare 190; intervention team 190; Learning Manager (Head of Year) and Assistant Learning Manager 188–189; multi-agency partnership 191; range of targeted support *189*; safeguarding team 190; Student Support Advisor 189
Emotional Literacy Support Assistant (ELSA) training 189
emotional regulation 31–32, 132–133, 135, 164
'The Enchanted Wood' (Blyton) 134
environment for development 76–77
epigenetics 29, 31
expert witness planning 90
extended family 81–82, 100–101, 108
extreme behaviours 96–97

Fagin, L. 41, 108, 165
family: adverse childhood experience (ACE) 46; Attachmentrelationships 8; averagefamily 7; Bipolar disorder 43–45; children behaviour 7; couple 9–10; cultural, social and religious beliefs 10–11; economic 11; emotional and physical needs of children 82; family life 10; family therapy 47; feeling of safety and stability 45–46; general family living hints 13–18; general principles for professionals 18–21; guilt 11–12; guilty 43–45; ideal family 7; Kids time 46–47; living together as adults 9; loneliness 9; lone parents 7; loyalty 12; meaning 6–7; parentingclasses/manual on child care 9; parents response to child needs 8–9; problems of family closeness 11–12; relationships 10–11, 14–16; resilience to problems 11; rupture and repair 44; safety and danger 9–10; secrets 13; stigma and shame 13; structures and functions 8–9, 16–18; supportive and understanding partner 9; suspicious rigidity 12; unsafe and threat 13; very close family 6
Family Action 88
Family Court 90, 97–99, 102
family resilience 99–100
Family Smiles 3
fear 19, 51, 58–59, 68, 123, 164
foster care 70, 73–75, 83, 86–87
fragility of mental health and its impact 58–60

Index   223

Francis, D. 205
Frier, A. 3, 4
frightening memories 102–105
Fromberg, D. 76
future relationship 91, 101

Garmezy, N. 37
genetics 29, 76–77
good enough (parenting) 43
good explanation about mental illness
    25–27, 54–56, 74, 87, 119–120, 164,
    177–178
guilty 11–12, 43–45, 49

'Hanse Merkur Innovationspreis' 209
healing power of good relationships 32
health, physical and mental illness in
    family and other relationships: adverse
    childhood experience (ACE) 40–41;
    brain development and functioning
    23; disease 21–22; emotion regulation
    31–32; family and professional
    intervention 35–36; feelings, thoughts
    and moods arousal 32–33; fight/
    flight mode 32; good explanation to
    children 25–27; healing power of good
    relationships 32; illness, definition
    of 21–22; Kidstime multi-family
    workshops 33–36; mental and physical
    experiences by individual 23; mental
    illness triggers 27–31; mental map
    24–25; 'Nature *versus* Nurture' 28;
    neutral explanation 27; Our Time 27;
    recognising, labelling and confirming
    child experience 26; resilience 36–40;
    wheel of causality 22, 28–31
holding person/environment 165–167
holidays 124–125
holistic, person-centred approach 48
home/parent unwell themes 138
honesty 48, 49, 82, 89, 217
honour 15
hospital themes 137–138
humour 12, 14, 37, 38, 45
hurdles and what helped: achievements
    as carer 64–65; to be selfish 60–62;
    defined and limited by illness 56–58;
    dynamic support network 57–58;
    fragility of mental health and its
    impact 58–60; lack of explanation
    and understanding 54–56; low self-
    esteem and self-critical 63–65; over
    responsibility 59; parental support

58–60; preoccupation with needs
    of others 60–62; realunderstanding
    55–56; resentment 63–65;
    responsibility without power 65–67;
    shame of being different 62–63; share
    with similar experiences persons
    62–63; strengths and capabilities of
    carer 67

ideal family 7, 94
ideas on mental illness 152–153
illness: definition of 21–22; behaviour
    98, 108; physical 1; psycho-somatic
    illnesses 32; trauma of child life and
    94–95
ill person behaviour 21–22
'The Illustrated Mum' (Wilson) 140
impact of parental mental illness 70–72
indirect contact 92, 107
inequalities of health 183
intergenerational influences 185
intervention 4–5
invalidation, of experience 19–20
Irwin-Ryan, G. 41, 165, 166
isolation 121–122

Jass film 176–180
Jugendamt 206

Kidstime in Spain: approach in engaging
    children 212; challenges 211–212;
    community project 211; future 213;
    Health System 211; improvement
    212–213; professionals 211–212; referral
    211–212; setting up groups 211
Kidstime model in Germany: challenges
    210; co-funding 209–210; concurrent
    evaluation 209; elements 206; families
    inviting others 208–209; funding
    205, 209; impetus 205; 'Kidstime
    Deutschland e. V' 210; limited
    information to families by referrer
    208; other parts of the country 209;
    problems of referral 209; referral
    routes to 207; reticence from
    professionals 207–208; reticence from
    the parents 207; social services 206;
    team set up 205–206
Kidstime workshops 3–4; achievements
    as carer 64–65; adolescents 120–121;
    advanced directive 67; advantages
    34; advocacy 74–76; age appropriate
    explanation of mental illness 55–56;

224 Index

aim 111–112; brain overload 33–34; children image and explanation 46–47; common anxieties 56; communication between children and their mentally ill parents 81, 84; confidence and resilience for future 49; connection to other people 73; cultural differences 125; dynamic support network 57–58; effects of medication on parenting 124; entrenched/reinforced schemas 55; explanations about illness 119–120; as holding network 165; holidays 124–125; holistic framework 49; ideas and hints 47; implications 35–36; isolation 121–122; learning from each other 56; members of staff 73; parental authority 116; parental hopes and expectations 123; parental mental illness impacts and risks 59–60; parent groups 112, 114–115; parents anxieties about their children 115–116; parent's world view 88–89; play 72; prejudice perceptions 123; resilience 68, 77–78; resources 112; safe environment 82, 84; school nurse 176; sense of belonging 73; to be selfish 61–62; separations 122–123; share with similar experiences persons 62–63; single parental responsibilities 116–118; storytelling and drama (see drama for empowerment); strengths and capabilities of carer 67; structure 112, 113; transgenerational influences 118–119; understanding 56

laughter therapy 137
learning mentor 178
lone parents 7; bonds with 100–101; children point of view 92–93; closure 98; contact reinstatement 97–99; contracts 92–93; direct personal contact 91; emotional involvement 90–91; explanation to children 164; extended family 100–101; extreme behaviours 96–97; family resilience 99–100; family secrets 116–118; frightening memories 102–105; future relationship 91, 101; indirect contact 92; love from child 91–92; mood fluctuations 95–96; power of an explanation 106; primary responsibility for care 96; resilience through narratives 105–106;

safe arrangements for contact 93–94; sharing child care 93–94; transgenerational influences 118–119; trauma of illness and child life 94–95
loyalty, constricting 17, 83
loyalty to ill parent: fallout on relationship 88; foster care 86–87; impact of parents' illnesses 85–86; lack of explanation about parent mental health 87; parent's world view 88–89; source of security/trap 12

madness 69, 72, 101, 103
'Making Sense of Mental Illness' 178
meaningful conversations on mental illness 152–153
medical practice, incorporate into 146
mental and physical experiences 23
mental health nursing 5
mental health service 183
mental illness 1–3; age appropriate explanation of 55–56; CAPRI 2; COPMI 2, 77–78, 175, 180 (see also children of parents with a mental illness (COPMI)); cultural difference on 69–70; dealing with parental 149–150; dilemmas with 110; education on 147–148; explanation for 74; good explanation about 25–27, 54–56, 74, 87, 119–120, 164, 177–178; ideas on 152–153; impact of parental 70–72; meaningful conversations on 152–153; short film on 171–172; stigma around 172; taboo about 1, 143, 151, 154
mental map 24–25, 164
Mental Processes Wheel 45; see also wheel of causality
mood fluctuations 95–96
multi-family model 4; see also Kidstime workshops

'Nature versus Nurture' 28
needs of children 168
NHS 78, 145, 161
'Niedersächsishce Gesundheitspreis' 209
Njoku, C. 35, 41, 81–84, 174, 219
normality, idea of 140–141

Our Time 27, 33, 157–158, 165
out of house parent 92–93; see also lone parents
over responsibility 59

Index 225

parental authority 116, 110, 116
parental hopes and expectations 123
parental support 58–60
parent groups 112, 114–115, 121, 125
parents anxieties about their children
  115–116
parent's world view 88–89
parity of esteem 1
personality disorder 114
Personal, Social, Health and Economic
  (PSHE) programme 186, 197, 198
person-centred approach 48
physical illness 1
play 37, 72, 76, 131
Plymouth City Council 183
Plymouth Report 183
post-divorce contact *see* lone parents
Post Traumatic Stress Disorder (PTSD)
  85, 151, 152
power of an explanation 106
practice for life 136–138
prejudice 123, 148, 164
preoccupation with needs of others
  60–62
pride 15, 64, 112, 139, 172, 176
priorities for COPMI 180
professionals doing family work: basic
  information to the family 48–49;
  child responsibility 18–19; conflict
  avoidance of uncomfortable topics 21;
  culture 79–80; difficulty in the work
  108–109; environment for child to
  think and respond 18–19; explanation
  for effects of illness 107; extended
  family/third party support 108;
  holistic, person-centred approach 48;
  invalidation of experience 19–20; level
  of conflict 19; narratives about the
  good 107; NHS 78; one person view
  of happening/has happened 20–21;
  points of view 18; positive attitude 18;
  possible avoid 20–21; power and rights
  in adults/children 19; power of human
  connection 78–79; problem in one
  individual 20; promoting resilience
  107–108; research 48; solid respect
  for the second family 107; tips for
  218–219; two family systems 107–108;
  valid view to express 21; whole family
  approach 47–48
psychological resilience 37
psychosis 53, 57, 65, 98
psycho-somatic illnesses 32

public awareness 152
public health in education 169
puerperal psychosis 94, 102, 104

realisation of the power of small
  interventions 3, 4
realunderstanding 55–56
recovery 49, 50n1, 166
relationship with audience 139–140
relatives with rights 2
religious exorcism 69
religious observance 154–156
resentment 63–65
resilience 2–4; active thinking 39–40;
  bounce back 36–37; children of
  parents with a mental illness (COPMI)
  77–78; concept 36; definition 36–37;
  factors 37; family and friend role
  45; family resilience 99–100; feel
  free 38; humour 37; play 37; positive
  difference in child 38–39; to problems
  11; professional 39; psychological
  resilience 37; self-esteem 37, 38;
  through narratives 105–106
responsibility 49, 51–52, 74, 77; without
  power 65–67, 115–116
rights of young carers 162, 173–175
role of parent (child in the) 51
Royal College of Psychiatrists 5, 110
Royal Foundation 1
Rutter, M. 3, 32, 110

safe arrangements for contact 93–94
safety and danger in family 9–10
schizoaffective disorder 147, 164
schizophrenia 37, 71, 119–121, 147
school and friendship themes 138
School-Based Adolescent Mental Health
  (SAMH) programme 189
school nurse: children's rights into
  practice 173–175; explanation about
  mental illness 177–178; Jass film
  176–177; Kidstime workshop 176;
  learning mentor 178; needs of children
  168; priorities for COPMI 180;
  research in the field 175–176; role 168;
  tips for schools 180–181; work diary
  169; work in schools 177–180; Young
  Carers' group 170–173 (*see also* Young
  Carers' group at school)
schools 146, 180–181; assemblies 186;
  awareness 185–186; curriculum
  enrichment 185–186; Dementia

Pioneer School 184–185; emotional category of student 188–191, *189*; implementation of Who Cares? Programme 200–204; inequalities of health 183; key areas of mental health 183–184, *184*; staff training 186–187, **187**; Stoke Damerel Community College 183; student support 187–188, *188*; support for young carers 195–200; Team around the Child (TAC) meeting structure *192*, 193–195, *194*; tips for adventurous schools 197–198; Who Cares? Project (*see* Who Cares? Programme); young carers' group 195; *see also* school nurse; Young Carers' group at school

scientism/pretend science 26
Scott, D. 98
self awareness 131–132
self-blame 164
self-esteem 37, 38, 63–65
self-harm 183
selfish 61–62, 81
sense of belonging 73
separations 122–123
shame 62–63
Shining Stars 195; *see also* Young Carers' group at school
single parent *see* lone parents
social isolation 171
social media and public conversations 152
social services 149, 211
social workers 72, 78
spiritual intervention 69
Spiritual, Moral, Social and Cultural (SMSC) programme 185
staff training 186–187, **187**
stigma 51, 148, 152, 172
Stoke Damerel Community College 183, 184, 196
storytelling 134–136; *see also* drama for empowerment
Streeting, J. 3, 181, 218
strengths and capabilities of carer 67
structures and functions of family 8–9
student peer support 187–188, *188*
supporting parents with mental illness: behaviour problems of children 110; dilemmas with mental illness 110; effects of medication 111; effects of medication on parenting 124; explanations about illness 119–120; holidays 124–125; impact of parental mental ill health on children 110, 111; isolation 121–122; parental authority 110, 116; parental hopes and expectations 123; parent groups 112, 114–115; parent point of view and feelings 111; prejudice 123; problems with adolescents 120–121; professional support 111; responsibility without power 115–116; schools 111; separation from children 122–123; single parental responsibilities 116–118; transgenerational influences 118–119

suspicious rigidity 12

taboo about mental illness 1, 143, 151, 154
Tahta-Wraith, K. 41
talking therapy 89, 104
Team around the Child (TAC) meeting structure *192*, 193–195, *194*
therapeutic conversations 159–160
tips: for children and young people 216–217; for parents 214–216; for professionals doing family work 218–219; for schools 180–181
training in nursing 5
training resources 219–220
transformational power of drama 128
transgenerational influences 118–119
trust 171, 181

UK National Society for the Prevention of Cruelty to Children (NSPCC) 3
United Nations Convention on the Rights of the Child 173

voluntary and statutory bodies 1

what is a family? 6
wheel of causality: concept 22; current environmental stressors 30; current family and environmental pattern 30; developmental family and environmental pattern 29–30; developmental strengths and deficits 29; diagram 28; epigenetics 29; genetics 29; mental processes 31; representation 28

Who Cares? Programme: benefit for school 204; 'dos and don'ts' for Young Carers 199, *199*; evaluation 203; feedback 203–204; implementation 200–204; modules delivery 198–200; online package 197; parent support 199, 200, 202; preparation 200; question box 198; rules and boundaries 199, *199*; students preparation 201; supervision 201–202; support for staff 201–202; support structures for students 201; synopsis of each module 202–203; tips for adventurous schools 197–198; tutorial programme 196; upsetting content 198, 200

whole family approach 47–48

Wilson, J.: 'The Illustrated Mum' 140

young carer: achievement 162–163; awareness 145–146; burden 142; conversation 165; conversations 160–161; coping with trauma 151–152; culture and community 153–154; dealing with parental mental illness 149–150; deal with stigma 157; definition 1–2, 143; depression and anxiety 151; 'dos and don'ts' for 199, *199*; education on mental illness 147–148; experience of caring 144; as experts 84; healthcare professional 146; holding person during frightening times 165–167; hope 157; ideas on mental illness 152–153; identifying problems 144–145; living with parent with mental illness 148; meaningful conversations on mental illness 152–153; national census 2; needs of 193–195, *194*; NHS 145; Our Time 157–158; personal beliefs 156; positive thinking 165; religious observance 154–156; resilience 166; rights 162; role 142; schools 4, 146; self-esteem 152; selfless dedication 145; social media and public conversations 152; social services 149; support 145–146, 195–200; talking openly 157–158; therapeutic conversations 159–160; understanding mental illness 143–144; in United Kingdom 4

Young Carers' group at school: activities 195–196; advocacy 172–173; Jass film and work in schools 176–180; key themes 175; mental health and illness 170–171; short film on mental illness 171–172; social isolation 171; Shining Stars 195; stigma around mental illness 172; as support group 170; trust 171, 181; Young Carer Champion and Students Support Advisors 196

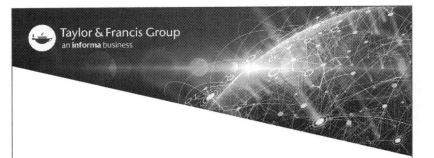